They
Think Again
Restoring Cognitive Abilities
Through Teaching

They Think Again

Restoring Cognitive Abilities Through Teaching

Carl Frankenstein, Ph.D.

Professor (Emeritus) of Special Education
The Hebrew University, Jerusalem

VNR **VAN NOSTRAND REINHOLD COMPANY**
NEW YORK   CINCINNATI   ATLANTA   DALLAS   SAN FRANCISCO
LONDON   TORONTO   MELBOURNE

Van Nostrand Reinhold Company Regional Offices:
New York   Cincinnati   Atlanta   Dallas   San Francisco

Van Nostrand Reinhold Company International Offices:
London   Toronto   Melbourne

Library of Congress Catalog Card Number: 78-17676
ISBN: 0-442-21646-7

Manufactured in the United States of America

Published by Van Nostrand Reinhold Company
135 West 50th Street, New York, N.Y. 10020

Published simultaneously in Canada by Van Nostrand Reinhold Ltd.

15 14 13 12 11 10 9 8 7 6 5 4 3 2 1

Library of Congress Cataloging in Publication Data

Frankenstein, Carl.
  They think again.

  Bibliography: p. 289
  Includes index.
  1. Socially handicapped children—Education.
2. Cognition in children.   3. Teachers of socially
handicapped children, Training of. I. Title.
LC4069.F7   371.9'67   78 17676
ISBN 0-442-21646-7

Preface

When we think of man's future, we look for relevant causal factors in technology, ecology, and global politics, but rarely, if ever, in human behavior. We may reject Marxism ideologically, and yet, almost compulsively, accept a deterministic view of man's basic attitudes as functions of so-called objective conditions. To say that man could be responsible for his future sounds to many almost childish and certainly unscientific (although psychoanalysts, in a similar context, have raised the question of man's responsibility for his repressions).

Even when we admit that a human attitude resulting from a set of "objective" circumstances is likely to reenter the individual's causal (developmental) equation as a modifying factor, we are reluctant to interpret the concept of modification so that it includes not only reinforcement or intensification but also change of direction. Hence most scientists' reluctance to accept the theory of reversibility; hence their quasihumanistic "benevolent" pluralism.

But education is more than a sum total of actions meant to help the individual toward self-realization. Education means liberation of his potentials, part of which may never have reached the level of actuality; part may simply have retreated into the fog of suppression or repression. Education means optimistic hope, sometimes even hope against hope, in the power to restore lost or impaired dispositions and abilities. Hence, a real educator, worth his calling, will, almost instinctively, and certainly often irrationally, reject clear-cut diagnoses claiming the right to limit his initiative.

This, we believe, is true for the education of every child, even the most gifted. The latter may not need cognitive stimulation, he may not even need intellectual "mentoring," but he certainly often needs someone who will make him aware of the personal meaning of learnable, so-called objective, laws and principles. He is liable to remain not only disinterested in, but, even worse, completely incapable of, discovering the human significance of scientific "truth." Many cases of mental decline after adolescence are due to the fact that the gifted child ceases to be productive because he fails to see the human dimension of facts.

Even more important is the problem of how to uncover potentials and how to activate them when we deal with children whose intelligence is impaired by certain environmental conditions. We have in mind those millions whose growth under the impact of indoctrination and conditioning, on the one hand, or an impersonal family atmosphere, on the other, did not allow their innate cognitive abilities to develop freely. Without the development of his potentials man is likely to become an automaton, as Erich Fromm would say, an automaton with its rigid rules of functioning, with its utter lack of freedom. Nor are the underprivileged the only ones liable to fall victim to the dangers implied in the loss of potentials. Many lose them because they *prefer* cognitive self-limitation, that is, a "comfortable" existence with less differentiation and still less inner responsibility. Thus, they think they will be able to lead a conflict- and tension-free life with the havable, with external values.

This study has two purposes: to show how certain life conditions almost inevitably produce an externalized life-style that may be detrimental to the intellectual development of many children born into poverty, neglect, or cultural ambiguity; and to show how teaching can help them find a way out of their predicament. Their predicament, we claim, is not only that they are compelled to fail but also, and mainly, that they are compelled to function beneath their level of potential abilities.

We propose to describe and analyze the essential symptoms of this condition, which we call "secondary retardation," to explain the principles and the methods of teaching meant to rehabilitate the thus handicapped pupils, and to show the intrinsic connection between individual treatment and teaching. Finally, a number of examples will illustrate the method, and we shall try to answer the question of how to build up a training system to produce the staff required for rehabilitative teaching and for counseling the teachers in the field.

We have already mentioned the seeming paradox between the

deterministic philosophy of most behavioral scientists and our optimistic claim that teaching methods can be worked out capable of restoring impaired cognitive potentials, if not to all, at least to the majority of secondarily retarded pupils. It can be shown that this paradox is indeed just a seeming one. It is true that certain objective factors, such as extreme poverty and want or value disorientation in cultural transitions, are bound to produce certain life attitudes, such as externalization of values and concepts. It is equally true that externalization, at least under certain personality conditions, is bound to handicap the child's cognitive development. But it is a serious mistake to translate causal inevitability into terms of irreversibility of results.

The teacher, in his or her personality, involvement, convictions, and methods, is a factor of determination no less potent than the social or cultural factors prevailing in the child's intimate environment. The study here presented is a testimony of faith in the teacher as a counter-determining force, the possible healer of one of the greatest social evils of modern society. The future of man depends not only on technology or on political developments; it also depends on the educators' courage to think and to imagine and never to accept the dictum of finality.

CARL FRANKENSTEIN

Contents

They Think Again

Restoring Cognitive Abilities Through Teaching

Part One

THEORY

1

Some Basic Presumptions

I. REVERSIBILITY OF SECONDARY RETARDATION

The Problem

In the past two decades, many studies have been undertaken and many papers and books have been published discussing the socially or culturally deprived, disadvantaged, underprivileged child and adolescent. In some of these studies and publications, the emphasis is on etiology, in others on a description and analysis of cognitive and/or social behavior. Some deal with problems of prevention through early treatment of the child's family and initial school environment. Others probe ways and means of compensatory education, adaptation of curriculum and methods, enrichment programs, social activation, technical skill training, and so on.

In this connection, the problem of reversibility is of the essence: most researchers agree that the child born with a low level of intelligence differs from the child whose originally normal intelligence was impaired following the consistent impact of certain adverse environmental conditions. (Thus, the poorly structured personality of the congenitally retarded, his primary emptiness and rigidity, are compared with the avoidance symptoms and the cognitive distortion in the secondarily retarded.[10,11]) Sometimes parallels are drawn between the socially or culturally handicapped and the child deprived of maternal care whose initially normal mental alertness declines as a result of this deprivation, particularly when the infant is placed in an institution with its more or less impersonal atmosphere in which genuine interaction is replaced by routine.[2,5,18,36] Other studies and analyses again emphasize the essential *differences* between these two types of "mentally impaired" children.[10] But in both cases the question of reversibility is asked.[2,6,25]

Educators and psychologists have little to offer to a discussion of the chances of reversing congenitally given mental defects (although biologists, neurologists, endocrinologists, embryologists, and students of genetics may not have given up hope). On the contrary: psychologists of education often try very hard to prove that not only primary but also secondary retardation is rarely, if ever, reversible.* Their conclusions are derived from either genetic studies or statistical evidence. Some of the genetic studies even go so far as to claim that the so-called underprivileged child is not handicapped intellectually because of his "disadvantaging" environment, but that this environment is the result of the parents' and therefore also the child's inferiority.[21] But since most of the genetic studies rely on statistical calculations as well, we should ask to what extent the latter are relevent at all for the question of educational reversibility.

Vulnerability

Certainly, restoration of impaired cognitive potentials is not in every case attainable through the application of what we shall describe in the following study as methods of "rehabilitative teaching." The chances of success depend no less on personality factors in the learners than on the teacher's skill to use these methods properly.

Moreover, the concept of reversibility refers not only to the ill effects of pathogenic traumatization or to the finalization of character traits. The high degree of vulnerability after rehabilitation, that is, an individual's proneness to "relapse," under the strain of later negative life events, is well known in the fields of both medical care and child rearing. But even non-finality of restoration of impaired potentials should not be used as an argument against the

---

*An interesting example of this, one could almost say, antieducational attitude of educational psychologists is offered by Kirk's critical evaluation of Bernadine Schmidt's experiments.[24,35] Kirk is much more interested in proving the reliability of accepted measurement techniques than in the welfare of the child and his chance of advancement.

justification or the effectiveness of methods of rehabilitative teaching. (The only correct conclusion we should and could draw from "vulnerability" and "regression" is that effective aftercare is an essential element of effective rehabilitative teaching.)

Poverty and Neglect

We could mention, and analyze, several varieties of externalization in which the ability to think in abstract terms, hence also the ability to learn complex subject matter, is *not* impaired (though personal involvement in objective and formal learning may be weakened). But since we are interested only in those social or cultural conditions that are liable to produce a variety of externalization which is characterized by other symptoms of behavior, and distort the basic categories of thinking, we ask: which environmental conditions are responsible for the simultaneous emergence of externalized behavior and impaired thinking?

Growing up under the impact of *extreme poverty and educational neglect,* on the one hand, and of *incompatibility of rigid value patterns with internalized values,* on the other, are considered to be the two main sets of causes for the ideal type of externalization accompanied by secondary retardation. Our question therefore must be formulated differently: when, under which conditions, do these basic elements of externalizing life conditions impair intelligence? So that the individual is forced to live on a level of functioning much lower than that of his potentially normal abilities?

We have already maintained elsewhere[13] that this is the deep meaning of the social-gap problem: not the injustice implied in environmentally conditioned inequality, but the tragedy of thousands and millions who are not helped to realize their potentials, the tragedy implied in this contradiction between an impaired but fatalistically accepted low level of actuality and an unreal, not realized level of potential normalcy or of latent talents.

Let it be said right here in no uncertain terms: seemingly democratic pluralism with its false ideology of equality between groups, between cultural patterns, is, more often than not, responsible for a truly reactionary perpetuation of the social gap in this psychological meaning of the word. In the field of social intervention, pluralism perpetuates inequality and injustice by means of compensatory education; it offers social, technical, artistic, or other forms of learning as compensation for the allegedly unattainable goal of abstract thinking, and thus for the exclusion from all high-status positions in our society.

But in view of the prevalence of externalization in modern society with its technological orientation, its ideals of "having," its status seeking, the aim of education is defined inadequately as developing the ability to differentiate and to think in abstract terms. Vital as the attainment of such aims will be from a social point of view, that is, as a means to bridge the social gap in its economic and its psychological meanings, education has a more fundamental and a more universal aim: to "teach" internalization and to teach it to all children, those whose cognitive functions are *not* affected as well as those whose intelligence *has* been impaired by adverse environmental conditions.

Practice has shown that the two aims are interlinked with each other, at least in part: to some extent, internalization strengthens, and internalization is attained by developing, the ability to think in abstract terms. And yet, it seems important to distinguish between the two as different aims: there are many ways of developing abstraction almost as a skill; and there are many ways of strengthening an understanding of living from within and a willingness to live from within, without participation of abstract functions. Hence, our emphasis on internalization as a distinguishable aim of education in our times!

To the extent that the teacher recognizes this as a legitimate (and essential) aim of, and as a regulating force in, his didactic efforts, it is justifiable to add: not the *contents* of teaching and not even the definition of teaching as compensatory determine the outcome, but this emphasis on internalization as the intrinsic aim of teaching (though it should be obvious that in this case, teaching and education are no longer "compensatory," and a unifying base is built on which "privileged" and "underprivileged" are capable of meeting as equals).

We have mentioned the nonscientific, pragmatic character of our attitude toward the problem of reversibility. We reject any theory or research method leading to the conclusion that secondary retardation is irreversible and that education can do nothing to restore lost or impaired potentials. *We define the function of education in this vital social-problem area as a series of ever repeated and ever modified didactic interventions aimed at the restoration of impaired cognitive potentials in as many underprivileged and socially or culturally retarded children as possible.* In the following chapters we shall try to describe the didactic principles of such methods and, later, to exemplify the methods by descriptions and analyses of class events, of lessons, of change processes in pupils and in teachers.

But the rationale of these methods cannot be made clear, cannot be understood, without a detailed analysis of how the essential *characteristics* of social or cultural retardation reflect their essential *causes*. This will be the purpose of the following section.

II. THE CAUSES OF SECONDARY RETARDATION

The Social Variety

The statement that poverty leads to deprivation essentially differs from the statement that deprivation is likely to lead to externalization, the symptoms of which will be described later (see pp. 18f.) It is universally known that poverty often produces physical malfunction through poor nutrition and overcrowding, hence also producing greater danger of infection and recidivism; that lack of privacy and lack of intimacy may produce general unrest and may be accompanied by sexual excitation from an early age on; that poverty often is conducive to truancy from school, to early school leaving, and to lack of opportunities to benefit from schooling, hence also a low level of intellectual functioning; that all these results of the pathogenic elements of poverty tend to reinforce each other and thus increase social deprivation.

At the same time, however, it is well known that a large number of successful citizens grew up under such adverse conditions. The causal equation connecting poverty in its "objective" (sociological) meaning and its measurable indicators with ill effects on the child's

---

*It is obvious that the chances of restoration decrease with the low level of initial, original, congenitally given intelligence.

mental development is ambiguous: it is exactly the large number of "marginal" cases, appearing in statistical research as correlation coefficients >1 or as standard deviations, that require questions of differential etiology.

We suggest that questions like the following be asked and answered:

(a) Is the parents' mind more or less exclusively directed toward, and preoccupied with the universe of material givens that are "*not given*," not available—that is, with want?

(b) To what extent do they conceive of the nonavailable as being *potentially* available, and to what extent do they expect all that they need and have not to be present one day, by chance and without any need for efforts to be made by them? In other words: To what extent do they fail to understand the causal connection between "having" and personal responsibility?

(c) To what extent is the parents' attitude not only toward their material conditions but also toward themselves, their partners, *and* their children characterized by weakness (or relative absence) of personal relatedness?

It should be already evident, from the wording of these three questions, that there exist many cases in which parents, though living under conditions of extreme poverty, do not spend their mental energy on want, on what they have not and could happen to be theirs one day, by chance. We have in mind those parents who are attached primarily to an ideology, a political or religious belief. Some of them may be so deeply absorbed in their ideology or belief that they fail to take adequate care of their children and even sacrifice the personal character of their family relationships on the altar of involvement with ideas and ideals. And yet, such parents' attitudes will not act as an externalizing factor on their children's development; some may produce more or less severe neurotic disorders, but they will have learned internalization from their parents' objective involvement.

In other cases, the parents' attitude toward life may be one of externalization, but they may (or at least one of them may) nevertheless remain genuinely concerned with their children's welfare. These are the cases in which at least some of their children endowed with a good congenital intelligence level will be able to keep their cognitive capacities, although they may simultaneously display most signs of an externalized value orientation (in imitation of their parents, as it were).*

We therefore are entitled to say that secondary retardation results from growing up under conditions of extreme poverty only when they are accompanied by educational neglect, that is, by an inclusion of the children as objects and not as subjects in the parents' externalized orientation toward the havable and in their chance-addiction. To the extent that the child can feel himself to be a subject within a less impersonal family atmosphere, the danger of "impaired intelligence" decreases.

The Cultural Variety

Secondary retardation is often defined as socio-cultural. However, it seems more appropriate to distinguish between the social and the cultural varieties of secondary retardation. Although the two tend to merge, in causes and in symptoms, the differences between them are clear enough to justify different methods of didactic intervention.

What is meant by the term "culturally conditioned retardation"?

Needless to say we are *not* concerned here with the anthropological aspects of "cultural primitivity." Neither do we intend to go into the complexities of comparing with each other different cultural value systems. We are dealing with one question only: what can education or, more precisely, what can teaching do to bridge the gap between the cognitive potentials and the low level of actual functioning in children who belong to the "underprivileged" ethnic subgroups? How is the coexistence of different cultural groups within a modern society conducive to the impairment of intellectual functioning? Why are the "solutions" offered by cultural pluralism and compensatory education inadequate? We must distinguish between two types of transition from one cultural value system to another according to the degree of complexity and differentiation characteristic of each system. If the transition takes

*We do not consider here the many cases in which parental apathy, feelings of worthlessness or of resentment, fatalism, despair, or aggressive rejection of the world as frustrating determine the parents' attitude toward their conditions of poverty, themselves, their family, and particularly their children.

place from one highly differentiated system to another equally differentiated one, conflicts, to the extent that they will appear at all, are the result of loyalty, rigid adherence to the contents of the old pattern, and unwillingness to give up something considered to be of superior value; in this case, we speak of "adjustment difficulties."

If the transition takes place from a "primitive," that is, a tradition-defined, relatively undifferentiated and rigidly patterned system to a more differentiated and more change-oriented system, two contradictory feelings emerge simultaneously: a feeling of superiority in one who belongs to a culture that somehow had been the locus of absolute truth and glory, and a feeling of inferiority, following failure and low status in the more differentiated society. This failure is translated almost automatically into one's feeling rejected, frustrated, and discriminated against. The results of the coexistence of these contradictory feelings are: a tendency to imitate some external manifestations of the dominant group's behavior, without understanding their meaning, and at the same time a strong rejection of the new world as hostile.

In both ways, the child's ability to relate adequately to his learning assignments is likely to suffer and the result is again secondary retardation. But, as we shall try to show soon, the symptoms of retardation are different in the cultural variety of secondary retardation from what they are in the social variety. (Here, it may suffice to mention the difference between cognitive distortions through concretism and lack of differentiation in the social variety, and manipulative instead of causal thinking and restriction of the time-consciousness in the cultural variety.) A parallel contradiction between attitudes appears in the child's perception of his parents, and particularly of the father: on the one hand, they are the prototypes of failure in the new society and, as such, are objects of contempt, shame, and rejection; on the other, they are objects of identification insofar as they justify rejection of the institutions that represent the frustrating present, first and foremost the school and the recognized leisure-time agencies. *This is the externalized version of ambivalence and of introjection*: passive expectations of learning (presented, as it were, by the parental culture of the past); and active rejection of parental values blamed for every failure in the present, which helps perpetuate and aggravate that failure, since it leaves the child without any direction from within. Belief in fate and in accidentality (chance) limit still more the child's ability to think selectively and critically.

A third version of this ambivalence can be found in the parents' attitude toward the school: they expect the school to help their children succeed in their scholastic achievements and to advance quickly toward full integration in the new society; but they do not understand the causal connection between achievement and natural abilities, on the one hand, or learning efforts, on the other, nor do they take into consideration the fact that successful adjustment to the school's and to the society's demands is likely to alienate the children from their parents' "culture of the past" (which, for them, remains the valid culture of their present, too). The parents are, of course, unaware of the inner contradiction between these expectations. Sometimes they reject this "alienating" school, although it continues to be, in their eyes, the "omnipotent instrument of integration." The result is a most frustrating lack of cooperation with the school, which sometimes may even take the form of open sabotage.

Configurations

Thus emerges secondary retardation of the cultural variety. Although it differs essentially from the social variety, the two tend to merge, because their essential causes tend to interlink. It is generally known that difficulties in value-adjustment following transition from one culture to another restrict the individual's economic adjustment chances—hence the high correlation between poverty and cultural ambiguity. In times of cultural value transition and ambiguity the affected adults wait for chances to solve their economic problems and wait for their culture's values, by their own force, to prove their superiority over, or at least their equality with, the values of the dominant (and frustrating) culture.

The poverty variety of externalization and secondary retardation with its typical emphasis on "having" and chance-addiction means that the adults affected by it live without being supported even by an illusion of cultural values, past, present, or future. When the two varieties merge, their main symptoms reinforce each other.

On the other hand, what we have said about the protecting force of poverty-stricken parents' genuine concern for their children's welfare, holds good also for the factor of family cohesiveness under conditions of cultural transition and ambiguity. Such cohesiveness makes it possible for the child to internalize values transmitted "from without" through a respected father's teachings or through the traditional family channels. However, these are atypical cases, just as children endowed with exceptionally well-developed intellectual abilities and thereby protected against even the most severely externalizing conditions of poverty and neglect or of cultural transition and ambiguity are exceptional.

It follows that externalization accompanied by secondary retardation cannot be explained adequately by relating it to one or two general causes, such as extreme poverty, want and neglect, or cultural ambiguity, unless we see these causes in configuration (a) with other modifying social factors such as the relative intensity of non-stimulation or of impersonality in primary relationships, or with *individual* modifiers; and (b) with the developmental stages through which a child exposed to the influence of those "general" causes has to pass until externalization appears in its more or less final (crystallized) form, usually at the end of adolescence.

Some of the most important individual modifiers are: type-conditions, constitutionally given thresholds of perception, vulnerability and congenital intelligence, but also the time-factor in the individual child's history of frustration and functional impairment, and availability of compensatory factors in the child's personality or in his environment.

III. THE DEVELOPMENT OF SECONDARY RETARDATION

The Problem

We now turn to the second question raised above, that of development. We shall try not to repeat what we have said elsewhere[10] on the specific contributions each developmental phase makes to the crystallization of secondary retardation in its two varieties. Most theories of development, such as those of Freud or Piaget, base their conclusions on observations of the middle-class child and disregard the essential differences in development under the impact of opposite conditions.

True enough: *every* infant needs the experience of regularity in the sequence of contradictory states (of tension and satisfaction, of movement and rest, of partiality and wholeness, of loneliness and protectedness). And every child needs this experience as mediated primarily by the mother or an identifiable mother substitute. In this way the child learns trust in the reliability of life and of his adult environment. He learns his first lesson in abstraction, namely to abstract from absolute absence and from absolute presence of protecting adults, that is, the meaning of nearness; he learns all about life situations never being "final," always being changeable, and about his own role as an active subject developing initiative to bring about such change. These are the preconditions of interpersonal as well as of cognitive relationships.

What happens when the child grows up under conditions that do *not* satisfy his needs for regularity, for personal relationships "meaning him," and, instead, feels himself treated as object among objects, depending on chance occurences rather than on constancy? What is apt to happen to the child's primary need for security when the environment neglects stimulation and meaningful communication? Inconsistency in the parents' attitudes and impositions, resulting from their never predictable orientation toward want and the "havable" is liable to produce a similar chance-attitude in the child, an attitude characterized by lack of differentiation. The child does not understand the parents' educational demands, which are rooted in their cultural traditions and patterns, rather than in their personality. As a result, he learns early how to accept authoritatively imposed norms of behavior and how to think in stereotypes.

Later on, when, ordinarily, ambivalence makes its appearance, creates conflicts, and accounts for the emergence of *inner* tensions (and internalization as a means to lessen these tensions), an essentially different behavior can be observed in externalization. Under conditions of poverty, want, neglect, chance-addiction, and parental inconsistency, we find external instead of internal tensions, univalent instead of ambivalent feelings, aggressiveness and resentments instead of mental conflicts. Under conditions of cultural ambiguity, as we have said, the place of inner tensions is taken by a strong conflict between dependence on the values of the old culture and a resentful recognition of the superiority of the new values. The child then tends to protest against the "old-fashioned" or "primitive" parents *and* against the frustrating environment; and he tends to depend on the past glory of the ethnic group and its customs, and on the representatives of the new culture, who are often imitated externally.

The developmental peculiarities of this phase are important for an understanding of later difficulties in the secondarily retarded child's causal operations: causal thinking has its emotional counterpart in relationships of mutuality, and the latter are often little more than an attempt to solve ambivalence-tensions. Hence the relative weakness of causal thinking in those children about whom we speak here.

Their secondary retardation becomes more evident with every phase through which they pass. Thus the relatively low intensity of interpersonal relationships in most lower-class families explains the weakness of so-called oedipal conflicts and therefore also the weakness of the child's incentive to internalize his parents, that is, their images. This means, again, tendencies toward externalized solutions are supported, solutions of personal as well as of cognitive problems.

The same weakness also accounts for the fact that the institutes of non-family learning, in our society kindergarten and elementary school, do not fulfill the dynamic functions they fulfill in the middle-class child's development: the latter needs these non-family agencies as neutralizing counterforces against their oedipal family tensions.* No such counterforce is needed in the developmental history of a lower-class, underprivileged child; his parents may welcome those institutes, since they take away from them the burden of care for their children, at least for some hours every day. But this does not mean that the parents are ready to cooperate with the school; on the contrary, they often continue to see in it a value-incongruent, even an alienating, agency.

This attitude is particularly characteristic of culture- and tra-

*In psychoanalytic terms: school readiness is a function of the "decline of the oedipal complex."[17]

dition-bound parents and their relationships with that child. It also reflects itself in the child's perception of his learning tasks and, first and foremost, in his attitude toward failure—not he is to blame for it, but the new culture. Chance-addiction is less characteristic of the cultural than the social variety of secondary retardation; its place as central symptom is taken by resentment and false pride.

Finalization takes place when the child reaches adolescence. Much has been written about the middle-class adolescent's contradictory behavior.[6] But developmental psychology usually emphasizes the adolescent's social behavior more than cognitive aspects. In secondary retardation, however, it is usually this second aspect that counts.

The educator, and particularly the teacher, must be aware of the "artificiality" that attaches to the introduction of a moratory period of learning into the life of an adolescent[7] who comes from conditions of poverty, want, externalization; he must be aware, even in a modern society, based on the democratic principle of "equal chances," that the addition of learning at this stage is bound to arouse tensions and, often enough, alienation. (We shall deal at some length with the educational conclusions that must be drawn from these facts.)

In spite of the mutual dependence of the main environmental factors that are responsible for the emergence of secondary retardation, the essential characteristics of the two resulting varieties become even more cogently evident at this stage of development: indolence, drivenness, associative thinking, and lack of initiative in any ego-transcending task can be observed to characterize the social variety; aggressiveness, resentment, denial, and stubborn defense of wrong answers—the cultural variety. It is needless to add again that the degree of intensity in which those or other symptoms appear depends on the configuration of the two main environmental and the many individual factors of causation, which we have already mentioned.

Thinking and Feeling

No feeling is imaginable without cognitive elements (though they may often be concealed), and no cognitive act, such as concept formation, induction, deduction and conclusion, problem solving, and so on, can be imagined without the participation of emotional elements.

It is true that man *learns* how to separate the two areas (although in conditions of stress this separation is often forgotten); but structurally and originally they are not only connected with each other, they are actually one.[33] The child who grows up in the impersonal climate of want and neglect or of cultural value ambiguity in periods of transition does *not* learn this separation. Non-separation (what we have also analyzed as "contamination") of thinking and feeling manifests itself in the ever present prejudices, stereotypes, and associative concretization in the secondarily retarded child's behavior and thinking. It is the function of rehabilitative teaching to rationalize feelings and to make the child understand and feel the essential difference between concepts and feelings.

For example, the experience of regularity in the sequence of contradictory states produces, so we have said, a feeling of nearness. This feeling is the basis of trust and courage, of understanding relationships of distance and nearness in space and time. Both are liable to be defective in cognitive relationships to the extent that the underlying primary experience of nearness is defective. Hence, it is the task of teaching to evoke and strengthen a feeling that the learnable facts and connections are reliable because of their comprehensible regularity.

Another example: When everything is experienced as being part of the "havable," that is, of things wanting that may be available one day, by chance, unconnected with man's personal involvement, everything is felt to be known, nothing "unknown" or "different." As a result, both, feelings and concepts are likely to be undifferentiated. *Developing* the ability to differentiate means helping the child recognize sameness in differences and differences in sameness, in feelings as well as in cognitive operations.

A third example: We learn responsibility in our feelings, our relationships, our behavior, our thinking through the early experience that we are subjects and not only objects among other objects to be manipulated by our parents, or that truth transmitted by tradition or authority requires application, and its relevance for our personal existence must be discovered. In other words, only by experiencing himself to be active when acted upon does the secondarily retarded child learn responsibility, and, with it, critical and formal (universal) thinking.

Parents and Children

To complete this brief discussion of how secondary retardation develops, we wish to add a few remarks of comparison between parents and children. It seems only logical to interpret the relationship between symptoms of externalization in terms of direct transmission and of imitation.

Lack of externalized parents' involvement in any ego-transcending task produces the well-known tendency in the children to seek immediate satisfaction of their ever-changing needs and to live out their impulses without leaving a reserve of tension and energy, as it were, for "delayed mental action." (This is different from a similar attitude in spoiled middle-class children.)

Children take over from their externalized parents: phraseologies, superstitions, prejudices, and the "unquestionable truth" of tradition—transmitted patterns of behavior and of judging (this has nothing to do with value internalization through identification).

The tendency to identify external success, particularly material or physical achievement, with strength and value, hence, to see such success as desirable, produces not only a similar attitude in the child, but it also produces in him, more than in his disappointed and frustrated parents, a strong tendency to imitate the external manifestations of such "successful heroes' " behavior. When that imitation does not bring the expected success, disappointment will often find its expression in an almost paranoid resentment. (This has nothing in common with what Erikson[7] calls role-playing in adolescence.)

In this respect externalized parents differ from their children—the latter may, at least, have something to look for and live for, to become free of the restrictions that are imposed on them as long as they are young and dependent. The adults no longer have anything left but disappointment, resentment, and their restricted and restricting reality.

On the other hand, it is exactly this difference that explains why externalized children take over from their parents a kind of pragmatic attitude toward problem solving: they don't waste time on the "mere possible,"[19] on alternatives, on imaginations, and, least of all, on hypotheses, illusions, the "As-Ifs." But since every learning act is based on the legitimacy of such As-Ifs, it is the externalized parents' pragmatic attitude that indirectly accounts for their children's low level of readiness for formal thinking and learning. And to the extent that an As-If *is* admitted into the mental world of an externalized child, it takes the form of wild fantasies, which not only fail to enlarge reality compensatorily—as genuine fantasies often do—but also take the place of responsible thinking. Similarly, the parents' "pragmatic" attitude manifests itself in their own and their children's tendency toward methods of simplifying the solution of cognitive problems by non-differentiation, dichotomies, concretistic distortions. Or we can see reappear in children the parents' way of what we shall try to describe as "manipulative" rather than causal thinking.

IV. COGNITIVE PATTERNS IN SECONDARY RETARDATION

The Problem

We define effective thinking by the following abilities:
—To distinguish between essential and accidental properties;
—To recognize newness in spite of similarities with the known, and to react to it with curiosity and interest, which implies comparing new phenomena with those that are known in their, seeming or real, similarity and discovering their points of difference, in appearance and in essence (this is also called the ability to differentiate or the ability to avoid patterns of simplification);
—To select emerging associations according to the degree of their relevance in a specific context, that is, to think rationally, critically, and responsibly;
—To mobilize that same ability of rational, critical, and responsible thinking against prejudices, stereotypes, and patterns that may impose themselves on the individual in his cognitive and evaluational acts;
—To recognize and respect the intrinsic laws of every phenomenon, every action, every process;

—To "leave" the concrete for the sake of concept formation, without, however, losing contact with the former (one of the essential elements according to K. Goldstein,[19] of abstraction);
—To see simultaneously different aspects of a certain phenomenon or process.

The effectiveness of thinking is different from individual to individual, not only in its degree but also in its field of preference. (That is why we speak of academic, technical, or social intelligence[39], although it is evident that not every one of characteristics applies equally to each of the three forms of intelligence.) In the cognitive structure of the secondarily retarded child, we find specific deviations in each of these characteristics. An analysis of these deviations allows us to distinguish between him and the "normal" and also the feebleminded or neurotic child. My study on *Impaired Intelligence*[11] was devoted partly to such phenomenological distinctions and comparisons. On the following pages an attempt is made to summarize them, with emphasis on secondary retardation of the social and the cultural variety.

Insufficiencies in the ability to differentiate, in the learner's responsibility for his thinking-acts, and in rationality are the most important symptoms of the secondary retardation. Each one is a cluster of traits and tendencies and can also be defined, described, and analyzed in terms of each of those traits, as we shall try to show. But in order to complete the list of symptoms (or clusters), we must add two symptoms that are often treated as separate "units" but should actually be understood as accompanying (or being included in) the third one, insufficient rationality. These symptoms are: the secondarily retarded child's and, in fact, every externalized individual's tendency toward concretistic thinking and his inability to understand the meaning of "As-If."

Insufficiency of Differentiation

In secondary retardation we see an overall tendency to identify similarity with identity and dissimilarity with otherness. The child growing up under the externalizing conditions of poverty and neglect or of cultural value-ambiguity (see above, Section II) comes to experience himself not as a subject but rather as an object manipulated arbitrarily by his environment.

We call this cognitive weakness also: lack of distinction between the essential and the accidental properties of a phenomenon, an object, a process, or premature and wrong generalization. As such, it is the first sign of the externalized child's inability to think in abstract terms.

The less the ability to differentiate is developed, the more the individual tends to use dichotomization as a means of organizing his universe of facts. The absolute, instead of fulfilling its function as a value criterion, becomes a characteristic of reality as such (one absolute as opposed by another absolute, black against white, etc.). It provides the individual with a false feeling of security—which, in turn, is derived from the illusion of being capable of organizing, bringing order into, the multitude of realities, precisely with the aid of such simplifying dichotomies. This is lack of differentiation in its social variety.

In culturally conditioned secondary retardation, however, dichotomization supplies the externalized child, and particularly the externalized adult, not only with the illusion of being able to organize a heterogeneous and self-contradictory reality but also with the illusion of knowing absolute truth and value: "valid" is what is "mine" culturally, what is rooted in my group's past and patterns.

In both varieties, lack of differentiation fulfills a function altogether different from its meaning in the life of a normal or neurotic child, where it may be an indication of fatigue and inattention or a defense against doubt, a denial symptom, and as such may be rooted in conscious or unconscious, deep-lying identity conflicts, but where it does *not* reflect a cognitive pattern. (Hence also the essentially different approaches to dealing with the symptom in the various cases.)

Weakness or Responsibility

According to our first hypothesis, insufficiencies in differentiation and tendencies to use simplifying methods of organizing cognitive material, for instance by dichotomization, indicate the relative absence of an experience and feeling of being a subject of determination. This explains our second hypothesis: that the secondarily retarded child, in his developmental weakness and lack of self-confidence, does not feel responsible for his acts of thinking and learning.* His thinking is associative, his reactions to a teacher's questions actually are little more than reflections of "the first thought that emerges," by chance, often dictated by remembering some irrelevant previous learning or by following automatically another child's remark or answer. In other cases the emotional or affective nature of the learner's personal experience is clearly responsible for associative and faulty answers. Again in other cases they may be determined by repeating what the teacher has said before, though in another context.

So far, the presumed sources of associative answers refer in particular to the social variety of secondary retardation. But the child's overdependence on authority (authority of the teacher, the text, a tradition) is equally representative of the cultural variety; the child expects the answer to the teacher's question to be given by those who ask and "therefore" know the answer, or to be found in the sources they, the teachers, use. Dependence on authorities does not mean that their representatives are accepted out of trust, love, attachment, or even identification. They are fundamentally impersonal, hence also easily changeable. Dependence does not mean a personal relationship (which is always based on the presumption that only two subjects can relate to each other). This is obvious particularly in the cultural variety, where associations determining the pupil's answer are more often of a cultural than of a personal character, dictated by generally accepted patterns or stereotypes rather than by their personal transmitters.

Absence of genuine personal relationships between externalized pupils and their teachers does not exclude an inclination on the part of some of them to imitate the teacher's behavior.** Although *reinforcing* dependence on authority, imitation proves a stronger degree

---

*Later, when we shall deal with the methods of didactic intervention, we shall have to answer the question why the here analyzed pattern of insufficient responsibility as manifested in associative thinking and in overdependence on authority, does not contradict the there recommended "noninductive" method of teaching but, on the contrary, comes to justify it.

**An inclination that belongs to the "arsenal" of externalization and its well-known identification of heroes with values, particularly in the cultural variety.

of activity than simple dependence. But because imitation by definition refers to the external, the observable traits only and excludes all understanding of the essential difference between their meaning in an adult's and in a child's behavior, it increases the frequency of inadequate and irrelevant answers.

Insufficient Rationality

Readiness to react affectively to apparently "neutral" contents of learning and thereby to distort their meaning is a well-known behavioral and cognitive symptom of externalization and secondary retardation. Often it is included in the large group of nondifferentiation due to the interference of irrelevant associations, because affective reactions are of a very personal nature. And since they restrict the learner's autonomy, we can also include them in the second group, of lack of responsibility.

We prefer to see in affective reactions parts of a specific pattern, alongside stereotypes, prejudices, irrational preferences, and belief in the "magic of words." All of these elements have in common not so much *dependence* on uncontrollable forces (that is, heteronomy resulting in lack of responsibility), as they reveal a kind of *identification* with the "non-ego" as represented by these irrationalities.

In the social variety of secondary retardation, it is identification with or, better, passive intake of a frequently changing and never unequivocally defined family-truth that the child feels to be a protective as well as restrictive reality. In the cultural variety it is identification with a superior truth, and, therefore, intellectual failure caused by such affective and irrational identification is accompanied frequently by overcompensatory aggressiveness. It is much more difficult to correct cultural than social irrationality, as every teacher knows when he tries to replace meaningless "big words" by more "modest" and more reality-adapted terms: in social retardation "big words" are used because their chance of better fitting seems so much greater than that of rationally thought-through concepts (it is their "bigness" that explains their attractiveness).

In the cultural variety, on the other hand, not only stereotypes and prejudices but also bombastic or scientific-sounding words without meaning are used frequently when the user, adult and child alike, wants to make an impression as one who is at home in the new (basically rejected) culture and its contents. The externalized nature of this pseudo-adjustment is quite obvious. But it makes almost hopeless every attempt to bring about changes of attitude by didactic interventions. Only a few who, even as children, depend on such maneuvers of irrationality for their self-inflating relationships with the environment will be accessible to objective teaching-and-learning experiences.

Concretistic Thinking

When Jung[22] calls perception and intuition "irrational functions" (as against thinking and feeling), he identifies rationality with active and conscious intentionality. In this sense, concretistic thinking with its emphasis on examples rather than on concepts, on the present rather than on time-sequence, on manipulation of givens rather than on recognition of intrinsic laws of universal validity, is indeed irrational.

We prefer to treat this cluster of cognitive traits as a separate unit ("concretistic thinking") because the didactic interventions required to deal with these manifestations of secondary retardation essentially differ from methods of dealing with the distorting influence of affective elements.

Examples occur; concepts are formed. The conscious and unconscious resistance to abstraction proves lack of courage and flexibility, proves fear of the possible and clinging to a perceptively mediated reality. So formulated, the definition is valid for concretistic thinking in secondary retardation. In "normal" children, preferring the concrete to the abstract has a different meaning altogether—it is indicative of over-imagination; the examples do not occur but are chosen, mostly as symbols representing ideas and not as their substitutes.

Closely connected with this tendency is the secondarily retarded child's identification of reality with what is present. It is almost impossible for him to understand that absence is not identical with nonexistence but may indicate a state of potential existence preceding later "emergence" or "realization." While this restriction of the concept of reality is typical of the social variety, it means, in cultural retardation, an opposite tendency, namely that of attaching value to the past only and thereby conceiving of the present as a non-committing reality.

An abstract understanding of time means understanding it as a continuum in which each present has its past and its future, real, remembered or imaginable, irrespective of its "place" in that continuum. When we speak of a "limited time-consciousness" as one of the symptoms of secondary retardation and particularly of the secondarily retarded pupil's concretistic ways of thinking, we have in mind his tendency to isolate each period of time and see it as disconnected from any preceding or following, past or future "moments." This disconnection, which restricts time to the concretely experienced present only, blocks not only an adequate understanding of development, in the personal or the historical sense of the word, but also that of causal sequence and that of temporal relationships.

While this is a definition of the concretistic time-conception in general, we should add that in the cultural variety of secondary retardation another distortion of the time-concept takes place: here the past is understood to be the only "real" time, the present its interruption, and the future its certain return. This not only explains cognitive distortions of historical events and sequences but accounts also for social-adjustment difficulties in the life of the externalized child.

But not only in the conception of time does concretistic thinking distort the externalized child's thinking and learning processes; we find a similar distortion in the understanding of intrinsic laws, especially the connection between cause and result. Normally, the child at a certain age understands that connection as intrinsic, and at the same time experiences *discovering* intrinsic laws as intellectual challenge.

The cognitive structure of the externalized and secondarily retarded child is different. We have already pointed out (see Section III) that the paucity of such a child's early experiences of being treated as a subject in his own right (with his specific intrinsic laws)—in other words, that the prevalence of experiencing himself as being an object among objects manipulated by his adults—makes it difficult for him to adequately understand universal laws as intrinsic to reality, among them, first and foremost, the law of causal connection. He has little regard, we say, for such connections; everything is arbitrarily connected with everything else and can therefore be "brought about" by manipulating objects or events.

It may sound paradoxical, and yet we can say, that the weaker the externalized child's ego and the less structured his personality, the more he will believe in the weak ego's ability to determine outcomes by learnable manipulations. Or: the less differentiated he is, the more he tends to conceive of every phenomenon as being "a case in itself" (hence not subject to causal interpretation, though exchangeable by another "case in itself"). Here we may recall the externalized child's weak ability to differentiate (which we have suggested should be explained as a reflection of externalized man's conception of reality as a universe of want and the havable). This weakness manifests itself not only in his relative inability to discover the partial identity of different phenomena but also in a parallel inability to discover the partial identity of seemingly different phenomena. This relative inability is reflected in the presently discussed difficulties of such a child to discover and accept intrinsic laws of causal connection.

The difference between the two varieties of secondary retardation are not very marked in this symptom area, perhaps with one exception: in the cultural variety, the concretistic interpretation of causal relationships finds its most striking expression in the externalized child's inability to understand the laws of historical determination in terms of interaction between different factors or in terms of processuality. Instead, history is seen as a multitude of personal manipulations, and even nonhuman factors of determination tend to be misinterpreted through personification. In this way, the affective (mostly aggressive) character of causal determination is more in evidence in the cultural variety than the accidentality that is the favorite category of quasi-causal interpretation in the social variety.

Inability to Understand the As-If

Concretistic thinking excludes an adequate understanding of symbols, analogies, metaphors, personifications, and similar forms of indirect expression of meaning.

Symbols are used in literature, art, and religion, as well as in mathematics and science, as substitutes for, or allusions to, meaning, which they condense and intensify. This is why analytical psychology[23] maintains that the influence of symbols on psychic processes is much stronger than that of concepts.

To a lesser extent, the use of analogies or of personifications in literature or in various forms of verbal communication is justified as a means of stimulating thinking beyond the level of conceptualization.

But when teaching aims at strengthening rationality, an unambiguous translation of symbols, analogies, metaphors, and personifications into concepts is considered essential, and their As-If character must be recognized as clearly as possible.

This translation encounters difficulties in the teaching of externalized and secondarily retarded pupils. It is their very concretism that actually *decreases* the intensity of the effectiveness of these forms because they are unable to distinguish between the dimensions of reality and meaning. Symbols, analogies, metaphors, personifications, are seen as identical with their expressed contents, not their alluded meaning. Instead of intensifying meaning, they give those who use them a false feeling of importance, particularly in the cultural variety of secondary retardation. On the other hand, the concretistic distortion of their function still further decreases the externalized child's ability to differentiate and to imagine possibilities.

A normally developed child may reject symbols or analogies or personifications because they contradict the learner's perhaps exaggerated expectation of realistic exactitude. Such children may accept symbols in mathematics or sciences as abstractions from complex thought processes, in which case, however, they give expression to their preference for formal operations.

This brings us to the last and perhaps the most important point in our discussion of cognitive patterns in the secondarily retarded pupil, his inability to think "operationally."

This inability, which, according to Piaget,[30,31] is characteristic of the younger age group, is a persistent trait in the externalized individual's structure all though his life. It can also be defined as "narrow realism" (hence, again, its close connectedness with concretistic thinking). Conceptualization and readiness for formal operations (for instance, in the theory of grammar and syntax, in mathematics, in literary analysis), as opposed to deep-rooted needs for exemplifications and applications, characterize, as is well known, the "less intelligent" learner, wherever and in whatever variety we may find him.

What is the meaning of the term "problem" in his mind and in that of a normally intelligent child? The latter knows that a problem is defined as "his problem," as a permanent challenge to his mental initiative and activity; the former considers a problem to be part of an external reality, and it ceases to be a problem when "someone" has solved it. And as a rule, he knows only such problems (in contrast to problems in his day-to-day existence, which are rarely, if ever, solved). Hence, his all-pervading expectation of someone in authority (some person or some printed text) to "tell" him, to "give" him the solution, which is supposed to be known to that person or to be contained in that text. Problems, for him, are little more than expected answers in the disguise of questions. They increase his dependence on authority instead of his motivation to think.

But how is this issue connected with the pattern we are discussing here, and which we have called "inability to understand the meaning of As-If"?

The answer is that operational thinking always is a kind of "playing with ideas." The easier it is for us to use abstractions as representatives of realities, the nearer our thinking comes to the area of the fictitious. Every concept is an As-If, whether considered from a nominalistic or a realistic, from an Aristotelian or a Platonian viewpoint.

Hence we can sum up what we have said about the cognitive difficulties of secondarily retarded pupils in a somehow paradoxical way: they are much more "honest," they take their thinking assignments much more seriously, than their so-called normal or intelligent classmates. Operational thinking is not only defined as abstracting from reality; it also means readiness to regard reality as a "second-rate" reality only. This, however, means that resistance to, or rejection of, operational thinking in secondarily retarded pupils, although undoubtably detrimental to their social advancement, can also be interpreted, paradoxically, as a sign of their (primitive) loyalty to the universe of immediately experienced reality. But we must not forget that this form of "realism" is rooted in basic insecurity, whereas a similar rejection of thinking in normally or more than normally intelligent children indicates a conscious or unconscious fear of the universe of everything nonfactual.*

V. SECONDARY AND PRIMARY RETARDATION

Before going into a detailed analysis of the methods of rehabilitative teaching meant to restore the impaired potentials of secondarily retarded pupils, we must face the question every teacher is likely to ask: How can I teach such children in a heterogeneous class? How can their cognitive needs be met by certain teaching methods while others in the same class need different methods of teaching and learning?

One of the main differences between primary and secondary retardation is that in the latter, experience and environmental conditioning are much more decisive than organic factors. But since the risk of minor brain lesions is greater in poor families, in which most secondarily retarded children are born and raised,** organic factors, such as disturbances of homeostasis, hypermotility, and so on, are liable to impair these children's intellectual development; the organic factors increase the danger of primary retardation emerging at last in addition to symptoms of secondary retardation. This is the reason why we find in many cases of secondary retardation an admixture of symptoms of genuine feeblemindedness (in different degrees of severity). As a result, it is often difficult, if not impossible, to formulate an unambiguous diagnosis.

Seen from the outside, as it were, the main symptoms of primary retardation are almost identical with those of secondary retardation. But the differences are of the essence:

---

*Comparable to this weakness is resistance to intuitive synopsis of whole-contexts as reflected, for instance, in the ability simultaneously to see and to react to different aspects of a cognitive problem instead of separating them from each other and dealing with each aspect as such, consecutively.

**Poverty as well as disorientation due to transition from one cultural value system to another are often responsible for traumatic irregularities in the birth process.

—Inability to select associations according to their relevance in specific contexts indicates, in the genuinely feebleminded, a structural defect and is not the outcome of a kind of an enjoyable "addiction to chance.'

—The latter is not identical with automatism of reactions, which make the use of the term "result" preferable to that of "reaction" in the feebleminded.

—Dependence on the illusion of "knownness" has little in common with the truly feebleminded individual's perseverations or with his basic unfamiliarity with the world.

—In place of perseveration we find inconsistency in secondary retardation.

—Weakness of differentiation, as expressed, for instance, in dichotomization, is a form of organization, though a rather primitive and inadequate one, but does not indicate organically conditioned defects in polarization as in the feebleminded.

—Replacing causal interpretations by a tendency to manipulate objects or happenings in order to bring about certain results is not identical with the feebleminded child's ability to see any connection as causal.

—In feeblemindedness, in contrast to secondary retardation, we find little evidence of intentionality, not even in the form of inadequate ego-extension through personifications or of inadequate ego-strengthening through limitation or use of stereotypes.

These are some of the essential characteristics that permit some sort of differential diagnosis of the two forms of retardation. But let it be said once again: cases in which admixtures of primary retardation appear in the behavioral picture of secondary retardation are not infrequently found in a class in which most pupils are classified as secondarily retarded.

2
Rehabilitative Teaching

I. PRINCIPLES

Introductory Remarks

We define the aim of teaching underprivileged children and adolescents whose cognitive abilities have been impaired by certain social or cultural factors as: restoring those potentially normal abilities to their optimal level. We call this type of teaching, which is different from that applied to children with unimpaired intelligence, "rehabilitative teaching." Pragmatically, that is, in terms of social aims, the method we are going to describe and analyze in the present study can also be defined as an attempt to make possible true integration of students coming from different social or cultural backgrounds and differing in their actual cognitive performances.

Thus the basic presumption is, as we maintained at the outset of the first chapter, that environmentally caused, hence "secondary," retardation is reversible. Rehabilitative teaching aims to replace false security (as it expresses itself in the externalized child's concretism and dependence on the illusion of the unknown to be known) by a sense of genuine security. The latter may emerge as the result of the learner's encouraging experience that he is able to orient himself adequately in a complex world of similar and different phenomena, through his own power of differentiation and generalization. This experience is the only reliable basis of a feeling of true social equality.

We already have referred to the other, more pessimistic conception of the aim of teaching underprivileged, externalized, secondarily retarded children, that of compensatory education. It is based on the presumption that even environmentally caused, secondary, retardation is irreversible. The optimal achievement we can hope for, claim the advocates of this educational theory and practice, is to soften the social ill effects of inequality. The methods recommended include: specially adapted curricula, special textbooks and programs, simplified and simplifying methods of teaching (such as making maximal use of audio-visual aids, concretizations, and so on), providing a multitude of enjoyable activities and "events" of the social or the artistic variety, adding technical training in preparation for a productive life in society. All these are interventions compensating the underprivileged child not only for the damage inflicted upon him by a discriminating and unjust social reality but also for the absence or the weakness of the child's ability to think in abstract terms or to benefit from an academic study program.

In rehabilitative teaching, in clear contrast to the basic presumptions of, and the methods used in, compensatory education, the teacher is the central force in the process of change, the teacher who reacts to his individual pupils and who uses his interventions actively to direct and to correct their thinking and learning processes. These interventions are based on the conception of each answer, faulty as well as correct, as the outcome of a specifically determined thinking process, which we can only guess, never know or prove.* The teacher must know how to adapt his teaching acts not only to his pupils' first answers but also to the mental processes presumed to have produced them. In this way, he satisfies the two seemingly contrary needs of his secondarily retarded pupils, their need for feeling secure and protected by a reliable—though never authoritarian—teacher and their need for showing (controllable and controlled) initiative.

---

*Or, better, as we shall try to show later, the only way of proving the correctness or the justification of a presumed interpretation of a certain answer, particularly a faulty one, is through the pupil's reaction and response.

Noninductiveness

Several didactical conclusions can be drawn from this conception of the forms and functions of rehabilitative teaching, the first of which is: it must be noninductive. It is a widely accepted tenet of modern education that a good teacher is able to help his pupils find, through their own initiative and inductive activity, the correct answer to a question, the solution to a problem, the formulation of a law or a principle "resulting" from observable facts or data. Reading, observing, experimenting, discussing, and putting the thus collected "information" in the proper order are the pupil's activities through which he reaches his conclusions.

A teacher trained in the spirit of this educational philosophy (which is most clearly represented by the so-called discovery method) will find it difficult to take the opposite method seriously or even to examine the theoretical premises. Teachers usually feel inclined to consider any noninductive method of teaching to be evidence of a reactionary attitude, whereas they themselves are unable to subject their inductive methods to the test of a critical psychological analysis. (What, for instance, are the psychological preconditions of inductive thinking, such as the ability to recognize independent objectivity and yet have the courage to venture into subjective interpretation and into discovery of possible, and alternative, meanings? It is sufficient to raise this question to reach the conclusion that inductive thinking requires a mental structure essentially different from that of the secondarily retarded child.) What do we understand by the concept of noninductive teaching?

One of the real dangers inherent in the method of inductive teaching is that of associative diffusion in the nonselective question-and-answer game that takes the place of a genuine and well-organized class discussion when the group is one of secondarily retarded pupils. They may enjoy the "illusion" that they are "active participants" in the thinking processes leading to the discovery of the correct answer. But there is really nothing to justify this illusion. On the contrary, the danger of self-deception is much greater than the possible advantage of that naive feeling that the class "should have a good time."

Instead, the teacher must know how to pose his questions as meaningfully and as intentionally as possible, must know when to interrupt the flow of associative answers. He must know when they are irrelevant to the subject under discussion and to his intentions. He must know it by *giving* the correct answer, *formulating* the law or the principle as exactly as possible. He should not fear that this procedure will frustrate his pupils, since immediately after giving the correct answer (meant to provide the pupils with an experience of genuine security through the image of a reliable and "knowable" teacher), he will pass on to the *second* phase of noninductive teaching. *This second phase will be devoted to activating the secondarily retarded pupils' cognitive initiative.* What happens in this second phase?

Here, the teacher will ask questions such as: Why was my answer formulated as it was? What would have been wrong with it, had I formulated it differently? Why was the answer suggested by me more exact than some of those suggested by you? Which data and phenomena are covered by the suggested law or principle; which other facts or phenomena are *not* covered by them?

This way of activating the pupils' ability to "think through" the possible application—and that also means the implications of what has been learned—and thus to face the multitude of the knowable and the learnable, serves a different purpose: it is meant to help develop the ability to think differentially, and it will help activate cognitive responsibility no less than the inductive teaching method claims to do. On the contrary, discovering the correct answer, the expected law, principle, or solution, tends to remain within the narrow limits of formal operations only; whereas application initiated and guided by a teacher who knows exactly the definable aims of his teaching, will be much more significant, for it will be based on the trust and the belief in the existence of a discoverable, inner and consistent, order of reality, in an experienced regularity of events and phenomena to which the lesson refers.*

---

*It goes without saying that the answers suggested by the teacher must be formulated in simple terms and not with an overemphasis on abstraction. We shall try to exemplify our thesis later, in the chapter on the forms and functions of didactic as against scientific, "philosophical" definition.

Branching Out

Closely connected with noninductiveness is a second element of rehabilitative teaching—it is more reactive than structured. It is impossible to give the teacher exact instructions as to how to prepare and organize a lesson, and at the same time to expect him to be open and to react to the pupils' associations. This means that instead of being focused on a specific and well-defined part of the subject matter taught, *rehabilitative teaching must be ready to "branch out."*

It is a well-known rule in orthodox teacher training that the teacher should learn how to prepare "his" lesson* by first learning its contents, its "material," and then sticking to his organizational plan. True enough, *every* teacher, hence also the one engaged in rehabilitative teaching, must be well versed in the contents of his planned lesson; but at the same time, this content preparation does not necessarily reflect itself in the actual execution of the "prepared" lesson plan, at least not directly. It often happens, particularly in rehabilitative thinking, that the teacher will come to see, in the course of a specific lesson, a quite different, and mostly no less important, problem emerging through and in his pupils' reactions to this or that—seemingly irrelevant—detail of the "material-to-be-taught." The reasons may be their being preoccupied emotionally with a certain problem, which prevents them from concentrating on the purely formal (objective) aspects of the lesson subject.

Such "branching-out" may lead the class discussion into another section of the subject matter taught, a part that was dealt with earlier. It may also find its expression in comparing the meaning of a certain concept in a presently discussed field of knowledge with its meaning in other fields of knowledge. And it may mean enlarging on *a certain part* of a text, a psychological, a sociological, or a historical problem, to the detriment of the *totality* of the subject

*The fact that we use the word "his" (and not "their") lesson indicates a teaching relationship in which the student is little more than an object or, better, a vessel of reception and not a subject of partnership. This is an important point not only in any traditional theory of teaching but also, as we shall see later, in any attempt to prove scientifically the validity of the method here suggested; the reactive character of rehabilitative teaching also implies the possibility—and even probability—of change ("in the middle of the way," as it were). But in the absence of an unequivocal and irrevocable definition of the method to be employed, its achievements can hardly be evaluated objectively.

matter problem under discussion (such as a piece of literature, a "creation" with its intrinsic gestalt), if and where it becomes evident that the students' mind is more involved in the personal implications of such a "creation" than in the creation itself and therefore justifies the "deviation."

In the first case, the branching out may help develop the pupils' weakly developed memory in a nonrepetitive but context-related, that is, meaningful, manner; they may learn in this way not only to remember details learned but also to understand their changing meanings in different connections.

In the second case, deviation is meant to help strengthen the pupils' insufficiently developed ability to differentiate: if a certain concept (for instance, that of "law") appears once as civil or criminal law, formulated in law books, another time as a basic law in physics or in biology, derived by research students and scientists from the interpretation of observable sequences of facts, a third time as a means of understanding historical events (and so on), the pupils may come to avoid misunderstanding their learnings under the influence of wrongly applied associations.

In the third case, "deviation" actually means "limitation" (and not enlargement); it means: limiting the class discussion to one part and one aspect only of the subject matter taught because it is thought to suit the teacher's purpose when he wants to help rebuild and strengthen a certain cognitive function in his secondarily retarded pupils. (We shall later come back to discussing the subject matter-oriented teachers' often affective rejection of this kind of "instrumentalistic" teaching, which, in their eyes, proves disloyalty to the essence of the subject matter taught, for instance a piece of literature).

Another form of branching out is the logical consequence of a basic presumption in rehabilitative teaching, which can be formulated as follows: in secondarily retarded pupils' faulty answers, specific cognitive patterns rather than simply "errors" find their expression. The teacher should take his pupils and their patterns seriously even when they seem to be retarded, or, worse, stupid and "hopeless." He should see in each of them a subject, a person with his specific mental structure, rather than an object to be manipulated at will. Error proves thinking, and the teacher should know how to delay his reactions until he has asked himself and his pupils what "hides" behind their answers and reactions, what manifests itself in them (see Section IV in Chapter 1).

The teacher must know how to suggest to each of his pupils tentative (or alternative) interpretations of the presumed thinking process underlying his errors. He must also be prepared to pass from one suggested interpretation to another if the first one fails to produce reactions indicative of insight and a more adequate attitude toward the specific question or specific learning assignment.

Obviously, such a teaching attitude requires imagination and flexibility. It also requires training in different areas of human knowledge, during the period of basic studies, through in-service training, extension courses, and continuous guidance. (See later.*)

Neutralizing Affective Reactions

Part of the second principle leads to a discussion of the third principle of rehabilitative teaching: the teacher must be ready to neutralize affective reactions to certain learning contents that are

*In two essays (on the training functions of a university school of education and on the genuineness of value education), both included in a collection of papers published in Hebrew,[15] the concept of branching out has been analyzed in regular teaching and value education, as a means of guaranteeing genuineness in learning.

There is no contradiction between the meanings of the concept in regular and in rehabilitative teaching. In both cases, the aim is one: to increase the effectiveness of teaching through and toward internalization of learning. In both cases, the teacher must learn how to detach himself from the contents of his specifically prepared lesson. The difference lies in the fact that regular teaching uses the branching-out method mainly for purposes of value education, but does not lose its raison d'être when it remains focused on a specific content and does *not* branch out into adjacent or associatively connected topics. Regular teaching *need* not define itself as value education, since the very process of internalizing content-learning (and learned contents) is already an integral part and an effective means of developing the learner's consciousness of values, at least his awareness of, and understanding the meaning of, intellectual values. Moreover, the regular, and particularly the intelligent, pupil is *defined* as being able to advance, on his own, from *intake* of learning-contents to "perceiving" their meaning and to understanding the principles "expressed" by them. (And when he makes a mistake in it, he easily learns, with the help of his teachers and through additional learning, how to correct his mistakes.)

The secondarily retarded pupil, on the other hand, is defined as one who has difficulties in understanding the meaning of learned contents. For him, the very process of learning *is* already a value education, not only in the intellectual field of values but, *through* it, in all fields of human behavior. Hence, the vital need, in his case, for the branching-out method of teaching, which is meant to help the secondarily retarded pupil, with his typical distortion of cognitive categories, to see the overall meaning of each of his particular learning-contents, that is, their life significance beyond their subject-matter meaning.

liable to emerge in the learner and impede his learning activities.

Such neutralization requires didactic reference to the personal and emotional aspects of a specific learning problem. But it is essential for the teacher to relate himself to these aspects *not* in their individual but in their universal significance. Moreover, the teacher must take care to use exact definitions in every stage of the discussion as best he can: the more important and deep-reaching the personal implications of an objective problem with which he deals, the stronger must be the emphasis on a rational approach, particularly when they bear an affective (and not only an emotional) character. This means that neutralization is meant to weaken the distorting influence of affects on thinking and learning processes. Here, again, the teacher should be ready to base his confrontations and interventions not only on clearly expressed affects but also on the "mere" presumption of their presence and impact.

The term "neutralization" is not used here in the meaning with which it is used frequently in common language; it is *not* identical with "elimination." When we speak of "neutralizing pain," we mean "benumbing" or "relieving" it. This semantic misunderstanding arouses strong objection in many teachers and educators (who feel and define themselves as progressive) to the here-suggested method; they see in the intervening affects a dynamic and, often, constructive force.

But here a basic error lies in their dangerous identification of rationally definable feelings (emotions) with irrationally erupting affects. As long as they are unable to recognize this misconception of the essential nature of affects, they will be unable to understand the intention and the suggested practice of rehabilitative teaching, its basic presumption being that it is precisely the teacher's disregard for the existence and the intervention of strong affects that makes it impossible for the secondarily retarded pupil to think differentially and to take responsibility for objective learning processes and activities.

Other educators claim that the mental health of a secondarily retarded pupil is liable to be damaged, or at least threatened, precisely by bringing up affect-laden topics, and they therefore conclude that it might be preferable not to touch "explosive issues." I believe this fear is unjustified, though only when the teacher knows how to deal rationally with the personal associations emerging from a learning problem and how to relate to their presumed meaning in their universal (not, or not primarily, individual) meaning.

Conclusions

What are the implications of these principles of rehabilitative teaching? What is the teacher's role in it? To what extent do we give him the training and guidance he needs to fulfill his functions adequately? One conclusion is evident: whatever training he may have received before beginning to work with secondarily retarded pupils, he will always be in need of continuous in-service and guidance. Spontaneity and flexibility, imagination and ability to improvise, empathy and reactivity, but also the ability clearly to define and explain the concepts he uses—all these are undoubtedly desirable qualities in every good teacher, but they are indispensable in rehabilitative teaching. Hence the teacher's need for guidance in didactics, in personal and intellectual matters. But while an ordinary teacher is able to benefit from such guidance even when it is anonymous, that is, when it is channeled through general instructions or refresher courses in subject matter or method, the teacher of secondarily retarded pupils needs it through constant *personal* contact: spontaneity and flexibility require control when we want to avoid the danger of associative diffusion. And the relative frequency of severe behavior problems in such a class population means a threat to every teacher and limits his didactic freedom.

Noninductiveness, branching out, and neutralization, these three elements of rehabilitative teaching are not only difficult to learn and master, they are also liable to arouse justified fears in every teacher: will he be able to "complete" the officially dictated curriculum?

His pupils, too, will ask that question. The more cognitive abilities are restored, the stronger will be their affective rejection of every attempt on the teacher's part to use subject matter for the purpose of developing their differentiation and rationality (that is, "functionally"), and the more outspoken they will become in their demand for enlarging their *massa apperceptiva* through learnable contents. Emphasis on this "material" aspect of learning will be particularly strong when they can compare their achievements in this respect with that of students in parallel classes (with a "normal" curriculum).

The teacher's fears, the fact that he is constantly confronted with the difficult task of interpreting mental processes supposed to underlie his pupils' inadequate reactions, his own cognitive insufficiencies, and his own affective reactions to his pupils' behavior disorders—all require intensive guidance. The ideal form is that of discussing and analyzing his and his pupils' behavior, as it can be observed during a lesson. (Group discussions usually remain only superficial, although they may serve a useful purpose as a means for clarifying theoretical issues.)

The next section will be devoted to a detailed analysis of the teacher's functions and problems.

II. PRINCIPLES ONCE MORE

Noninductiveness

We have said that the first principle of rehabilitative teaching, noninductiveness, implies transmission by the teacher of correctly formulated answers to the very questions or problems he himself has raised. Here the question-and-answer period does not precede but follows the answer given. But in order to enable the teacher in that period to ask questions meant to help his pupils understand the main intention, that is, to teach them how to differentiate, he must know himself how to think logically and how to define his concepts as exactly as possible.

But it would be a mistake to emphasize only the logical or conceptual aspect of the method; the teacher is not a philosopher and should never even try to play that role (just as he should not try to play the role of a psychologist or a therapist). We shall come back later to discussing the essential difference between didactic and scientific definitions. But what we have in mind here is a problem much wider than that of exact definitions; it is that of teaching differentiation.

The teacher of secondarily retarded pupils must learn, with the help of as many examples as possible, to become as familiar with differentiation as he wants his pupils to be. After he gives them a feeling of basic security through formulating for them "the" (or, better, one of the alternative) answers, they are better prepared for the tasks of active thinking than before. It is then much easier for them to relate in a well-focused (not associative) way to questions such as: "Why is the answer I have suggested more correct than the one given by you?" "What would be wrong in my answer, had I left out, or changed, or formulated differently part of the question?" If more than one answer is possible, or if someone else has suggested another, equally correct answer, the question would be: "What is the difference between the two answers, and when is the one preferable to the other?"

After explaining the intention of an analogy, the teacher may suggest another comparison and then ask: "Why are both legitimate, what is emphasized through the first one, and what through the other?" In case an unsuitable analogy is used either by the author of a text or by one of the pupils, questions of "Why?" may be raised again, and the teacher must be ready to give the answer when he feels the danger of associative diffusion approaching.

It is useless, it may even be dangerous, to base the teaching of secondarily retarded children on "progressive programs," containing, as they do, elements of activation, experimentation, observation, and concretization (through the use of audio-visual aids, pictures, graphs, and so on). In their case, the teacher must take responsibility for translating everything that may have been expressed, observed, done, experimented with, concretized, into terms of meaning. Again, the use of exact formulation and definition is of the essence, and again, the teacher must not hesitate to help his pupils, even when it means "doing the job for them."

Under no circumstance should the teacher of these children consider it his main task to "entertain" his class, to give his pupils a good time, to make the learning process into something called "fun" (a word used often today in so-called compensatory education). All these things may be legitimate in regular classes, that is, in the teaching of intellectually well-developed children who do not need these doubtful inventions of "progressive education" (or, on the other hand, in the teaching of the feebleminded). For the millions of children *we* have in mind here, the most meaningful experience which the school can give them is that of being able to function well and productively in cognitive tasks requiring differentiation and responsibility, to function on a level comparable to that of the so-called normal children.

Our thesis contradicts a generally accepted tenet in the theory of teaching: most teachers feel that it is precisely the normally or more than normally intelligent child who expects and demands from him that he should be able to make each of his statements as exactly and as clearly as possible. The ordinary teacher is sensitive to, or even afraid of, those pupils' readiness and ability to find out with ease even a slight inaccuracy in his formulations. He knows, of course, this very attitude proves that for the success of their learning efforts they do not depend on his accuracy; they are able to correct him, whether he is at fault or they disagree with his formulations.

The secondarily retarded pupil, on the other hand, is liable either to take in and accept even a wrongly defined concept and, consequently, misunderstand the problem and its solution, or to feel confused when the teacher does not make clear enough an answer, a solution, or a concept. It means that the importance of exact definitions and formulations is much greater in rehabilitative than in ordinary teaching. The former is much more difficult than the latter, requires much more preparation and responsibility, precisely because underprivileged children so much more depend on the teacher.*

In this context, two questions are likely to be asked: whether the here-discussed part of the noninductive method does not contradict one of the basic aims of rehabilitative teaching, the aim of counteracting the secondarily retarded pupil's tendency to depend on authority, in this case represented by the teacher's "transmitted" formulations, and whether the method can also be applied to mixed groups, to heterogeneous classes.

There is little danger that the child's dependence on authority is increased by a teacher who "transmits" his answers (instead of "producing" them, step by step, inductively, through using the

---

*When we analyze the ordinary teacher's motivations and fears, we are likely to find that he is more concerned with his image in the pupils' eyes than with their objective needs. This is one of the reasons why experience in ordinary teaching often is more of a liability than an asset for rehabilitative teaching. We shall deal later with the complex problem of training and of attitude change when a teacher decides to work with secondarily retarded children.

question-and-answer method) and immediately afterward proceeds to much more complex demands—to compare different answers with each other, under a variety of criteria, to recognize the limits of the suggested answer's validity, to experiment, as it were, with changing conditions. The mental effort demanded for these purposes far outweighs the danger there may be in the initial receptiveness of the learner. To some extent, this answers our second question as well—accuracy in definitions and explanations surprisingly proves to be advantageous didactically in a heterogeneous class. Everyone knows the objection raised when teaching in so-called integrational groups is suggested, groups in which not only children from different social and/or cultural backgrounds but also children of different levels of formal or abstract thinking are instructed jointly: that it is almost impossible to give the intellectually disadvantaged student an equal chance to participate productively in a lesson conducted in accordance with the question-and-answer method. He will always be slower than the "normal," the "advantaged" child with his high degree of mental mobility and quickness. He will, therefore, seldom if ever enjoy the experience of being able to compete successfully with others, that is, the experience of equality.

This applies also to questions meant to produce definitions. But when the emphasis is less on defining concepts than on defining nuances, on justifying the choice of certain words and formulations, *knowing* the correct answer will not be sufficient. Nor will quick adaptation without depth help the "advantaged" child prove his superiority in this task situation, no more than will that intellectualistic sophistication which so often characterizes his cognitive attitude. The teacher must also be ready to use inaccuracies in the formulation of such apparently sophisticated answers (or disregard for certain human or social aspects with which the child may not be familiar), in order to help the "disadvantaged" child see the objective limits of displayed superiority, and thus gain confidence in himself, with or without the teacher's support.

It has been our experience that mere coexistence of pupils of different social backgrounds and different levels exercises little integrating influence (notwithstanding the seeming evidence of it in certain statistical studies such as that of Coleman).[6] The advocates of this form of integration claim that the example and the daily experience of the ways in which "normal" children function lifts up, encourages the disadvantaged, liberates potentials, brings to the fore hidden abilities, at the beginning through imitation, later through internalization of their modes of operation. On the basis of our experience in the field of teacher guidance, we have come to a different conclusion: the "disadvantaged" child's vital need of experiencing potential equality with his "disadvantaged" classmates requires active interventions on the part of the teacher. When teaching in a heterogeneous class, he must know how to use the principles of noninductive teaching (as outlined here and exemplified later) to demonstrate the objective difficulties inherent in every cognitive operation; he must also know how to demonstrate the disadvantages inherent in the world of experiences and in the cognitive structure of the so-called normal child when it comes to a certain type of question and problem, the answer to which requires, for instance, life experiences that are often alien to him.

(Thus, the essentiality of a specific expression in a piece of literature may be understood much more adequately by a child less inclined to abstraction than by his normally intelligent classmate. But in order to bring this difference to the consciousness of both pupils, the advantaged and the disadvantaged, the teacher must again be ready to offer an abstractly "exact" definition of what the latter wanted to express. We should not forget that the conceptual and the existential adequacy of definitions and interpretations are *not* one and the same. Here, again, the central role of the teacher in noninductive teaching, particularly in a mixed group, becomes evident, and this not only for the sake of the pupil in need of rehabilitative teaching but also for the normally functioning who may be in need of discovering another dimension of meaning.)

Teaching based on such presumptions and principles puts the teacher under a heavy obligation: in this case preparing himself for a lesson is not identical with what we are accustomed to call "preparation for the subject matter to be taught." Here, the preparation for the psychological aspects, presumed (but never known) to be implied in a certain teaching assignment, requires not only isolating critical concepts and defining them as exactly as possible, comparing with each other alternative definitions, but also imagining possible difficulties and misunderstandings, recognizing aspects that are likely to be neglected as the result of an exclusively formal (logical) approach to defining the concept and the content under question, and other aspects that are apt to be overlooked under the influence of affective elements.

Here we come to the last point of relevance in a discussion of the noninductive method. We have emphasized, in various contexts, the importance of exactitude in defining concepts and ideas precisely in rehabilitative teaching. On the other hand, nothing would be further from the truth than identifying definition in its didactic meaning with definition as it is used in scientific research. We have already mentioned that teachers should not play the role of philosophers. There exists a difference in principle between didactic and scientific definitions: the scientist *bases* his research on defining his concepts and his hypotheses, since this is his way of guaranteeing optimal congruity between his methods and findings, on the one hand, and his research purposes, on the other. The teacher, on the other hand, *accompanies* the formulation of teaching aims as well as his suggested answers and solutions by optimally exact definitions. But these definitions not only must be partial and preliminary only, it is *desirable*, from a didactic point of view, that they be partial and preliminary.

We should bear in mind that rehabilitative teaching is not only noninductiveness (including, as it does, giving definitions to the pupil before analyzing their implications and applications), it is also branching out. We shall try to explain the meaning of that concept later in this section. In the area of definition, the branching-out character of teaching finds its main expression in the way teachers and pupils together (that is, through interaction) supplement the initially suggested definition with the help of the material they bring up reactively. In this way, the original definition grows and "expands," until it reaches its optimal form and formulation (optimal from a didactic viewpoint).

There is another way of approaching our problem: defining means identifying and verbalizing the essential characteristics of a certain phenomenon (object, process, property, concept, approach, attitude), emphasizing the necessary as against the possible elements. Thus, defining prepares differentiation, particularly between similar yet different givens. It helps the learner, the researcher, the actor to orient himself in the multitude of phenomena that he encounters in his learning, his research, his activities. This orientation is sometimes called "understanding," though it actually does not do more than prepare the ground for deeper penetration into the meaning of the defined phenomena. The same cognitive aim can also be attained by the use of exemplifications, that is, of finding and describing as many examples as possible, each illustrating a different nuance of a certain phenomenon. Most people, adults and young alike, thus learn how to "find their way" in the bewildering multitude and multiplicity of meanings, called "reality," and only a few need definitions for this purpose. As a result, most people find it extremely difficult to define "their" phenomena, although this difficulty in no way limits the effectiveness of their activities, practical or theoretical.

In this respect, the teacher is no exception; even if he knows his definitions, he does not necessarily teach "through" them. Exemplifications and explanations are likely to establish closer connections than definitions between the learner and the facts of learning, between his facts and their explicable meaning (which, as a result, will in the end turn into understanding). Defining in the didactic, not the scientific meaning of the term *accompanies* exemplification, though its primary function in teaching and particularly in rehabilitative teaching is to develop and to strengthen accuracy of expression, to prevent the use of words without meaning, to avoid distortion of learning contents. Didactic definition is much less content-oriented than it is function-oriented; even the optimal accuracy of defining concepts or contents, which, we said, is an essential element in noninductive teaching, is not only compatible with but actually *requires* exemplifications for the purposes of comparison and differentiation.

Later, when we shall describe "class events" and lessons in order to show the ways in which the here-discussed principles of rehabilitative teaching can be and are being applied to the teaching *practice*, we shall see yet another difference between scientific and didactic definition: while it is essential in scientific definitions to aim at completeness and comprehensiveness, the opposite is characteristic of didactic definitions—they grow and expand in the interaction between the teacher and his secondarily retarded pupils. The addition of elements, in reaction to the pupils' reactions to a "partial" definition, makes the latter meaningful. It is this dynamic character of definition in noninductive teaching that serves its purpose: developing and strengthening differentiation.

Branching Out

We have mentioned four varieties of deviation from the topic to which a specific lesson may be devoted: into some other part of the same subject matter, which may have been taught previously; into other fields of knowledge, in which a certain concept or idea presently dealt with may appear in different connotations; into details of one aspect only of the topic under discussion, details chosen (though it may mean neglecting the "totum" of that topic) because the teacher considers them relevant for developing an important cognitive function in his secondarily retarded pupils; and into discussing a certain mental pattern that, the teacher believes, has produced a faulty answer.

The first two of those varieties of branching out are self-explanatory. We have said the first one helps recall a subject matter already learned, though in a different context. In this way, not only will the memory, which is known to be structurally weak in secondarily retarded children, be strengthened and developed; the children will also learn how to distinguish between knowing and learning, that is, between intake and internalization. They will find through experience that the mere fact of having dealt with a certain matter does not mean remembering or understanding its significance, and that true remembering requires comparing with each other matters learned in changing contexts, and under changing viewpoints.

Theoretically, all this is well known to every teacher. But he often forgets the particular importance that attaches to the cognitive handicap in the learning process of the pupils we have in mind here: their resistance to "coming back" to what seems to them to be known because they remember having learned "about it" (not learned "it") is very strong; their need for always "new" (that is, additional) subject matter is but a different expression of their externalized conception of learning, against the background of their "illusion of knownness." Hence, the importance of this form of branching out into already learned material as an integral part of rehabilitative teaching.

It should be added that the form of branching out does *not* mean "losing time" or even abandoning the context of the specific learning assignment that the teacher may have chosen. Under no circumstances should he try to make his pupils recall past learning (which would indeed mean wasting precious time). He should give them in a brief summary the essence of past learning and add, *in his own words*, an equally short explanation of the difference between the two approaches to the same subject matter, the one in the past and the other today (our presumption being that remembering past learning is meaningful only to the extent that the "illusion of knownness" is weakened if not destroyed).

The same applies in principle to the second variety of branching out, into different areas of knowledge in which a presently used concept or idea appears in different meanings. We have mentioned the concept of "law" and its different meanings: in *civics* (the civil and the criminal law as laid down in law books to be consulted and interpreted by lawyers and judges in court cases); in *biology* (the Mendelian laws, the laws of phylogenetic and ontogenetic development); in *history* (the laws as interpretational constructions in different schools of historiography); and similarly, though in each case having different meanings, in *physics*, in *mathematics*, in *logics*, in *philosophy*.

Needless to say, the choice of examples from other areas of knowledge depends on the age and level of experience of the students. But the most important point to make is that the formulation of differences of meaning should fulfill two purposes at one and the same time: it should make the learner aware of the need for thinking about any subject of his learning in configuration with the condition in which it is embedded, as it were, hence also as changing its meaning when conditions are altered; and it should satisfy the secondarily retarded pupil's needs even more than those of a "regular" pupil. The latter, we have already said, is much more at home, and much more easily "plays," with concepts than the former. The former, in his inability to think in terms of the As-If, rather than the latter, in his readiness to use concepts "at will," needs those added examples offered in the branching-out method of rehabilitative teaching.

But the method will be legitimate only when the teacher using it knows how to avoid the danger of "gliding" into an adjacent field of knowledge and thereby losing contact with the lesson subject from which he started out. All deviations should be well-defined and limited in scope to make possible a quick return to the main topic, again by way of emphasizing points of similarity and difference (just as the branching out was based on comparing a detail of the lesson taught with associatively connected details of other subject matters).

The two other varieties of branching out are not subject-matter oriented. In the third variety, the teacher decides to isolate a certain aspect of a story or a poem, a biology problem, a historical event, a hero, a movement, and so forth. Every curriculum is, of course, selective, and the selected parts should be representative of a larger number of nonincluded subject-matter items (although in most cases their representative character is far from being self-evident). But in rehabilitative teaching, it is not so much the selection of certain items in favor of others, that determines its character; it is the emphasis placed by the teacher on a specific idea (more or less arbitrarily isolated from the whole-context) through which he tries to develop and strengthen the understanding of a certain concept or a certain cognitive function, a function he considers to be essential for the rehabilitation of his secondarily retarded pupils' cognitive abilities.

Thus we can speak of a functional approach to teaching. Many teachers object to it although they may be convinced that they are faithful to the principles of rehabilitation. There exists a difference in principle between primary loyalty to the aim of restoring impaired cognitive abilities and primary loyalty to the formal aspects, for instance, of teaching literature, a story, or a poem.

Isolating a certain idea because of its presumed but definable personal relevance for the disadvantaged pupil may perhaps mean restricting the scope of literary (formal) analysis, which is still considered by many to be the essence and final aim of literature teaching. But it will, on the other hand, help make that specific creation much more relevant for the learner; he will learn how to associate it with a specific cognitive difficulty that may distort his interpretation not only of that creation but of others as well. And still more important: the child will learn how to apply his learning to problems of daily concern. There exist, of course, alternatives to each aspect chosen and isolated; but all of them have personal relevance in common (and the same is true for all, though primarily the humanistic, subject matters).

This leads us to a discussion of the fourth variety of branching out. It has *in common* with the third one: emphasis on the personal aspects, in this case of cognitive patterns, presumed to be responsible for faulty answers. It *differs* from it, however, insofar it is focused on thinking processes; and any transfer to the area of day-to-day contexts may be an outcome (over a prolonged period of time) of life experience and almost always unconscious application, but not of intentional directives built into the very teaching process by the teacher.

We have mentioned (pp. 18f.) insufficiencies of differentiation, responsibility, and rationality, concretistic thinking and inability to understand the As-If, as the main clusters of symptoms that indicate secondary retardation. We have made a point of differentiating between secondary and primary retardation (pp. 28f.), by emphasizing the distorting intentionality of the former as against the structural deficiencies of the latter. To what extent, we ask now, should the teacher deviate from the specific topic of his lesson into referring to this or that pattern of distorting thinking?

The answer is: to the extent that he is genuinely concerned with his pupils' thinking processes more than with the integrity of the subject matter he teaches; or: to the extent that he is convinced of the priority of the "subjective" approach as a precondition of objective, formal thinking and understanding. But what we have said before, about the need never to lose contact with the subject matter under discussion, holds good here as well: branching out into brief references to the presumed sources of faulty answers does not *contradict* teaching the essentials of a specific subject matter, but *supports* it. A few examples may help us to understand this point.

When the teacher has reason to believe that associative interferences of personal or cultural patterns with a thinking process make it difficult for the child to understand the essence of a story or, for that matter, even of a mathematical problem, he must give him to understand that he is aware of the determining force of that pattern. Thus, a pupil could not understand any explanation offered by his math teacher that $14 - (-14) = 28$. He rejected the solution as "unjust." The teacher reacted by saying that he could understand his resentment and protest against what seemed to be discrimination in favor of the positive (that is, in the boy's value system, the successful, the privileged). But he was sure the boy was well aware of the fact that mathematics had nothing to do with social injustice. The boy smiled and thereby acknowledged that the teacher's interpretation had been correct.

Some pupils defined "courage" by quoting the manifestations of courage in the hero of a story. The teacher brought up other expressions of courage, in other persons, different in many respects from the hero of the story. He even included one of the pupils who had recently shown courageous behavior of an altogether different type (by admitting responsibility for some mischief in which the whole class had been involved). What common elements could be found in the different behaviors mentioned? She showed them in this way the assets and liabilities of concepts *versus* descriptive examples: that a concept is economic but omits differences in details. When the discussion returned to the story, the depth of differential understanding in most of the pupils was remarkable.

We have mentioned the various ways in which a secondarily retarded child tends to simplify his cognitive problems: by mechanical dichotomization, by overlooking nuances, by using "empty words" or stereotypes. Here, it is the teacher's task to show his pupils that differentiation is worthwhile because it helps discover new aspects that are bound to be lost as the result of simplification. A few examples follow.

Man's inability, objectively to judge his nation's enemies is a universal weakness, an affective limit to his intelligence. But normally functioning children are able to accept relativism, at least in theory, in order to harmonize nationalistic with humanistic values. The secondarily retarded child does not even see the contradiction between his knowledge of something he may have learned, perhaps the beauty or the wisdom of a foreign culture and its creations, and his affective rejection of that culture as something "belonging to the enemy." In such a case, branching out into a discussion of prejudices and stereotypes in general is of the essence: the pupils must be helped to recognize first and foremost negative elements in the value system of their own group and culture, perhaps elements that their families reject as evidence of discrimination, alien, or frustrating. Another form of deviating from the original topic of the lesson is the use of different criteria of judging. What does it mean, for instance, when we call a certain piece of "primitive" art "beautiful"? In order to learn differentiation and to give up his methods of simplification the pupil must learn as much as possible about the coexistence of different value areas and criteria.

We have mentioned the secondarily retarded child's over-dependence on authority as indicative of his lack of self-confidence and his need for unambiguous solutions. One of the didactic interventions best suited to weakening this irrational dependence on authority is for the teacher to react to its manifestations by branching out into alternative interpretations, as they may be offered by sources or persons of equal authority. Another means is, to show his own doubts and hesitations; again another one, to bring up a text difficult to understand or a problem in sciences not yet solved.

In all these ways he actually proves the legitimacy of uncertainty. He must, therefore, be prepared for reactions, such as: "Why study, if in the end we are told by you that even you, the teacher, do not know the answer?"

Here, once again, the importance of the principle of noninductiveness becomes evident. We have tried to show that, according to this principle, the teacher *does* give the answer as clearly defined as possible. In other words: the attacks on the pupil's over-dependence on authority, as suggested here, should be added carefully and not too frequently to the experience of reliability (of the universe of facts *and* of the teacher)* combined with that other experience, namely, that he, the pupil himself, is able to examine the validity of the answer given by the teacher (see p. 42).

We recall what we have said about possible distortions of causal thinking by preferring manipulation to processuality: events are connected not in a relationship of causes leading to results (that is, of

---

*We should not forget that dependence on authority is weakened by each of the other didactic means of rehabilitative teaching as well; increased differentiation and rationality also contribute to weakening overdependence on authority.

gradual process) but are interpreted as the effects of arbitrary interventions (manipulations). Had the latter been different, the result—for instance, in history or in biology or in human development—would have been different (automatically).

Here, the importance of branching out again is clearly evident. When teaching biology, the teacher must be ready to give examples from other areas of knowledge, such as history or psychology (and vice versa). One pupil explained phototropism as forcibly produced by the sun. He even suggested that something must be done to counteract this undesirably violent interference, to protect the "weak" plant. The answer shocked the teacher, particularly because he had explained before, and in detail, the chemical processes responsible for the phenomenon. He therefore decided not to return to his previous explanation, but to branch out into another field, history. He mentioned the essential difference between the causal effect of natural or economic processes and that of planned human intervention. Such intentionality, he said, can be attributed to human minds only, not to natural bodies such as the sun or, better, to such neutral forces as light (see p. 48).

We can also interpret this kind of branching out as an attempt to reinforce thinking in terms of cause and effect. Quoting an example from another field of knowledge is sometimes more convincing than adducing additional arguments from the subject matter under discussion.

And, finally, let us make a few remarks referring to one of the essential symptoms of distorted thinking, the secondarily retarded child's difficulty in distinguishing between the dimensions of reality and the As-If. We do not intend to repeat here what we have already mentioned about the child's failure to understand analogies or symbols. Still more important is his inability to understand the implications of formal thinking and its cognitive value, particularly in such fields as geometry, climatology, or grammar.

Formal thinking, by definition, excludes exemplification—which is why it cannot be made meaningful to a secondarily retarded child as long as his cognitive abilities remain restricted. In other words, adequate learning in these fields of knowledge is possible only *after* rehabilitative teaching has achieved success. And yet the curriculum does contain subject matter taken from these areas in which the secondarily retarded pupils are known for their weakness and their frequent failures. Thus the subject matter is considered to be an instrument in its own right to rehabilitate cognitive potentials* and, in particular, to restore the ability to understand the As-If character of formal operations.

It is in these parts of the curriculum that the principle of branching out does *not* apply (in clear contrast to practically all other areas of knowledge and learning, in which the As-If character of, let us say, personifications, metaphors, analogies, or symbols can be made comprehensible through the here-described methods of rehabilitative teaching).

We mentioned above (p. 34) that branching out from the original context and purpose of a planned lesson into a discussion of the cognitive patterns possibly underlying a faulty answer requires not only much imagination and courage on the part of the teacher but also readiness to pass from one suggested interpretation to another one, should the first (tentative) interpretation fail to elicit proper reactions in his pupils. We shall give a concrete example of such flexible branching out in the second part of our study, when we shall describe the course of lessons. We shall see then also how this type of "deviation," though initially caused by a pupil's faulty answer, is related to all pupils.

Another issue, closely connected with the here-analyzed element of rehabilitation, is also mentioned above (on p. 50), the fact of many teachers' affective objection to what they call lack of loyalty to the spirit and wholeness of the creation or of the problem taught. Most outspoken in this objection are literature teachers. They know, of course, that loyalty to the spirit of a creation does not contradict differences in its possible interpretations, nor does it contradict personal preferences. But their emphasis nevertheless is on objectivity and inner discipline, on the efforts made to penetrate through the texts into their intrinsic essence and meaning.

Here it seems justified to ask: does "loyalty to the spirit of a context" find in these attitudes more convincing evidence than in the teacher's and the students' courage to express individual convictions in differential (and often alternative) interpretations? More than in

*See, for instance, the illuminating paper on geometry teaching by Mrs. Yael Shefi, in reference [14].

their imagination, when they dare to use even facts of history or of biology, even mathematical laws, to arrive at their "speculative" discoveries?

In literature teaching, the question should be formulated differently. Since every piece of literature has different meanings and allows for different interpretations, we ask the following two questions: (a) Does there exist a hierarchical order of possible interpretations according to their degree of nearness to the author's presumed intention and according to their degree of inner consistency? Is the teacher able to discover this hierarchical order on his own or with the help of those among accepted commentators, with whom he, the teacher, decided to agree? (b) Does the teacher have the right to prefer one interpretation to another on the basis of *didactic* considerations of the benefit his pupils may derive from his preferred interpretation for the development of their cognitive abilities or their personality?

Those who ask the first question feel responsible primarily to contents and values; those who ask the second question consider contents or values to be instruments more than aims in themselves. The first tend toward absolutistic, the second toward pragmatic, interpretations of their functions as teachers.

Suppose a certain poem gives expression to the tragic nature of life ending in death. The specific problem through which this existential tragedy is exemplified is that a child's love for his country may lead him, when grown up, into death for his homeland. The same is true for the children in the enemy country. Both enjoy life today, both admire their country's beauty, both may die one day, because of their love and identification.

In a regular class, the tragic nature of life as an existential problem may be emphasized, while the tragic nature of national identification is shown to be an example only. In rehabilitative teaching however, other functions take preference: developing the secondarily retarded child's concept of time and of the causal connection between present and future; strengthening his understanding of the meaning and function of analogies or symbols; protecting him against the danger of using stereotypes or of falling victim to phraseologies; helping him to think rationally. It would seem that, to attain these aims, it is essential to branch out from the central idea of the poem (its existential aspect) to the periphery of the example (here the national-identification aspect), because of its greater degree of realistic significance.

To sum up: It is essential for the teacher to be aware of the multitude of meanings to be found in a specific piece of literature. He should be able to understand not only the *existence* of different aspects (hence also alternative approaches to teaching, say, a certain piece of literature), but also the *hierarchical order* in which the different aspects relate to each other. However, when this awareness is reached, choosing and emphasizing one aspect only or a number of applications (or actualizations) are equally essential, at least in rehabilitative teaching with its principle of branching out. (By the way, every teacher should remain aware of the fact that even in a most comprehensive analysis—one usually heavily laden with formal elements—his teaching, in a regular class, is bound to be selective, hence subjective.)

Neutralization

Most secondarily retarded pupils come from socially and/or culturally deprived families. In the first chapter we briefly analyzed the essence and the causes of the social and the cultural varieties of cognitive deficiencies (see pp. 7f.). In that connection, we mentioned, though in passing only, the concept of contamination, meaning inadequate separation of concepts from feelings. It is in the light of this contamination that the third element of rehabilitative teaching becomes understandable and meaningful, that of neutralizing affects (p. 36).

Feelings of being discriminated against by society or by fate and reactions of aggressiveness and envy or inferiority feelings and indolence are parts of the family climate in which these children grow up. Hence the frequency of affective associations interfering with the learning process. We see their results in what we are used to calling weakness of motivation for learning that does not lead immediately to the experience of its usefulness, that is, for learning assignments that require an ability to plan ahead and to think in abstract terms. No less affective is the parents' lack of cooperation with, or their open rejection of, the value-alien school. Or the pupils' tendency both to resent success of others and to interpret their own failure as proof of injustice. Affects of aggressiveness, fear, inferiority are responsible for many absurd distortions of contents, distortions usually accompanied by particularly strong affective involvement. Or even for a generalized rejection of the establishment as such, hence also of the school as a representative of that establishment.

These affects exercise their restrictive and distorting influence on cognitive processes irrespective of whether the children are placed in heterogeneous (mixed) or homogeneous classes. Personality factors will determine the "choice" of their negative reactions, aggressiveness and resentment in one case, inferiority feelings or despair and withdrawal in others. But the class environment is a reinforcing factor and, as such, of equal importance; it finds its main expression in a tendency of secondarily retarded children to reject the methods of rehabilitative teaching as proof of discrimination. In a homogeneous class, they may resent being considered inferior and therefore in need of special teaching methods; in a heterogeneous class they may react to the success of others as well as to their own failure by "giving up." That is why we say that personality factors and class environment are liable to reinforce each other in their restrictive and distorting effects.

We shall deal again later with the question of class composition and its bearing on curriculum planning and method selection. Here we intend to mention another aspect of that problem, that of extrinsic, mostly political, factors reinforcing the families' and the pupils' affective objections to the introduction of differential teaching methods. Spokesmen of the underprivileged as well as research students have claimed they can prove that the potential abilities of these underprivileged have better chances to develop fully in mixed ("integrational") than in separate and homogeneous groups. Others have added the well-known arguments against the distorting influence of prejudiced low expectations on the individual student's achievements. (Some even claim that "positive prejudices" are likely to produce better achievements.[32])

Even without taking into account the political, often demagogical nature of arguments in favor of integration as a *means*, not an aim, of bridging the social gap, we should remain aware of one rather disputable element in defining the concept of integration. We mentioned this element, pluralism, in the first chapter. It cannot be emphasized often enough that when the concept is transferred from its original area of application (cultural pluralism) to the area of social achievement and social status, it not only loses its raison d'être but is likely to turn into an indicator of reactionary attitudes (perpetuating inequality under the pretext of tolerance).

In teaching, its equivalent is called "individualization." As long as the latter is used as a method of teaching only, it is indeed an intrinsic part of every good teaching. But it would be dangerous to conclude that individualized teaching prepares all the pupils for different vocational functions of equal social value, and that it therefore solves the problem of inequality and social gap. Individualized teaching starts out from the *actuality* of each pupil and tries to develop his "given" abilities to their optimal level; it does not aim at restoring his potential abilities and does not reserve judgment as to his future career until such restoration has been achieved (or not). In particular, individualized teaching does not try to develop the ability to think in abstract terms, since it does not give preference to abstraction and to operational (formal) thinking (just as pluralism does not see in them preferable functions, in spite of the fact that access to high-status positions and respected achievements depends on their availability).

Individualized and rehabilitative teaching have one tendency in common: to bring each pupil to a point where he can feel that he is actually or potentially equal with others, although he differs from them in the *type* of his achievements. But rehabilitative differs from individualized teaching in practically every other aspect: it emphasizes potential equality in the major cognitive functions and not actual equality on the basis of objective achievement in different activity areas (irrespective of their prestige value in society); it emphasizes elimination of affective factors as possible sources of restriction and distortion of thinking; it emphasizes the supreme role of differentiation and rationality in the child's learning. To the extent that we find in it individualization, the latter takes the form of "following" each individual pupil with his specific cognitive patterns, supposed to be responsible for specific faulty answers.

We now return to discussing the concept of neutralization, when an affect-laden association emerges in a faulty or inadequate answer given by a student. It is not at all easy for the teacher to react naturally to such answers. Not only must he know much about his externalized and socially or culturally retarded pupils' family backgrounds and their culture-conditioned value systems (and about their deep-rooted disappointments and resentments, fears, and unrealistic expectations); he must also be ready and able to relate critically to the manifold expressions of personal involvement. We have added the word "critically" on purpose, since we do not accept as educationally valid the idea of "unlimited acceptance"— understanding the causes and dynamics of strong personal involvement in a stereotype, a traditionally transmitted pattern, a culture-sanctioned prejudice does not make it respectable. On the contrary, it only comes to prove the need for a critical analysis of that pattern, stereotype, or prejudice.

This is part of the *neutralization* process. We have already pointed out in several places that there exists a basic difference between teacher and therapist. Both come across affective expressions of fear and guilt, of aggressiveness and resentment, of inferiority feelings and shame, following conflicts of ambivalence or alienation, following experiences of discrimination or failure. But the therapist, at least the one who believes in the value-free nature of therapeutic relationships and interventions, tries to help his patients give expression to their affects in order to "get rid" of them. The teacher tries to help his pupils, at least those among them whom we call secondarily retarded, to become aware of alternative views.

The main tools the teacher uses for this purpose are comparing and defining: comparing with each other customs and habits of various ethnic subgroups, defining advantages and disadvantages of achievement and nonachievement; comparing with each other personality traits according to their assets and liabilities; judging events or attitudes according to different criteria and defining the latter.

In these respects neutralization resembles differentiation in general, though it refers only to affect-laden situations as reflected in the pupils' reactions and therefore is bound to encounter much stronger objection than differentiation in general. How can the teacher* help a child see the positive traits in the images of his parents when he feels ashamed of their "primitivity"? How can he make him see the relative validity of a cultural pattern or prejudice believed to be absolute truth?

The need for neutralization (through rational methods of comparing and defining) arises much more frequently when some humanistic subject matter is discussed (civics, history, literature, and so on), but presents itself also in the teaching of sciences such as biology. We shall return to this problem in the second part of this study, when we shall try to analyze certain lessons in which affectively laden, "explosive" issues emerged. We shall show then also the importance of didactic guidance as an essential element of rehabilitative teaching. It is precisely in this area that mistakes made by the teacher are fraught with danger to the pupil's cognitive functioning as well as to his mental health.

We have mentioned the concept of contamination in Section III of Chapter 1, as well as in another study.[11] We maintain that, normally, the child's cognitive development starts with a phase in which emotionally relevant experiences constitute his first steps toward abstraction. (The concept of nearness, for instance, which is relevant for the emotional development of relationships as well as for the cognitive development of relations in time and space, is "mediated" through the infant's vital experiences of the mother "coming near" or "going away," according to his needs. This nearness can be called the child's first "abstraction," from the mother's absence *and* presence.) Similarly, the child's first emotions are closely connected, in fact merge, with his perceptions and, at a later stage of development, with his apperceptions.

To the extent that the child experiences himself to be a subject of relationships with his immediate environment (and not only an object of manipulation), differentiation grows as a by-product of security, trust, and initiative, and, with it, differentiation between

*The objections may be so strong that the teacher will feel not competent enough to deal with them in the class, (particularly when only a few among the pupils struggle with such affective problems); he may then prefer transmitting responsibility for neutralization to a counselor or a discussion group specially composed for this purpose. It is obvious that in this way the discussion is likely to lose its importance as part of rehabilitative *teaching* (though not of therapy).

feeling and thinking takes place as well. But in the development of the child who grows up under conditions of poverty, want, and neglect or of cultural value-ambiguity, there is no or, at best, only insufficient experience of regularity and intentionality in his parents' relationships with him. He experiences himself not as a subject but as an object only. In this case, the development of clear separation between feeling and thinking is impaired, and we speak of a primary contamination of the two functional areas.

(This should not be identified with what we call, in a later stage of development, "illegitimate interference of feelings and of unconscious complexes with thinking processes," as we know them from the psychopathology of pseudo-feeblemindedness. In such cases, separation between the two functional areas *did* take place early in life, and only later, as a result of certain traumatic experiences, of an intimately personal nature, regression, repression, and neurotization occurred.)

Contamination, as defined here, finds one of its main expressions in the distortion of thinking and learning processes through affective, irrationally autonomous, "irruptions." It is here that the teacher's responsibility for correcting such distortion through methods of rational neutralization of the distorting affects begins.

But, strangely enough, many teachers of secondarily retarded pupils, though they may have chosen working with them, perhaps even according to the principles of rehabilitative teaching, show many signs of equally distorting contamination. They may object affectively to these principles: noninductiveness, they say, impedes the child's initiative; imagining the possible sources of their pupils' mistakes contradicts their self-image as intellectually subject matter-oriented transmitters of knowledge, as representatives of absolute values and principles; relating to one pupil is liable, they claim, to frustrate the rest of the group; taking a pupil's faulty answer seriously (though only in order to discover its underlying cognitive pattern) may be interpreted as dishonesty. They are not properly prepared, they say, for a method that requires studies in psychology (of thinking and of personality), studies in logics (to define concepts exactly), and studies in different fields of knowledge in order to be able to branch out. Some teachers may even go so far as to demand detailed instructions, although they know, theoretically at least, that the methods of rehabilitative teaching are based on responsiveness, imagination, improvisation.

The discrepancy between their declared willingness to work with disadvantaged children according to the principles of rehabilitative teaching and their affective rejection of almost every practical implication of those very principles could perhaps be interpreted as a sign of their feelings and their thinking being "contaminated." It would seem that they experience difficulties similar to those of their pupils in keeping their rational decisions apart from their irrational fears, their affective stereotypes, their patterned self-images.*

III. THE TEACHER AS A PERSON, HIS CLASS AND THE CURRICULUM

Type Differences and Contamination

Not every teacher is suited for the functions implied in rehabilitative teaching. Some are so rigid (not to speak of the undifferentiated ones) that they will not be able to learn from training, in-service training, or didactic guidance meant to change their attitudes. Others may be afraid of any expression of ambiguity and uncertainty, which requires imagination. Again others perceive themselves as being content- or science-oriented intellectuals and, as a result, are interested only in teaching "gifted" children. It is obvious that all these teachers will never succeed in rehabilitative teaching with its intrinsic emphasis on reactivity, empathy, imagination, and readiness for improvisation.

Then, there are teachers who are able to apply the principles and the methods of rehabilitative teaching only to young age groups; others are interested in the older age groups only, students in junior and senior high schools, where they can and must apply these principles and methods to subject matter teaching.

And yet, it would be a mistake to identify such preferences with

---

*One may ask whether it is justifiable to use the term contamination when speaking of a grown-up person who has reached a fairly high level of differentiation in most of his personal and interpersonal contexts (with one exception, that of his professional functioning). Would it not be more adequate to see in these cases evidence of quasineurotic disturbances, primarily of the projection type? But most of these teachers show no supportive evidence of being neurotics, at least no more than does any other so-called normal adult.

genuine suitability, with natural gifts for dealing with those age groups effectively. They may be little more than reaction-formations, that is, defense mechanisms against irrational fears or aversions. Thus, the woman who prefers young children may seek in her devotion to them substitute satisfaction of frustrated maternal needs. She will be likely to reject the emphasis on differentiation, this essential element of rehabilitative teaching, and may claim that it is much too early to start with differentiation at this age, and that enjoyable experiences in a secure and playful environment are much more likely to help *every* young child, the underprivileged in particular, to acquire a basic sense of reliability through regularity. The teacher we have in mind here is unable to see that understanding regularity as inherent in the universe of objects or happenings is an experience of no lesser impact on the secondarily retarded child's growth than any game may be. (We shall come back to that problem soon when discussing the relative merits of prevention versus rehabilitation.)

Those who prefer the older age groups may do so because they are not secure enough in themselves to accept imagination as a cognitive function no less legitimate than analyzing and explaining contents of learning. It is not the older age group that attracts them, but it is their own, conscious or unconscious, fear of regressing into a condition of lesser differentiation that accounts for their preference of content teaching, but, of course, at the same time also for their failure in rehabilitative teaching.

Here is the place to come back to what we have just said about contamination and to analyze the teacher's suitability for the type of teaching here recommended, with the aid of this concept.

No one is entirely successful in the process of separating his thinking from his feelings or his feelings from his thinking (so that he can relate one to the other freely)—which is the same as saying that no one ever reaches full autonomy. The practical conclusion we must draw from that inevitable limitation, which is particularly in evidence when we discuss the specific difficulties of teachers of secondarily retarded children, is *not* to see a case for therapy in every such teacher but to provide him with adequate guidance services.

The functions of the didactic counselor can be summarized in one, that of neutralizing affective reactions in the teacher, in order to prepare him for his—similar—function in teaching. Rehabilitative teaching is, in the last instance, the sum total of interventions meant to neutralize irrational fears, patterned expectations, aggressive prejudices. Noninductiveness and branching out, we believe, are essential to prepare the ground for affect-free, rational, differentiating, and responsible approaches to each learning assignment.

When the teacher claims that noninductiveness is liable to paralyze the child's initiative, he actually shirks his responsibility for the later stage of noninductiveness, the stage at which he is supposed to help his pupils apply a transmitted solution to varying conditions and thus help them recognize the *relative* validity only of that solution. He may justify his objections rationally, but actually he does so only because he fears the consequences of the method of noninductiveness.

When he claims that imagination needed to recognize the sources of his pupils' mistakes contradicts his intellectual and moral self-definition, he actually fears the cognitive effort he must invest in his teaching when he accepts imagination as legitimate.

When he claims relating himself to one child may frustrate the other children in the class, who then may feel frustrated, he forgets that the method recommended is *not* identical with individualization (and certainly is not meant to establish a "dialogue" between him and the pupil), but is auxiliary only to neutralization and, as such, forms part of the total, class-oriented lesson.

When the teacher condemns taking seriously the pupils' mistakes (by seeing in them evidence of thinking), when he sees in it a sign of lack of honesty, he actually hides his lack of empathy behind a false absolutism: in fact, he does not *want* to take mistakes seriously because he feels so much more secure as long as he can use quasirational dichotomization ("correct" versus "wrong" answers, as determined by him and the prescribed curriculum).

When he defines his teaching functions "intellectually," he often fails to give himself account of the contradiction between this self-definition and his seemingly modest self-resignation to his "lack of knowledge" and to his insufficient training in logical thinking or in the art of defining concepts or phenomena.

The Teacher's Background

We have presented in two ways the teacher's difficulties in rehabilitative teaching: as evidence of type-conditioned or acquired preferences in their overt and their covert meaning, and as evidence of residual contamination of feeling and thinking. In both cases, the main question to be raised is: to what extent are the teacher's resistances, preferences, and handicaps reversible, if he is given adequate guidance? This question will be dealt with in one of the next paragraphs. But before that, we must mention a number of other problems concerning the teacher as a person: what is the impact that his origins may have on the way in which he conceives of his responsibility vis-à-vis his pupils and vis-à-vis the curriculum that is imposed upon him? And what is the impact that his function as a teacher in general, and as one engaged in rehabilitative teaching in particular, is likely to have on his personality?

We often hear that a teacher with a cultural background similar to that of the underprivileged child has better chances of understanding him, his fears, his expectations, and his ambitions, than one coming from a different environment and culture. Is not the latter bound to remain a stranger in the child's eyes, one representing a world to which he does not feel committed? (A similar question is asked, of course, in other fields as well, for instance social work.)

But experience teaches us a different lesson altogether. Often, it is precisely the teacher from a comparable social or cultural background who is not only oversensitive to but also extremely intolerant of the secondarily retarded child's weaknesses. Intelligence and strong character enable many sons and daughters of underprivileged families to overcome the intellectual handicaps that endanger growth processes under the externalizing conditions of poverty, want, and neglect or cultural ambiguity (while many coming from the opposite backgrounds fail to realize and develop their potentials). But the wounds inflicted early in life are liable to make themselves felt painfully much later, and particularly as affective oversensitivity or emotional vulnerability when they are faced with representatives of their own past.

Thus, we may encounter a tendency to deny the existence of essential differences between the ordinary learner and the secondarily retarded child, to deny the need for different methods of teaching. We have already mentioned the claim of cultural pluralists with their false equality ideals. Here we have in mind a more dangerous claim: that full equality of achievement in abstract learning can be the result of one and the same teaching method because the pupils are essentially equal; that all need the same—enlargement of their *massa apperceptiva*—and that the difference is only one of the "quantity" of the effort to be invested for this purpose.

True enough, the very concept of secondary retardation is an "ideal type" construct and is represented in reality by a "more or less" only. But it would be wrong to jump from this reservation to the conclusion that the existing differences are not *qualitative*, are not essential. They are, and not only when we compare extreme cases. Their essentiality is the result of cognitive and social behavior, of a process in which patterns of distorted thinking and their behavior equivalents reinforce each other.

This is the reason why so many teachers coming from backgrounds similar to that of their underprivileged pupils fail to recognize the need for special methods (of teaching, of social education, of treatment) meant to prepare the ground for the genuine equality of functional abilities. It is, apparently, as difficult to get rid of a past self-image produced by early experience of injustice and social failure as it is for a neurotic person to get rid of his (or her) fixations to early stages of libidinal development.

However, no one can ever hope to overcome affective reactions to direct or indirect encounters with his past unless he is ready to face it not as a part of, but as different from, his present identity. It requires courage to look at our past from a distance, as it were. No one can accept it as a reality toward which he feels committed as if it formed part of his actuality. It is precisely this courage that characterizes a rational, mature person.

Hence, we can say, though it may sound paradoxical, that there is no difference in essence between the teacher who comes as a "stranger," from a different social or cultural background, to his underprivileged pupils, and the one whose roots are similar to theirs. The latter, too, will be suited for his function only to the extent that he is able to accept the values that he wants to teach and impart, particularly those of differentiation, responsibility, and rationality, and to accept them as committing. And yet, both he and the other, the "stranger" must be aware of the need not to impose those values, from without, in the name of a general, a universal, and an "anonymous" curriculum; he must learn how to build them into his pupils' mental structure by way of constantly confronting them with his pupils' reactions, by relating the existing patterns of his secondarily retarded pupils' mental structure to those "culture-alien" values.

In this respect, both types of teacher will have the same difficulties: the "stranger" because he must overcome his personal resistances, the "near-one" because he must overcome his deep-rooted dependence on his social or cultural past. And for both there exists the same problem: overcoming the past should never be interpreted as giving up loyalty to that past. It is the tension created by this didactic coexistence of freedom and loyalty that characterizes a good teacher, whatever his origins.

We shall see later, when discussing the problems of teacher training and teacher guidance, what the implications of the presently analyzed difficulties in rehabilitative teaching are in training and counseling. One aspect (which actually can be fully explained only after we have dealt with the place of the curriculum with its rigid demands in rehabilitative teaching) may be mentioned now—the teachers' fear not to do justice to the curriculum.

The Teacher Facing the Curriculum

In many places this problem is solved easily. To the extent that the curriculum demands are individualized, as in the so-called open schools, tensions of this kind are avoided with respect to both the pupils and their teachers. Compensatory education, too, particularly in the so-called comprehensive schools, eliminates the problem with equal ease. But where the ultimate aims are equality in abstract thinking and success in matriculation examinations to make possible continuation of studies on a university level, tensions and fears seem almost inevitable. It is first and foremost the second element of rehabilitative teaching, that of branching out into relating faulty answers to cognitive patterns presumed to be responsible for their emergence, that arouses doubt and fear because it seems to consume too much time. At the same time, the branching-out into this kind of "psychologization" is open to attack by many teachers who are afraid of the amount of imagination they are supposed to use for this purpose. It is therefore easier to reject it on the grounds that it is much too time-consuming than it is to admit the underlying fears.

Another argument against the seeming neglect of subject matter and curriculum content in favor of functional development is that the pupils, particularly in the higher grades, will feel frustrated when they compare their own achievements in quantitative terms of material covered with that of students in a "regular" class. This argument is often heard when secondarily retarded pupils are concentrated in homogeneous classes. It is certainly the most legitimate argument, since the children's doubts and fears are not groundless at all.

There are two ways in which the teacher, with the help of adequate didactic guidance services, should react to such fears in himself and in his students—one objective and one subjective, one methodological, one psychological.

Much of the material included in the official curriculum is not essential and can therefore easily be omitted without any serious damage done to the learner. This is at least true for humanistic subject matter. Although practically every curriculum planner claims that he uses as his own criterion of solution the representative value of the specific content chosen, closer examination of the nature of such selection reveals that its nature is, to say the least, doubtful. Criteria may be purely formal, as, for instance, in planning literature curricula in which every form must be represented and much too little attention is paid to the ideational and educational suitability of the creations chosen.

Concentration on the secondarily retarded pupils' ability to think differentially and in abstract terms may indeed restrict the extent of the subject matter "covered." But there exist perfectly legitimate ways to make up for that "material loss" by devoting the time immediately preceding an examination to training the class in the techniques of answering questions likely to be asked. True enough: this is not an intrinsic part of rehabilitative teaching or, for that matter, of any good teaching. It has little to do with the internalization of knowledge, with adequate understanding, or with the development of vital cognitive functions. It is meant solely to help the secondarily retarded (and therefore particularly "failure-prone") students overcome that hurdle called "examination" and thus enable them to continue their studies at a higher level.

Besides that, it can be shown that functional rehabilitation makes even quasimechanical memorizing toward an examination easier; one of the implications of the former is the pupil's readiness to take in subject-matter details that can be learned only when we do *not* insist on asking questions of meaning. This may sound paradoxical, since *not* asking questions of meaning actually is the opposite of internalization and therefore characterizes primitive forms of learning. And yet we can understand this seeming contradiction when we remember what has been said about the ability of thinking in terms of the As-If. The teacher who has succeeded in restoring this ability in a secondarily retarded pupil's cognitive structure should also dare to give up temporarily his primary concern for the sake of such essentially meaningless, yet practically necessary forms of learning.

Thus, we see how the objective aspect of guidance meant to help the teacher overcome his fears is interlinked with its subjective aspect. The student's fears may be of a rational character and should be dealt with as such; but the teacher's fears are much less rational, are much more rooted in his personality structure and his professional self-perception. It therefore falls upon the didactic counselor to refer to this aspect, though without assuming the role of a therapist: the teacher must be flexible and courageous enough to insist on the principles of rehabilitative teaching *and* to give them up, when his pupils' needs require it.

A few remarks should be added here on the influence rehabilitative teaching is likely to have on the teacher's personality (see pp. 64f.).

Some claim that the use of the here-described methods of teaching requires so much intellectual concentration, so much differentiation, and so much imagination that the whole personality is bound to be affected. The attitude changes brought about by deliberate, well-planned, conscientious application of those principles we have tried to analyze, often transcend, according to many teachers' evidence, the area of their professional functions, and make themselves felt in their relationships with their own children as well.

One can hardly say the same of other teachers—many well-functioning kindergarten teachers are known to be overanxious mothers; excellent subject-matter teachers in high schools are compulsively rigid with their own sons and daughters; many teachers successfully engaged in open schools produce neurotic children. The same happens, undoubtedly, to teachers in rehabilitative teaching as well. There are not a few who invest their whole being in what they believe is good rehabilitative teaching. But when its principles turn into the internalized and genuine conviction that it is the teacher's primary function to rescue and restore potentials buried under heaps of failure and disappointment, the teacher's self-conception is bound to change; they will see their human environment as well in the light of that fundamental nonidentity of what appears with what lies underneath the surface, its potentialities, of reality and its possible enlargement.

This, in brief, is the most important and the deepest effect successful practice in rehabilitative teaching may have on the teacher's personality.

Prevention versus Rehabilitation

When rehabilitative teaching is discussed, it is inevitable that the question of prevention and its preferability will be asked. Is it not much easier to create conditions for the normal and adequate development of cognitive functions than to correct the distortions caused by a more or less prolonged period of negative environmental conditioning? Why not teach the mothers of underprivileged children how to speak to their children from the earliest period in their life on, in a more differentiated way, and thus avoid the emergence of the most serious handicap in secondary retardation, poverty of language and verbal expression? Is it not reasonable to hope that, even in later stages, enlarging the child's *massa apperceptiva* through offering him as many details of information as possible and repeating them as often and as possible will strengthen his ability to distinguish between essentials and accidentals, that is, to be differentiated and to think in abstract terms?

As regards the first claim, it is this belief in the possibility and preferability of early prevention that has led to the elaboration of a number of valuable methods, such as neighborhood activities with an emphasis on systematic education and guidance of mothers.[38] Basil Bernstein's proposals[4] should be mentioned in this connection. And yet, no evidence can be adduced to prove the *long-term* preventive effect such methods have had on children who grow up under the externalizing conditions of poverty and neglect or of cultural ambiguity, or children who are exposed to their combined impact. Although the *short-term* effect proves that the underlying principles are sound, the destructive influence of continued externalization in later stages of development proves the inevitability of distortion, the narrow limits of prevention. As long as the destructive influence of a negative environment continues to make itself felt, cognitive potentials will always tend to be endangered or impaired, and restoration of lost abilities will remain indispensable.

This should *not* be interpreted as criticism of the philosophy of prevention as such.* But it does mean, as we said at the beginning of this study, that prevention will never be able to create structural conditions of immunity against a negative environment. Moreover, and this is the most important point in the present discussion, conscious confrontation of the learner not only with the contents but also with the modalities of his thinking and learning, confrontation which, in turn, is the basis of change, of development, of internalization, is the essential precondition of rehabilitating impaired cognitive potentials.

This is, indeed, paradoxical, but there is no way out of it: structurization implies, in our case, that of secondary retardation, that the categories of thinking have become distorted and distorting; but it also means that the learner has become a person, that is, a subject of confrontation, a fact that may make possible genuine change, with the help of rehabilitative teaching. The latter will be effective to the extent that the teacher is ready and able to relate to his secon-

---

*One point, however, cannot be stressed often or strongly enough—that it is practically impossible to change the environmental conditions of an underprivileged child's growth, to change his adult's cognitive behavior toward him. Parents may learn more differentiated modes of speaking; they may even learn how to change their value-orientation in relation to their children. But it is more than doubtful to what extent such changes in the child's meaningful adults are deep-reaching enough to affect their educational expectations and reactions also when he reaches a higher age. Cooperation with parents is essential for the success of rehabilitative teaching but does not come in its stead, as we shall try to demonstrate in Chapter 3.

darily retarded pupils as such, that is, as subjects with their structurized and yet changeable patterns of thinking. In other words, though no less paradoxically formulated, responsibility for thinking and learning can be developed only in persons who have reached a phase in their life in which they are potentially able to understand the meaning (and the burden) of responsibility, hence also the purpose of *avoiding* responsibility.

This also explains why enlarging a child's *massa apperceptiva* through transmitting information is not an efficient means of preventing secondary retardation—intake of knowledge is relevant for cognitive development only when the act is a responsible operation implying screening and relating details to each other in changing whole-contexts in which they become meaningful. Passive intake of knowable details, on the other hand, remains functionally irrelevant and does not even help develop the basic functions of remembering and even less of recalling at will.

This, in turn, accounts for the fact that rehabilitative teaching based on the principles of enlarging the *massa apperceptiva* is, to say the least, of doubtful value. Knowable details learned not only tend to remain isolated and therefore meaningless, they also support some of the secondarily retarded pupils' typical attitudes, that of identifying understanding with knowing details and, even worse, that of having "learned" details with knowing them. In this sense, attempts to rehabilitate impaired intelligence through the transmission of knowable details not only are bound to fail, they also counteract their aim, since they strengthen the *illusion* of understanding.

Alternative Methods

The principles of rehabilitative teaching—noninductiveness, branching out from a specific content for the sake of functional development, and neutralization of affects—are valid for every age group. What differ are contents *to* which, and media *through* which, the methods are applied. We have emphasized that the concept of secondary retardation is an ideal-type construct only, and that the cognitive behavior thus labeled develops gradually during the various life stages, during which an externalizing environment acts as a conditioning factor on the crystallization of the child's patterns of thinking.

The reality of the classroom of every group of learners is heterogeneous, we have said. Before coming back to the crucial issue of homogeneous versus heterogeneous classes and, with it, to the problem of so-called integration, we propose here to add a few remarks on the teacher's attitude toward rehabilitative teaching in the various age groups and in classes of different levels.

The younger the pupils, the stronger is the emphasis on concretization and activation as essential elements of teaching. Even the teacher of "ordinary," more or less well-functioning children is so deeply convinced of Piaget's tenets concerning the sensorimotor beginnings of meaningful thinking and learning[36] (even without having studied his theory or understood its implications), that he cannot imagine a young child as being able to think abstractly. He identifies the latter ability with formal ("operational") thinking, an understandable mistake when we think of many learning theories in which the same mistake is found.[31]

Hence the teacher's preference for using quasi-experimentation, concrete examples, audio-visual aids, activity programs. Seldom does he ask himself to what extent the concretized is understood correctly, an omission that, indeed, is not very dangerous as long as we have in mind the ordinary or even the gifted child: they find their way with the help of their enriching and supportive environment or their own well-developed intelligence, from concrete phenomena to discovering meaning.

We have interpreted this ability as a symptom of "structural differentiation," between subject and object, between ego and non-ego. We can speak of a genuine subject-position as against the universe of perceivable phenomena and learnable contents, to the extent that the child is able: (a) to conceive of the essential difference between a phenomenon and its meaning, and (b) to try to find and understand that meaning. In this respect, the secondarily retarded child essentially differs from the "normal" one. It would be as fallacious to define secondary retardation as a state in which the child is irreversibly fixated to a so-called preoperational stage of cognitive development, as it is to define a primarily retarded child in terms of mental age, thereby declaring him to be "younger" than his chronological age.* Although a child's secondary retardation manifests itself, inter alia, on the concrete (perceptual) basis of his experiences, in overdependence on what he believes is known to him, these manifestations are reversible. It is the function of rehabilitative teaching to bring about that reversal, to help the secondarily retarded pupil trust in the regularity, the reliability, and the explicability of phenomena, of objects, processes, events.

This means, however, that emphasizing the use of concretization, experimentation, and exemplification is contraindicated in the teaching of secondarily retarded pupils even at an early age. For, even then the teacher must make every possible effort to accompany each example, each discovery seemingly "resulting" from it automatically, by a counter-example, in order to avoid the danger of the pupil's identifying that "concretum" with the law to be taught. It is obvious that such a conception of the function of "teaching" requires constant active intervention on the part of the teacher, not always and not necessarily by way of frontal instruction, but in any case by way of explaining the meaning of what has been concretized and exemplified.

For the same reason, simplifying the curriculum does not solve our problem. We have in mind those curriculum planners who work out shortened textbooks in simpler language, in accordance with their conception of secondary retardation as irreversible, or, at best, demand more repetitions and concretizations to accompany the chosen curriculum. In this way, they cause a considerable slowing down of the process of teaching, even if they agree to omit certain chapters of the prescribed curriculum. The critical question is not how to save time, through restricting the sum total of topics taught, but how to use the time saved: for repetitions and examples or for structurizing explanations. In both cases, resistance to slowing down the process will be felt and voiced;[3] but the decisive difference between the two is one between defining secondary retardation as irreversible or as reversible (or between seeing the environmentally handicapped child as potentially equal or as essentially and permanently inferior to the "normal" child).

The teacher should be aware of this double meaning of restricting

*Compare the author's arguments against the concept of "mental age."[11,37]

the extent of the curriculum contents taught: if the time gained through omitting certain parts is used for the development of understanding the essentials and for differentiating between various aspects of laws, principles, or solutions learned, then we can no longer speak of simplifying. On the contrary: it makes the process of rehabilitative teaching much more complex and complicated than is even the ordinary way of using the curriculum material in teaching ordinary pupils.

There exist two more methods of rehabilitative teaching: working out textbooks with elaborated instructions as to their use in a class of secondarily retarded children, and working out exercises with problems based on words and sentences or on forms to be manipulated.

The contents of specially prepared textbooks may be chosen according to what their author considers either material suited to the mentality of the pupils he has in mind, or as being representative of more comprehensive and more complicated material contained in ordinary textbooks. But the method is not identical with that of "simplification"; its essential characteristic lies in the elaboration of detailed instructions given to the teacher to guide him in the use of the contents. As a rule, the teachers are also given special courses meant to prepare them for that task, and they sometimes are accompanied by didactic counselors who supervise them in their day-to-day practice.

To the extent that such—printed and/or verbal—instructions are meant to enable the teacher to use his texts in a flexible manner and to use them with imagination, the method resembles that recommended here. But usually their intention is different—the instructions are worked out in great detail because their authors believe in the power of universally valid and understandable textbooks and instructions rather than in the teacher's ability to react intelligently and intuitively to his pupil's overt and covert thinking processes. But if this is the case, the method, whatever its merits may be, is the opposite of the kind of rehabilitative teaching analyzed here (and demonstrated later). Reliance on the teacher's reactions and improvisations, on his empathy, courage, and imagination, requires the availability of didactic guidance but excludes any kind of uniform instructions claiming general validity.

Usually exercises meant to develop and strengthen cognitive functions are based on principles similar to those that underlie the construction of intelligence tests. The pupil is asked to find the correct order in which mixed-up letters or words or sentences will make sense; to choose from among similar forms the one that will complete an incomplete form (and to find the formal principle according to which the choice will be easiest); to find the exceptional item or word from among a series of items or words (and to explain the criterion according to which it is exceptional); to imagine the continuation of a sentence or a story or to translate the drawing of a facial expression into words (and again to justify the "translation"); to recognize the absurd points in a story and to explain their absurdity; to understand the meaning of a proverb, a fable, an analogy, and translate it into the language of logics and realism; to understand the rationale of practical (technical) actions.

These and many other varieties of exercises are, of course, graded in difficulty and complexity. Although some may be of doubtful value functionally, the underlying principle seems sound and valid: the ability to differentiate, to understand the essentials of a phenomenon or a problem, their meaning and their implication, to express their understanding clearly formulated, to distinguish between reality and imagination—all these are, indeed, relevant cognitive functions. Each of them can be developed through the kind of exercises we have mentioned here, exercises attached to tests of information or of literature, provided the pupil is asked to explain in his own words why he has chosen a specific answer to a specific question asked.

The disadvantage of the method lies in the fact that exercises never form an integral part of the ordinary curriculum but are additions to it, separate units of learning. It is, therefore, legitimate to ask to what extent the lessons learned from them and the functions developed through them are being transferred to the regular learning process.

Let us return here briefly to rehabilitative teaching in the lower grades of the elementary school with their relatively limited subject-matter orientation. It is in these classes that we find *teaching programs* meant to further the child's intellectual development, programs that are borrowed or derived from Dewey's and Piaget's theories:

Efforts are made to use the child's sensorimotor functions, to bring the subject matter as near as possible to his reality, to facilitate experiencing, doing, discovering, and self-expressing and to proceed from movement to observation, from sensory experience to manipulating forms and directions, from there to classifying objects (what is understood to be the most important concretistic or manipulative equivalent of abstraction). Many textbooks, particularly for science teaching, are worked out according to these principles, and instructions are given to the teacher as to their use. Learning is declared to be fun, the naive presumption being that the enjoyment of experiencing and experimenting is conducive to internalization of knowledge. At the same time, the importance of individualization, activity programs and group work is emphasized. *Individualization*, for instance, is considered to be essential for the optimal development of skills, in writing, reading and arithmetic, in accordance with each child's individually different dispositions and needs. Activity, or, better, *activation programs*, are believed to help develop learning-motivation and increase the learner's "creativeness" (whatever this rather loosely used term may mean). *Working in small groups* is said to be good for socialization. And all these elements together are declared to be relevant for strengthening the learner's emotional involvement in his cognitive assignment.

These are undoubtedly excellent programs and methods, greatly stimulating—particularly for those children who don't need this kind of stimulation, or, better, who are capable of finding their way into the intricacies of knowable facts and meanings, irrespective of the methods used by the teacher. These are the children who, to put it paradoxically, are able to learn contents, to internalize their acquired knowledge and to develop the cognitive functions required for the process, *even* if these tasks are presented as fun. These are the children who understand that the term "fun" should not be taken too seriously, that learning actually is meaningful only when it is experienced as the opposite of fun! These are the children who grow up in more or less stimulating environments, who participate in everything the school does, supplementing it or correcting its mistakes and omissions.

Learning, we maintain, is more meaningful when it includes *over-*

coming resistances and task-alien tendencies in the learner's cognitive structure. True enough, reliance on the better-developed functions, one of the basic tenets of individualized teaching, helps the child acquire basic skills, and every teacher should be aware of their existence; but at the same time, he should be aware of the need to strengthen precisely the "*less*-developed" functions, if he wants to avoid one-sided developments, which are bound to restrict the scope of possible learning.

Now, while all this may be important but is not decisive in ordinary teaching,* it takes on a different meaning in rehabilitative teaching of secondarily retarded children. Here, the teacher's function is the decisive factor. He must know, even in the playful atmosphere of a kindergarten or in the activity-oriented setting of the lower school grades, how to help his pupils detach the perceived results of his actions from their actuality; for this purpose, he must help them translate their experiences or "discoveries" into the language of *comparable generalities*. Without the teacher's active explanations, interpretations, definitions, a secondarily retarded child will not be able to move from percepts to concepts.

There is no need to add that the teacher's interventions will be of a much simpler, much less complex nature in these initial stages of learning than later. But *all* interventions have one element in common: the secondarily retarded pupil, at all stages of his development, must be helped to distinguish between reality and meaning. For him, this is the most meaningful "discovery." To the extent that he has learned this distinction, he will have overcome his cognitive handicap. The earlier such attempts are being made by the teacher, the better. But they must be continued all through the pupil's school years, until his potentials are restored. Only then will the principles of the discovery method or of activation programs become meaningful. And again, it can be said, paradoxically, that only when the pupil is no longer in need of specially adapted methods of teaching (because his cognitive functions have been restored to their originally normal level) will such methods become applicable.

---

*Or, better, becomes important and decisive to the extent that the child cannot rely on his inner, self-regulatory forces or on the compensatory and corrective activities of his environment, outside the school.

Heterogeneous and Homogeneous Classes

For many years, in Israel and the United States, particularly after the publication of the famous Coleman Report in 1966,[6] the discussion of how to teach the underprivileged and secondarily retarded child has been almost identical with a discussion of integration. The socio-political connotation of the latter concept has obscured its meaning as an educational method. We mentioned the issue when we discussed the method of noninductive teaching (see pp. 39f.); we have also made an attempt in another paper[13] to submit the concept of "integration" to a general analysis.

"Integration" means the creation of a new, or the restitution of a lost, whole. In its social connotation it means the creation of a meaningful unit in which each part relates to all other parts as well as to a hypothetical, almost metaphysical, center of unification. In its educational connotation, that is, in the composition of a class, it should mean that qualitatively and quantitatively different pupils relate to each other in relationships of mutuality and interact; which would mean that cognitive changes take place in *all* and not only in the weak ones, the underprivileged.

But no one takes the concept seriously to such an extent—which comes to show its basic falsity: the advocates of integration through teaching a mixed group mean, of course, nothing more than making the weak ones benefit from their coexistence in one group of learners with the strong ones, and from the latters' undisputed positive impact. At best, a note of condescending pluralism is added, which, however, means, if anything, social, certainly not cognitive, equality or tolerance to be learned from each other. As a rule, this note is so feeble that it is lost in the loud and arrogant claim of cognitive improvement.

Genuine integration is *not a means* to bring about functional equality but *presupposes* equality—that is, freedom to choose those with whom you *want* to associate or to be friends and those with whom you do *not* want to have anything to do, whatever their level of intellectual function or their social status may be.

The advocates of school integration, particularly in the United States, claim that the disadvantaged pupils' scholastic achievements go up as a result of conscious or half-conscious imitation of their more adequately functioning classmates. But they did not ask questions about the intellectual preconditions of the former's success (perhaps only the most intelligent among the disadvantaged, or, as we prefer to say, the secondarily retarded, did benefit?). Nor did they ask why the integration programs, claiming to be so successful, did not manifest themselves in structural changes of the American society. (We shall come back to this question when we deal with the problem of evaluation criteria.)

What is meant by the terms used in a discussion of school-integration programs? What is the meaning of "homogeneous" and "heterogeneous" classes?

Homogeneous means a class in which most pupils, though coming from different social or cultural backgrounds, are intelligent enough to learn according to the principles of inductive teaching. To the extent that some are less intelligent and others emotionally disturbed, their presence in a more or less homogeneous class does not require the introduction of specialized teaching methods. (If it does, the class ceases to be homogeneous.)

Homogeneous, on the other hand, means a class in which the majority of the pupils are secondarily retarded, though in different degrees. Some genuinely retarded may remain in that class without disrupting its homogeneity; such retarded children usually belong to the "submissive type"[11] without being properly diagnosed as such but also without disrupting the class homogeneity as regards the teaching methods chosen to meet the needs of the majority. (If they do, the class ceases to be homogeneous, though in a different way from that mentioned before.)

Heterogeneous means a class in which the two types are represented in substantial numbers (whether the proportion is 1:1 or 1:2 "in favor" of this or that type). Where one group forms a small minority only, any uniform teaching method becomes almost impossible. And yet, we shall have to deal with this variety of heterogeneity, which, empirically, is part of the school reality almost everywhere in the world.

Another form of heterogeneity is found frequently in classes of secondarily retarded children intermingled with some problem cases of the severe, mainly aggressive, behavior-disorder type. The latter may not be, and, indeed, often are not, retarded at all, but, on the contrary, may be highly intelligent though unable to make constructive use of their intelligence. They can be defined as "able but unwilling to learn," whatever the method of teaching may be. Their pathology is defined as affective (aggressive) rejection of the adult world as hostile, including, of course, the school teachers (or any other educator) as its principal representatives. They are frequently found in a group of secondarily retarded children (in spite of their intelligence) because the environment responsible for the emergence of these behavior disorders, as we have tried to show in another study,[12] causally resembles that responsible for the emergence of secondary retardation.

In the light of these brief remarks on the essentials of heterogeneity it will be obvious why all we have said about the principles of rehabilitative teaching should be understood to be an ideal-type construct only (just as the secondarily retarded child is no more than such an "ideal type"). The reality of the school is different when we deal with the disadvantaged child and his learning needs. (Normally intelligent and adequately functioning learners could actually be *defined* as pupils who are more or less independent of the teaching methods to which they may be exposed; their "adequacy" finds one of its clearest expressions in their ability to adapt their thinking to those changeable methods and to benefit from each of them, according to its specific intentions and directives.)

Homogeneity is an illusion. In one case, there may be not a few intelligent pupils in the class who could perhaps benefit from inductive teaching methods as much as, or even more than, from rehabilitative teaching. How can we avoid frustrating or even damaging them? In another case, the numerical proportion between normally functioning and secondarily retarded pupils may be such as to make every method contraindicated for a substantial part of the class population. In a third case, it will be the presence of pupils with disruptive behavior disorders that will limit the applicability of rehabilitative teaching even when all pupils in the class are secondarily retarded.

It follows that one of the main problems in the use of the here-recommended teaching methods is that of how to apply them in a way which will not be meaningless for those pupils for whom they are not intended, at least not primarily. This becomes particularly difficult in the teaching of sciences because of the resistance to formal (operational) thinking often displayed by secondarily retarded children. We have already mentioned that the ability to think in terms of equations and formulas is by no means identical with the ability to think in abstract terms. Differentiation, understanding nuances and meaning, comparing with each other forms of human behavior or concepts relevant within well-defined problem areas, understanding the difference between imagination and reality—all these and many other forms of abstraction may be, and indeed often are, more developed through rehabilitative teaching than the modes of operational thinking in physics or mathematics. As a result, secondarily retarded pupils, after some years of rehabilitative teaching, often surpass their highly intelligent classmates with their ability to think "formally."

Many regular and gifted students, particularly those with a strong inclination toward so-called exact sciences, tend to hold in contempt humanistic contents and values. Some may even identify the kind of abstraction required adequately to work through those subject matter and values with empty phraseologies. To the extent that they "learn" them, they do so without personal involvement. Others may replace adequate human and humanistic differentiation and abstraction by strict formulations, thereby demonstrating their "scientific" orientation.

All this comes to show in which way rehabilitative teaching can be applied to heterogeneous classes: it helps the secondarily retarded develop genuine involvement in humanistic contents and values, to a point where the "rehabilitated" can rightly feel superior to the "formalist"; it should show and even prove the practical value of their superiority when it comes to choosing a career; it shows the inadequacy of depreciating or distorting those contents and values under the influence of the "pure science cult"; it shows the latter's limitations. At the same time, science teaching, in the proper sense of the word, may have to be postponed to a relatively late stage of learning (perhaps the last three or four years of the secondary school), and the abstractive abilities developed in the meantime with the help of primarily humanistic subject matter should be used for learning scientific thinking.

A few words may be added here on the value of the so-called

discovery method with its emphasis on experimentation. Without repeating what has been said previously, we maintain that the use of experiments, particularly in the younger age group, as a way to exemplify, concretize, or confirm a verbally explained fact of nature, has been shown to be of doubtful value unless it is again accompanied by verbal interpretation. The experiment pretending to help the pupil discover (better: rediscover) a law of nature or the meaning of an observable occurence may help the ordinary and particularly the gifted student increase his interest and involvement, provided he is taught simultaneously the rules of scientific research (which often has much less to do with experimenting than with planning or with calculating).

But what is the use of all this "playing around with science," when it comes to teaching secondarily retarded pupils, particularly at the higher age levels? If our suggestion is accepted that science teaching with its emphasis on formal operations should be introduced only in the last three to four years of learning, then the question should be asked: how can the teacher make optimal use of the limited time that will be at his disposal? The answer is: by relying as much as possible on audio-visual aids to exemplify and concretize his verbal explanations in the area of supplementary, though not necessarily extracurricular, activities, at the expense of other, enjoyable but less vital, activity groups.

Where the adequately functioning pupils represent a (small) minority, the teacher must make every effort to involve them as actively as possible in finding and formulating exactly worded and differentially valid definitions. They will soon come to see that this is an intellectual challenge of the first order and that much learning is required here to function intelligently (just as the *teacher* should be aware of the fact that offering his pupils adequate definitions of phenomena or concepts requires careful preparation). Thus, the noninductive method of teaching becomes meaningful for the well-functioning as well as for the secondarily retarded pupils: the former may take a more active part in *preparing* definitions, while the latter can concentrate more on *applying* them.

It has also been suggested that the teacher should make use of some among the adequately functioning pupils to act as tutors for some of their secondarily retarded classmates. Such tutoring, however, will be meaningless, or even harmful, if it is seen as part of a mutual aid program or is meant to advance social integration. It is meaningful only if it is carefully planned as part of a cognitive rehabilitation program. For this purpose, the "tutors" should receive guidance individually adapted to their "pupils'" needs. Then, and only then, tutoring, in addition to being a valuable tool of rehabilitation, may help change the class climate, and thus prepare the ground for the introduction of effective rehabilitative programs.

We have mentioned that the political aspects of "integration" tend to obscure the educational implications of school heterogeneity. Actually, a class composed of pupils from different backgrounds and of different cognitive abilities and needs is far from being an integrated class. "Tracking," "grouping," the introduction of various vocational or academic or other trends within the framework of a so-called comprehensive school—all come to prove that integration is an ideology rather than a reality. We should not speak even of "equality of opportunities," and certainly not of pluralistic acceptance of differences, before we have exhausted all possibilities of restoring lost or impaired potentials in individuals functioning on different levels of intellectual effectiveness.*

On the other hand, it is precisely the fact that in every group of secondarily retarded children various degrees of impairment—from genuine retardation to near normality—are represented, that gives the concept of heterogeneity another educational connotation: it makes a flexible teaching practice possible, one in which inductive *and* noninductive teaching can be tried out simultaneously or alternatively, on an experimental basis, as it were.

The most difficult form of heterogeneity is that of a class of secondarily retarded pupils with a few severe behavior problems among them. Their aggressive attitudes against all adult values as such, including those implied in the teachers' learning-demands, jeopardize every attempt to teach them together with other children, particularly children with a weak ego-structure and weak defenses.

---

*Here, again, is the place to raise strong objection to compensatory education. Those who, according to the arbitrary judgment of diagnosticians and planners "require" compensatory education, are thereby declared to be inferior: they are declared to be unable to benefit from that type of education that has the highest prestige value. Compensatory education therefore radically contradicts integration or even equality of opportunities.

(Such children may be easily seduced by the aggressive ones into avoidance of discipline and away from their learning assignments, although they *want* to learn.)

The aggressive children need an educational setting meant to restore in them a basic trust in the adult world. But even if this primary aim has been attained, they may not be able to benefit from a teaching method aimed at strengthening their power of differentiation and their rationality. They may then need either a regular program with emphasis on discovery and activity, or a special program with emphasis on "acting out" and as many opportunities as possible to satisfy their strong and often overstrong motility needs (irrespective of whether their behavior disorder is primarily, that is neurologically, or secondarily, that is reactively, connected with symptoms of hypermotility).

In extreme cases, there may be no alternative to removing them from the class, and be it only to protect the basic interests of the majority, who may be willing and able to benefit from a program of rehabilitative teaching. But in less extreme cases, the potentially destructive influence of the aggressive types on the other children *can* be counteracted, though it requires a permanent availability of services of individual treatment and auxiliary teaching. These aggressive children need a maximum of personal attention though they may not be ready to accept it. (Is it worthwhile to give up, though perhaps in part only, my negative world-conception? Are they trustworthy, these adults who pretend that they want to help me? Or are they interested in their values more than in me?)

It may be argued that this is a psychotherapeutic rather than an educational function, and that few, if any, teachers will be found who are able and willing to give that kind of support and treatment to their aggressive pupils. This may be so. But then, no solution is in sight to the problem of heterogeneity as a result of the presence of such disruptive elements in a class of secondarily retarded pupils. It would mean that we would have to give up from the start any hope of restoring the impaired cognitive potentials in those many children who are secondarily retarded because of the socio-cultural conditions under which they grew up. There is no way out from inequality and injustice into rehabilitation and integration unless we are ready to take seriously every aspect of heterogeneity and draw from it the appropriate conclusions: homogeneity as *preparation* for heterogeneity, accompanied by, supported by, appropriate methods of teaching and treatment.

Criteria of Evaluation

The ultimate aim of rehabilitative teaching and the main criterion of its success is the pupil's ability to take upon himself the responsibility for his thinking and learning processes. It can also be called differently: "relative autonomy" or "internalization." It should be obvious that no quantitative measurement-techniques can be worked out, and that any attempt to prove the validity of the method statistically must remain inconclusive. It is one of the essential characteristics of responsibility, autonomy, and internalization that they manifest themselves not necessarily in that same area in which they have been achieved, scholastic learning in our case, but perhaps in another area and only much later—for instance, in social behavior, work attitudes, civic responsibility, interpersonal relationships. Hence, the irrelevance of achievement or attitude tests, not to speak of final examinations.

And yet, every effort should be made, as we have already said in another context (see p. 68) to help the pupils overcome that external hurdle called the matriculation exam. Cognitive rehabilitation is not an aim in itself but is a weapon in man's struggle for social improvement, for more justice and more equality. These aims may require, or justify the use of, certain additional practices, but under no circumstances should they determine the methods of rehabilitative teaching or its direct purposes.

We shall come back to the issue when we ask what implications our definition of aims and criteria has for teacher training and guidance. Here we restrict ourselves to adding a few remarks on its implications for the teacher's basic attitudes. What counts is his ability to see himself as an acting and reacting subject, while knowing that he is at the same time an object of his pupils' relationships—his ability to see his pupils as potentially equal, to learn from them about the hidden motives and dynamics of their thinking. The teacher must be able and willing to see himself as a subject also in his relationships with his counselor, though not as a self-identical but as a changing subject, ready to overcome his rigid and restrictive self-image, to overcome what we have called his own residues of contamination of feeling and concepts, to free himself from the domination of his fears and principles, his prejudices and stereotypes.

It is a slow process, never fully successful in every area of the teacher's activities, never equally successful with all groups of children, never permanently successful. And yet, we can define the essential criterion of success in the counselor's work with the teacher, exactly as we can define that of the teacher's work with his students or with that of the students' work with their learning assignment: ability and readiness to act out as a responsible subject and a responsive object at one and the same time, requiring, as it does, imagination, openness, and flexibility as well as systematization and rationality.

I have been engaged in a number of projects with underprivileged and secondarily retarded pupils in junior and senior high school classes. The following results could be found and confirmed in each of these projects:

—Homogeneous classes proved to be more suitable than heterogeneous classes for preparing secondarily retarded pupils to continue their studies in mixed groups, at the high school or the university levels.

—The seeming success of so-called integrational classes (if it was achieved) could be observed more clearly in the lower than in the higher grades, in technical more than in academic high schools, in rural more than in urban areas.

—To the extent that changes took place in the cognitive and the social behavior of the underprivileged children within mixed groups, they were accompanied, in almost every case, by a feeling of inferiority, which, in turn, seemed to be responsible for frequently emerging and undesirably strong tendencies to imitate the "privileged." Such tendencies are a negative indication of seeming success only. They are observed more frequently in younger than in older age groups, and they coexist with opposite feelings, feelings of being discriminated against, of resentment.

—It is, therefore, extremely difficult to determine unambiguous success-criteria of rehabilitative teaching in the younger age groups. Theoretically, the most reliable criterion would seem to be: the pupil's ability to continue his study courses, of a technical or an academic trend, in mixed groups and to be able to benefit from "inductive" teaching methods. But experience has shown that the majority of underprivileged children, even after graduating from junior high school, require a continuation of teaching aimed at strengthening their cognitive functions and not only at enlarging their *massa apperceptiva*, their knowledge of facts and laws.

—Feelings of being discriminated against are found at every age level among the disadvantaged, irrespective of whether their class is homogeneous or heterogeneous. One of the criteria of genuine success is the extent to which such feelings can be overcome or, better, transformed into topics of rational analysis and self-confrontation. This transformation usually is a by-product of growing differentiation and responsibility. The latter express themselves, as we have said, not only in the areas of learning but also in a basic change of the student's self-conception, in a realistic attitude toward his own future and past, toward his family and culture.*

—It could be observed that genuine friendships between children from different social or cultural backgrounds emerged only in a few cases, more frequently in older than in younger age groups and then mostly between boys and girls rather than between boys or between girls. Such friendships had better chances of survival and of permanence after the school had completed its task of rehabilitating lost or impaired potentials, and graduates met either during their army

*We shall see in Chapter 3 that social work and individual treatment are intrinsic parts of rehabilitative teaching and not only auxiliary services as introduced in most schools. When analyzing its functions, we shall have to deal also with the question of "explosive issues." These are topics such as fears and resentments, aggressiveness and prejudices, compulsions and cultural patterns, individual freedom and its limits, which should be discussed independently of the curriculum, that is, not only by the teacher with his neutralizing interpretation of different contents, but also in groups in which students of different levels and coming from different backgrounds participate under the direction of an experienced discussion leader. When such extracurricular activities bear fruit, it will be difficult later to find out to what extent class teachings and to what extent group discussions have contributed to the successful attitude-changes in the pupils. But this distinction, of course, has little significance here where we try to define the *criteria* of success and not the types of intervention best suited to bringing about the changes.

service or in their subsequent university studies. This again comes to prove that coexistence is not an instrument, but a result of successful rehabilitation, one of the criteria of its success.

—Educators still continue to define the aim of an academic high school program as "developing a well-balanced orientation in various areas of knowledge." This is also their criterion of evaluating the individual's success. Accordingly, the number of graduates passing the test of such "overall orientation" (with as little personal involvement as possible) serves as the criterion for evaluating the *school's* success. In rehabilitative teaching, the criterion is exactly the opposite: not an overall orientation based on provable though superficial knowledge of basic facts in different fields, but internalized knowledge and readiness to look for the meaning of facts and laws out of personal involvement. In other words, cognitive potentials are restored when the learner is able to concentrate his mental energies on one or more fields of knowledge to which he feels personally attached, where he feels responsible for "doing justice" to, for discovering the meaning of, specific problems in his fields of preference. The acrobatics of jumping from one branch of the tree of knowledge to another may be characteristic of formal operations but certainly contradicts genuine involvement and meaningful internalization.

—What are the *negative* implications of these success-criteria? What are the failures almost inevitably accompanying successful rehabilitation?

(a) There is the danger that a student will not pass a final examination in one or more subjects and consequently will not be admitted to a higher course of learning. Internalized knowledge will not be translatable with equal ease to fields in which skills or mastery of formulae are of the essence. (Hence the need for introducing into rehabilitative teaching programs auxiliary services such as tutoring partly unsuccessful students even *after* graduation.)

(b) Differentiation may be functioning unusually well in understanding intrapersonal processes, interpersonal relationships, social problems, and configurations; but the student may be unable to make use of these abilities in the more formal learning assignments to which his final examinations relate. (Hence the need for working out alternative examination forms or for nonschematic, not purely quantitative calculations of examination papers).

(c) We have observed that sometimes the rehabilitation of the ability to differentiate was too much of a success, as it were; some students gave the impression of being oversophisticated in their fear of regressing into their former *lack* of differentiation, in their attempt to avoid every form of an absolute answer, even when it was the correct solution of a problem, in mathematics or physics, for instance. In such cases, the method, though successfully employed by the teacher, produced inadequate results due to a still remaining basic insecurity.

—It would be a mistake to define as a criterion of success the pupil's ability to withstand the harmful impact of a negative environment and to maintain what they may have gained as a result of successful rehabilitation teaching in spite of the unfavorable conditions with which they may have to live. Vulnerability is a collateral of rehabilitation, a problem we mentioned at the beginning of our study. The damage done to the child's mental structure is liable to make itself felt long after it may have been "healed." A valid criterion of success in rehabilitative teaching would therefore be: the students' and the graduates' ability to understand the meaning of the social workers' support and to cooperate with them in order to preserve and protect that cognitive tension which is the precondition of any cognitive gain.

In other words, the criterion of success here envisaged is the learner's ability to react realistically to the services offered. Actually, this realism means that he has come to see himself as a subject, not only in his learning tasks but also in his self-perception and his interpersonal relationships. This revised position requires trust without dependence, and—again—internalization. It is one of the criteria of successful rehabilitation.

—When speaking of any method of human intervention, we should remain aware of the fact that it may be contraindicated in certain cases (and this in spite of a certain degree of individual success). We have already mentioned that in every class, hence also in every seemingly homogeneous class of secondarily retarded pupils, some will invariably be found who do not "belong" to it. Some may be of normal learning ability, and the noninductiveness of the teaching method may unnecessarily delay their possible progress; they should be transferred to a regular class. But the advocates of a primarily integration-oriented school system and teaching method are often reluctant to "give up" such a bright child and, as a result, cause great harm to the less capable students, the so-called slow-learners.* But then, the advocates of a primarily integration-oriented system of schooling reject, as a rule, the methods of rehabilitative teaching recommended here. It would, therefore, be self-contradictory to see in such cases (of bright children not benefiting from a teaching method that is not meant for them) proof that this method has failed.

— We have mentioned the case of the bright pupil to show the limits of rehabilitative teaching (reference is made also to what has been said above, on pp. 78f., about the problem of class heterogeneity in general). Still more serious is the limitation of the method and its applicability when there are present in the class a number of aggressively disruptive children. Although we shall come back to that problem in the following chapter, where we shall analyze the social worker's functions within a rehabilitative teaching program, it must be admitted here that dealing with such cases, even successfully, is *not* a success-criterion of rehabilitative teaching: teaching as such is not capable of reaching the deep-lying personality roots of severe behavior disorders. This can be achieved, if at all, only in a therapeutic group, specially designed for this type of pathology, but certainly not in an "open" class setting in which the majority have different needs and expectations but are, on the other hand, weak enough in their ego-structure to be drawn away easily from concentration on learning by their disruptive classmates. But for the same reason, failure of a rehabilitative teaching program due to their disruptive presence should in no way be construed to be evidence against the validity of the idea and the methods of rehabilitation.

---

*Needless to explain again why we consider this to be a misnomer: it is a concept much too comprehensive and undifferentiated to allow for adequate diagnosis or for differential didactic interventions.

Let us now sum up what we have said on the subject of how to evaluate the outcome of rehabilitative teaching.

It can be said to have been successful to the extent that the child will relate himself to his cognitive assignments as a subject responsible for his acts of thinking and learning. It aims at bringing the learner to a point where he will no longer be satisfied with taking in passively what the teacher may want him to know or understand but will be able to distinguish between content and meaning. This requires the use of special teaching methods. Hence homogeneous groups are preferable during a "preparatory" period. In such groups, the child will be less exposed to the dangers of external imitation of so-called regular learners.

The often emphasized advantage of improved intergroup and interpersonal relationships, that is, of so-called social integration, particularly in the younger age groups, seems doubtful: true nearness between human beings requires the experience of existential, though not necessarily functional, equality: as far as the secondarily retarded child is concerned, this experience requires a more realistic self-perception or self-evaluation.

Such a basic attitude-change results, in turn, from the child's frequently repeated experiences of being taken seriously in his thinking processes, even when they result in "wrong" answers. The most important manifestation of this attitude change is the learner's personal involvement in discovering the differential meanings of specific subject matters learned.

This, however, excludes an effective, though superficial and impersonal, overall orientation in many areas of knowledge as required in most types of final school examinations. Hence, partial failure in such examinations, though from a social point of view a negative result of rehabilitative teaching, should not be interpreted as proof against the validity of the method.

The method is not defined adequately by an analysis of its three constitutive elements (noninductiveness, branching out, and neutralization of affects). No less intrinsic to it is the availability of a number of supplementary services: contacts of the teacher with individual pupils, when it becomes evident that class discussions will not meet their needs; social-work contacts with each child and his parents; intensive aftercare; group discussions of "explosive" issues, jointly with so-called regular students; facilities for the early transfer of very bright pupils to regular classes and of disruptive behavior-disorder cases to special treatment settings; and, of course, adequate teacher training and guidance.

This means, as we have already pointed out (see pp. 66f. and pp. 85f.) that independence and cognitive freedom should *not* be considered an absolute success-criterion of rehabilitative teaching. Preventive interventions at an early stage in the child's life, optimal stimulation during his elementary school years, rehabilitative teaching in the junior high school—none guarantees that freedom of thinking which we call "normal"; they should follow each other and lead to continued support.*

Thus, when the child, at the age of 11 or 12, enters junior high school, he may have reached a stage in his development in which "the synthetic function of the ego" (to quote a term used by Nunberg[27] is strong enough to make self-confrontation with learning contents possible, but where the ego is also flexible enough to change his attitudes to learning, if properly guided. But this does not mean that when he has reached the age of 15 and is ready to enter senior high school, he will be "rehabilitated" to such a degree that he will be ready to join a regular class and to continue his learnings according to a generally accepted, inductive, and content-focused method of teaching.

---

*Nonacceptance of this tenet is one of the factors that explain why most statistical evaluation studies lead to pessimistic conclusions; it is indeed true that no single method of intervention produces changes in the child's cognitive structure that enable him to proceed unaided.

3
Social Work and Teaching

I. THE SOCIAL WORKER'S FUNCTIONS

The Functions

A school teacher must ask himself, before he takes upon himself individual treatment functions, whether he thereby increases his effectiveness as a teacher or, perhaps, jeopardizes his teaching role.

We see this problem from a specific angle only: that of the socially or culturally retarded child or adolescent at school. True: *every* school benefits from a social worker's cooperation; every school needs supplementation of its educational service through some form of treatment services. But a school for the disadvantaged is much more in need of a social worker, and not only because of the relative frequency of social and economic problems in the families of these children and adolescents; the main reason is their need for guidance and treatment when externalizing life conditions endanger or impair their mental capacities.

Never should a teacher take upon himself treatment functions that require dealing with the intimate aspects of family relationships. Let it be said again: we are speaking of the disadvantaged child and his family. A teacher entering such a family and trying to influence the parents' educational attitudes by referring to their hidden as well as to their conscious motives, is liable to lose in their eyes his status as cognitive authority. He should not know "too much" about what is going on inside the family, yet he could not guide them effectively *without* knowing highly personal details. But he will never be able to discover such details: since the parents of socially or culturally deprived children are, as a rule, more rigidly tradition-oriented and more rigidly patterned in their attitudes toward life, they expect the teacher to remain at a distance, as it were. But since, on the other hand, genuine changes depend on the parents' readiness to cooperate without self-restriction or reservations, the teacher is usually *not* the most suitable person to deal with problems that cannot be approached without personal nearness.

This does not mean, of course, that the teacher as an educator cannot and should not fulfill certain very important treatment functions—but he can do so on two conditions: the behavior problems with which the *teacher* can deal effectively must be such as to have some bearing on the total class situation, and they should not require treatment of unconscious complexes, in either the child or his parents.

The teacher's interventions are restricted to the conscious-ideational level. As soon as personal problem areas are touched, the parents feel justified and compelled to conceal vitally important motivations, value patterns, and beliefs in order to please the teacher and live up to what they believe are his expectations. Obviously, treatment is bound to remain ineffective when the parents pay lip service only to certain principles and attitudes that they consider "are expected." We know how difficult it is to recognize what a certain behavior means to a person and what motivations may lie behind it. Much learning goes into their recognition, and much courage is needed to venture into ever uncertain assumptions. But as far as the teacher is concerned, even learning is not enough. Even if he knows well how to diagnose behavior and how to guide adults, including his pupil's parents, he is bound to lose status in their eyes as soon as he starts assuming the role of a therapist.

It is doubtful, to say the least, whether functions of teaching and educating (with their orientation toward the child's and the parents' conscious minds) can ever be combined in one person with treatment functions; the latter requires abstraction from the manifestations of consciousness and concentration on the forces and contents that may hide behind them. It is precisely for this reason that the social worker is the proper person for such treatment functions—the parents do not identify him with teaching or with education, and they are accustomed to seeing in him someone who is familiar with their weaknesses. It is much more natural for them to trust the social worker and to have confidence in him; it is easier for him than for the teacher to reach their true perception of themselves and of their children, of their past and present conflicts and their expectations of the future, without being misled by the impression they try to make on others.

Obviously, the social worker must be careful not to fall victim to the externalized person's attempts to manipulate him and to exploit him for the attainment of certain immediate advantages. But it is relatively easy for a well-trained social worker to handle such attempts, since it is part of his training to learn how to distinguish between different demands made on him, whether legitimate or unjustified, and his functions.

What, then, *are* a social worker's functions within a school for socially disadvantaged and retarded children and adolescents? His functions include personal contacts with the parents and the pupils, group discussions with the parents, group discussions with the students, individual contacts with the teachers.

Individual Contacts with the Parents

One of the major aims of these treatment contacts is to help the parents understand their sons' and daughters' age-conditioned personality difficulties. Most of the parents will find it extremely difficult to accept all implications of a long-term study program, particularly with a nonvocational, academic, orientation. Acceptance of a "moratorium" (in Erikson's use of the term), particularly for their adolescent children, is never as natural for them as it is for the ordinary middle-class family in a Western or Westernized world. Moreover, nonrealistic expectations of full and quick success are almost unavoidable under these conditions. Clinging to traditional demands, particularly with girls, is another expression of the parents' externalized attitude toward values and social goals and of their limited time span. Such attitudes are, of course, liable to have a negative impact on their children's learning. The apparent contradiction between these limitations and the parents' willingness to accept and support the school's program is part of the behavior picture called "externalization."

Another group of problems requiring a social worker's intervention is that of personality weaknesses in one or both parents. Such weaknesses or defects are known to be pathogenic factors in the school career of any child, but their weight increases when they operate in conjunction with poverty and educational neglect or with cultural transition and value-ambiguity.*

In what respect do the child's behavior disorders differ when they result from the parents' personality disturbances only, from what they are likely to be when the primary factor is externalization and personal difficulties are auxiliary causes only? What is the parents' behavior like when the two factors operate independently of each other and when the latter appears as *the result* of the former? It is obvious that if there exists an essential difference between those two constellations, treatment interventions, too, must be different.

But did we not claim that what children with secondary retardation need is a teaching method conducive to the rehabilitation of their impaired intelligence? Why, then, should the *school* provide treatment services meant to change the parents' attitude, or to deal with their personality problems? Would it not be sufficient to use existing community services for this purpose?

We claim that the integration of treatment services offered by a social worker with rehabilitative teaching is an essential element of the latter and not a more or less dispensable addition. As long as children or adolescents continue to live in those very social conditions that had been responsible for the climate of externalization and for the impairment of their intelligence, they are exposed to their pathogenic influence—which is liable to counteract whatever the school may be able to repair. Moreover, the inevitable alienation of the children from their parents, particularly as the result of an intensive course of high school studies, increases the danger of environmental frustrations and, through them, endangers the learning process. Hence, the addition of social-work treatment is not only

---

*In many cases urgent material needs require assistance, either directly or indirectly, that is, by referral. In other cases, brothers or sisters require counseling services, guidance, help with vocational plans, and so forth.

justified but even indispensable in any school project aimed at rehabilitating socially or culturally impaired intelligence.

Group Discussions with Parents

The main purpose of group discussions is to make the parents see the similarities between the difficulties they experience with their children and those experienced by others, and to make them aware of the common age factor.

Group discussions with the parents also serve to improve their ability and readiness for cooperation with the teachers. The problems discussed then often become subjects of discussion in the individual contacts as well. In this case, the group has important preparatory functions.

When one is working with adolescents it is of the essence to secure *inner* consent on the part of the parents to the teaching project, its aims and methods. Their conscious confrontation with the implications of consent, in the presence of other parents, is likely to diminish their resistance.

Toward the end of the study period another problem comes up in these group discussions, that of how to choose a proper career for the child after the matriculation certificate—continuation of studies at the University or going to learn a trade or a vocation! Here again, group discussions do not replace but prepare individual contacts. Receiving accurate information on the multitude of individual varieties helps many parents understand the need for taking into full consideration their children's specific inclinations, abilities, limitations, expectations. The objective needs of the economy and the individual's chances of striking roots in a particular profession or vocation should be discussed; so should the problem of personal satisfaction to be found in occupational functions and its dependence on the level of possible earnings, on social status, on personality factors.

Such discussions should be held frequently, not only to correct faulty attitudes, but also to foster a feeling of sharing common problems. Discussing the future of their sons and daughters, their hopes and expectations, and the need to give up certain demands or attitudes in which they had seen part of their cultural identity—these are effective means for changing the parents' externalized perception of their parental roles and their children's future. Group discussions, to be really effective tools of education, and attitude change, must gradually become a responsibility of the participants, who should even take the initiative for organizing the meetings and choosing the topics to be discussed. This, however, presupposes readiness, on the part of the participants, for self-confrontation with personality problems—which is rarely found in externalized or "tradition-directed" adults and never in "problem parents," for whom self-confrontation is a threat to their rigid self-perception.

Many adults suffer from strong resentments and feelings of being frustrated when children are included in a separate class unit. Why are they not admitted or at least transferred to a regular class after a short period of preparation? What is wrong with them? Are they, the parents, to blame for it? Group discussions with parents are, as a rule, much more useful instruments of interpretation than personal contacts.

Individual Contacts with the Pupils

Underprivileged and secondarily retarded children and adolescents often feel ashamed of their "primitive" parents, who, tied to poverty and distress, are not free for those values that the school represents and are, in any case, strangers in that world of values. But shame is essentially different from conscious rejection of the parents as may result from strong independence-needs in many middle-class adolescents. Both types, it is true, may not want the school to cooperate with their parents, but revolt does not necessarily impair intellectual acuity and certainly not the ability to differentiate in spite of possible distortions. Shame, on the other hand, easily impairs cognitive initiative and activity, since it manifests itself in two equally strong but contradictory tendencies: to belong to the parents and to be different from them—an inner contradiction that is liable to paralyze thinking processes. When rejection and revolt increase, there may be a need for therapy to prevent extreme pathologies. But when we deal with secondary retardation, it is an integral function of *teaching* to consider the ways the child's rejection of his parents' mentality manifests itself in his thinking and learning processes. The contradictions between the learning attitude that the school endeavors to create in its socially retarded pupils and the inner tensions produced by their negative and yet unacceptable perception of the parents as "primitive" is liable to jeopardize their cognitive abilities—hence the need for a social worker to deal with the many problems that are likely to result from this inner contradiction.

(Obviously, it is not enough to add a social worker to the school's services, if we want to prevent serious disturbances. Other services are needed as well, and particularly guidance of the teachers with a view to deepening their understanding of the pupils' inner conflicts and the bearing these conflicts may have on the learning process.)

The situations necessitating a social worker's interventions may be similar to those known from school social work in general. Yet these situations have an altogether different meaning in the life of middle-class children from their meaning for an externalized child or adolescent.

The intensity of the conflict increases, it is true, in each of the two types when the parents show lack of understanding for their children's phase-dependent conflicts and behavioral peculiarities. But while the generation conflicts and tensions are part of a middle-class child's growth process, the crisis resulting from similar conflicts in lower-class, and particularly in externalized, families, has a different meaning: it is liable to produce increased externalization in the child as well—as if he felt a need to translate his personal problems into the language of his parents' externalized life-patterns.

Group Discussions with Pupils

Such discussions can be organized by the social worker, the class teacher, or both. The responsibility of each worker depends, of course, on the subject discussed. The treatment of intimate personal issues should be and remain the social worker's prerogative, while the teacher should deal with the cognitive and value aspects of those issues, in group discussions no less than in personal contacts. When parent-child relationships come up in a group meeting with the social worker, there may be a frank discussion of feelings (fears, hopes, expectations, doubts). The very same topics in discussions with the teacher remain somehow associated with contents of learning, with concepts and principles—no doubt an important enrichment of objective learning as well as of personal self-confrontation.

Another topic frequently discussed is that of the separate class unit. Feelings of resentment, of being discriminated against, come up in ordinary class discussions as well, and can therefore be considered suitable for discussions under the joint leadership of the teacher *and* the social worker. Whereas negative behavioral expressions of those negative feelings can better be discussed by, and with, a teacher (in the class or in subunits), it is the underlying affectivity that should be analyzed with the help of a social worker. It is obvious that the affects connected with feelings of being discriminated against will not as easily be expressed in the presence of the teacher as they may be in discussions with the social worker.

Another problem area is that of sexual feelings and relationships. The teacher should undoubtedly take an active part in sex education, provided he has received adequate training in its techniques. The social worker can discuss open and hidden fears of sex, misconceptions and fantasies, expectations and disappointments, both in group discussions and individual contacts. How are sexual experiences and feelings connected with a child's, and particularly an adolescent's often distorted, self-perception?

These are some of the problems that come up in group discussions led by a social worker who is not associated with any formal function or setting but is, on the other hand, intimately and intensively connected with the family. The social worker, though emotionally "near," is often much more convincing as an image of competence than the parents; he combines the qualities of reliability and usefulness with a nonjudgmental attitude.

Some comments may be added here:

Group discussions, here as in any treatment setting, may prepare a participant for individual contacts. Many children are unable to overcome their resistance to discussing personal problems with any adult, and even the best-skilled social worker may not be able to break their resistance. But it is precisely in such cases that the experience of similar or contrary problems as they appear in classmates will make it easier for them to discuss such similarities or contrasts as topics suitable for objective analysis. The fact that these discussions are no longer confined to the esoteric friendship group, but are controlled by a trustworthy adult, in this case the social worker, makes them much less dangerous, more "objective." This objectivity, however, opens the way for a continuation of discussions, on a one-to-one basis, in personal contacts with the social worker.

We know, of course, of opposite cases as well, of children and adolescents who refuse "on principle" to discuss personal problems in the presence of an adult because they fear loss of status. These are mostly adolescents whose greatest problem is their need to wear a mask. They, therefore, must be offered an opportunity to establish personal contacts with a trustworthy adult, and to maintain them often for a considerable length of time, before they will be able to participate in group discussions "without a mask."

Another function of group discussions is bridging the gap between a child and his family. Here, too, recognition of the universality of a seemingly unique problem, which helps the child perceive the parents more objectively, will be easier and more effective when the issue is being discussed in groups. We must not forget that we are speaking of youngsters who have grown up in a tradition-directed or in an externalized environment. For them, a noneffective or, at least, a less affect-laden perception of their parents' reality and values, is vitally important because affective fixations stand in the way of attaining the ultimate aim of education and development, individuality and independence.

The social worker will be able adequately to fulfill the here-specified functions only to the extent that he succeeds in maintaining his image in the eyes of the adolescent as both near and neutral: the student may see in the social worker a representative of the values identified with the school; he may then consider the social worker to be an extension of the school authority and will therefore try to keep at a safe distance from him. It goes without saying that the latter cannot work usefully without changing this distorted and distorting perception. He does *not* represent the school, even though he works *on behalf* of the school. This fact, better perhaps than any other, throws light on the essential difference between the social worker's and the teacher's functions in a total treatment plan for socially deprived and secondarily retarded pupils. The question of "belonging" will never be asked with regard to the teacher, but only in connection with the social worker's interventions. He is in contact with the home. Can he be trusted? Or does he serve the interests of the parents only? Much skill is needed, indeed, to gain and to keep the child's trust without losing that of the parents; it is the parents' confidence that makes the contacts with the child meaningful.

We have not yet mentioned another possible function of group discussions, that of social values, which is, of course, primarily one of the teacher's main functions. Outstanding among such value discussions is that of social justice. The latter is most closely linked with feelings of resentment over being discriminated against that is, with the experience of—objective or imagined—injustice. Their aim is to strengthen in the participants self-confidence and social trust, those preconditions of overcoming resentments.

It would seem that one of the most useful means of dealing with the problem here analyzed is to conduct discussions of social values, of justice and injustice in all their objective and personal implications, in which both the underprivileged and the regular students take part. Alleviating the inner tension produced by affective interpretations of social differences, social justice, and injustice is one of the preconditions of effective rehabilitation of socially or culturally impaired intelligence. Intellectual achievements will be more reliable and more meaningful for transfer of learning to other, practical as well as cognitive, areas, when they are supported by affect-free self-perception in social contexts.

Furthemore, no one will ever be capable of overcoming his negative affect-reaction to the experience of social differences on a purely intellectual level* or through discussing emotional reactions only. Conceptual interpretations and explanations must be accompanied by personal confrontations with the representatives of the "other side." Needless to say such discussions contain explosive material, and those responsible for leading them must be well trained in methods of handling human conflicts and tensions. It would seem that neither the social worker nor the teacher should take upon himself this function.

---

*See the later discussion of "explosive issues" and their treatment in class lessons.

Contacts with the Teachers

Here, where we analyze the social worker's functions with regard to the teachers, we have in mind contacts aimed at helping them understand their pupils' socio-cultural background and behavior patterns. Everyone will agree that the teacher needs guidance in this vital problem area, but it is an open question whether he will be ready to learn from a social worker's experience how to relate himself to his students and how to understand each child's individual needs. Contacts between the teacher and the social worker have a double aim: to help the social worker understand how the facts of the child's background are reflected in his learning, and to help the teacher toward a more adequate interpretation of his pupil's behavior and thinking, in the classroom and outside. What is the impact of personality factors, specific family relationships, and socio-cultural patterns on thinking and learning processes? This is a question that cannot be answered unless social worker and teacher pool their experience.

But at the same time, we must warn against a danger in this very cooperation: it has happened quite often that a teacher, after receiving relevant information from the social worker, has made unallowed use of it by giving one of his pupils to understand that he knows "secrets" about him or his family which he could have heard only from the social worker. The teacher must not only be careful to keep such critical information to himself, he also should never forget that, being a teacher, he must refrain from trying to "treat" a pupil's problem. He could not continue with his teaching objectives if he became engaged in such intimate treatment-functions. Securing the teacher's cooperation is of the utmost importance for the social worker—so much so, in fact, that it may sometimes be preferable to do *without* that cooperation if there is reason to suspect the teacher may overstep his professional limits.

On the other hand, the case of one specific pupil may have to be discussed jointly by a number of teachers and the social worker. Such discussions, which resemble clinical conferences in other settings, are capable of bringing to the fore general problems of causation or symptomatology as well, and here too, the social worker's possible contribution is of vital importance.

Another aspect is that of the teacher's need for understanding the psycho-dynamics of his conscious and unconscious motivations which determine the way in which he perceives his functions and his students. This is the area of what is commonly called "mental hygiene in teaching." It is an important part of teacher training and teacher guidance in every school and doubly important in a school for socially underprivileged and retarded adolescents. But it certainly is *not* a function of the social worker within a certain institution to deal with the mental health problems of the teachers who work within that very institution, either individually or in groups, even when he is properly trained for such near-therapeutic functions. It is unthinkable to entrust one and the same worker with the two equally important functions of dealing with the students' needs, on the one hand, and those of their teachers, on the other.

Intensity of Treatment

Degrees of intensity of the social worker's contacts with his "clients" differ. Sometimes treatment centers on the pupil only or on one of the parents only. In the majority of cases, however, the child within his family, that is, both the child and his parents, have to be treated. Similarly, in most cases, contacts have to be maintained, for one reason or another, throughout a prolonged period, although not always at the same level of frequency and intensity. These are the cases that could be classified as belonging to the "high intensity" group. "Intensive," however, can also refer to short contacts that require the mobilization of several services within a limited period of time, sometimes renewed after a few months or even a year, for the same or for different reasons.

On the other hand, many cases require peripheral interventions only, usually directed to the child only, or to one of the parents only, and not to the whole family. But even these more or less superficial contacts often have important preventive functions.

In every group of secondarily retarded children many will need no treatment contacts whatsoever. A relatively high degree of integrational abilities in the child and harmonious family relationships will make solutions of whatever problems appear, possible without a social worker's assistance. When the latter meets with such a student or with one of his parents, the purpose and content is support rather than treatment. Here, the restoration of environmentally damaged cognitive abilities is a function of the specific teaching process only, unaided by any form of "auxiliary" treatment.

Some pupils will not receive the treatment they need, because of some kind of deep-rooted personality disorders or family pathologies. General indolence, for instance, may be responsible for weak participation in the learning-activities and/or the social life of the group. Passiveness, however, does not always cause concern because the child does not disturb. It may well be that deep-going therapy would discover the hidden roots of these disorders and, if successful, could help the child reach a more satisfactory level of intellectual or social activity. But there are always more pressing demands on the social worker's limited time, a fact that explains why he tends to neglect those few, indolent and relatively inefficient but somehow "bearable," cases.

Ideally, the aim of social work is to eliminate the pathogenic factors in the child or one of his parents or his socio-cultural background. More limited, less ambitious, aims are to help the child and his environment understand the implications of the learning process, and to reduce intrapsychic and interpsychic tensions (which, as a rule, limit understanding).

But we should beware of any overoptimistic evaluation: the vulnerability of a socially or culturally underprivileged and therefore intellectually impaired pupil constitutes a threat to what can be achieved unless social support is secured for the graduates. We are aware of the difficulties implied in this reservation, since the social worker cannot, as a rule, control the ways in which society absorbs them. Hence the importance of including aftercare services in any project meant to rehabilitate impaired intelligence.

Aftercare

Its main function is to reduce to a minimum the vulnerability that can express itself in regression to former patterns of externalized behavior and thinking and in losing all interest in continued studies. To the extent that such regression is likely to take place, it is not due to cognitive deficiencies or to structural defects but to lack of continued educational support. Such support has two functions: to help preserve the acquired ability to think differentially and responsibly, and to keep alive the self-image of "one belonging to the community of learners." For these purposes, contacts have to be maintained with the graduates and their parents (although the latter, for obvious reasons, become less decisive in planning their grown-up sons' or daughters' future, and much more depends on the latters' self-conceptions and decisions).

The social worker must start working with the students in-dividually as soon as possible: one graduate may need help to improve his matriculation test marks where there have been partial failures; in another case, arrangements should be made for admission to a specific preparatory course of studies; often, contacts have to be used for the sole purpose of developing reading habits or stimulating interests in a specific area.

In all cases, the social worker must help the graduates toward a more realistic conception of their plans for the future. They must come to accept the fact that university studies essentially differ from the high school experience because now the students have to bear full responsibility for their own maintenance; they are not given another "moratorium"; they may have to work, in addition to studying, even if it means adding a year or two to the period needed for completing their course.

In one of our comprehensive projects the most unexpected success was the fact that most of our graduates chose an academic study course after completing their army service,* that is, two to three years after they had left high school. The girls preferred social work, laboratory work, physiotherapy, occupational therapy, or teaching in elementary schools, but some also chose university courses in humanities or in natural sciences with the intention of becoming high school teachers in these subjects. Most of the boys chose computer science, law, economics, or dentistry, in addition to high school teaching.

But even in these cases, aftercare was of considerable importance. Its main purpose and function was supporting the students' ability to maintain their intellectual initiative and to resist the detracting force

*Which, in Israel, is compulsory.

of environmental factors. It was, indeed, no small achievement for them not to have chosen other ways of preparing themselves for some sort of "easy jobs," which would have yielded a good income without much preparation. Some who did go into clerical work because they had decided to found a family as soon as possible and therefore had to earn money, immediately attended relevant continuation courses, in banking and economics, and succeeded extremely well.

II. SOCIAL WORK TREATMENT AND TEACHING

The Teacher's Educational Functions

One of the symptoms of externalization and one of the recurring difficulties in the learning processes of secondarily retarded children, of all ages, is the inadequacy of their reaction to failure. "I have made great efforts," such a child will say; "how come that I received such a low grading?" And then, according to mood or temperament, he may go on saying: "No use making efforts! I give up. Learning is not for me." Another one, inclined to more aggressive reactions, will blame the teacher for having had a bias against him, though he might not be able to support his feeling of being discriminated against by any factual evidence. (But then: disconnecting a feeling from the context of objective behavior and not seeing another person's behavior as part of a system regulated by inner consistency are indications of externalized attitudes.)

The educator may then discuss with such a pupil the criteria for assessing the quality of achievements: the effort made (and its evidence), the objectively comparable results, the degree of internalization (as against chance success). He may try to discover, together with the pupil, the reasons for his failure and the inadequacy of his aggressive or resentful reactions—all this, however, without going into an analysis of personality tendencies that may be responsible for a general inclination to perceive the adult world as hostile. It may be rooted in the parents' failure to provide the child with a sense of trust and security in reaction to their own disappointments or personality deficiencies. But the teacher should not take the initiative for dealing with such—repressed or suppressed—experiences. The pupil would be at a loss to understand how one and the same person could simultaneously fulfill two obviously contradictory functions: to speak in the name of contents and ideas, values and cognitive methods, and to discuss, without judging, human weaknesses, as they appear not only in the child but also in his parents, those primary representatives of value and authority.

Another problem area in which the teacher and educator will feel competent is that of "responsibility" and its different expressions and applications. A pupil may have taken upon himself a task for the benefit of his class, and he may fail to take seriously the ensuing obligations. The teacher will discuss with him what he should have done, but he would *not* tell him that he has not been involved in the task he took upon himself as strongly as he would have been in another, more drive-determined task. For comparing with each other degrees of ego involvement in self- and other-centered tasks would inevitably lead to the question of "value judgment versus psychological understanding": Can the teacher accept as an excuse the fact that a child may not be motivated strongly enough to act responsibly in a certain task situation? Can he draw the conclusion that while trying to create a stronger motivation he may have to give up, at least temporarily, his role as a value-oriented educator whose duty it is to confront the pupil with value-directed demands? It would seem that a teacher can never give up this role even when he accepts comparison of values as a legitimate method for improving thereby his students' ability to differentiate and to think rationally.

It often happens that an educator must take a definite stand in dealing with a pupil who is trying to deny his guilt for some offense he has committed. For the teacher, denial of guilt is much more serious a problem than committing an "ordinary" offense. For him, courage and honesty are absolute values, and he will use all methods at his disposal to convince his students that accepting these values is not only a pre-condition of human, but also of intellectual integrity. The social worker, on the other hand, and still more so the therapist, will ask why a child lacks courage, why he needs defense through lying, and how he could be helped toward a different self- and world-perception, one that would make lying unnecessary; for him, courage is a value because it indicates genuine (not compensatory) security.

There are, of course, those many attempts made by great educators and child psychologists to strengthen a pupil's feeling of belonging, his sense of trust, his "courage to be," and thus, incidentally, also his honesty. But these attempts are, as a rule, made within a comprehensive life setting, a group or an institution, whereas we are speaking of day schools for socially deprived pupils in which they are not exposed to the same extent to a "therapeutic environment." Their teachers must therefore rely on the supportive treatment of a social worker, while they confine themselves to activities meant to strengthen the adolescent's consciousness of values and principles.

Still another expression of responsibility can be found in the child's attitude toward school property. One of the well-known symptoms of man-in-externalization is his relative inability to recognize anonymity; he respects the rights of others when he knows them personally, and the better he knows them, the more he will be prepared to respect their rights. Public interests, on the other hand, are far removed from his mind; they are abstractions that do not commit him personally. This holds good for school property as well, at least as long as he does not feel attached to the institution. He may feel attached to a teacher but not to an institution. Hence, the educator may try to "teach" him attachment-in-the-abstract, as it were, but he should not indulge in illusions of success. The externalized child must have experienced great success in his cognitive activities before he can feel attached to something as impersonal as a school building or property.

Some teachers have strong feelings about the way in which the pupils use their occasional earnings: they consider it "irresponsible" that they spend their earnings on luxuries such as expensive (and showy) clothes and accessories or on a motorcycle. In this respect, however, the teachers must revise their value-orientation if they want to reach their pupils; they must accept as natural what at first seems to them proof of irresponsible behavior. Any attempt to bring about changes in the scale of preferences through intellectual means only is doomed to failure, since it does not take into account the dynamics of externalization: the "havable" will become less attractive only when successful learning produces a feeling of security and self-reliance.

This raises the question of whether the teacher can (and whether he should) become a party in the socially deprived child's struggle with his neighborhood patterns. These patterns include fixation to the known and immediacy-orientation, preference for external status symbols, and inability to establish and maintain relationships built on mutuality. Rejecting these patterns may be the result of a slow process of internalizing the values of learning; it may be the expression of a positive alienation, of a gradual withdrawl from the values of the neighborhood. But giving up a pattern of evaluation and behavior should not become in itself a content of learning; *teaching* change of values breeds falsity. Only when such value changes become the by-products of internalized learning, will they be reliable.

This does not mean that the teacher has no function to fulfill in the very process of value-change that goes on in his pupils under the influence of teaching and learning. To the extent that changes can be dealt with as topics of analysis and differentiation, the teacher can do much to support change processes by strengthening awareness. But he should never believe that changes can be *induced* by intellectual analysis only.

The same applies to the many problems of relationships with parents and siblings, with friends in the class and the neighborhood, with teachers and workers in the school. Only to the extent that a clarification of behavior trends and their meaning or an open discussion of questionable attitudes alleviates inner tensions, are these forms of educational intervention significant. Easing tensions prepares, it is true, the way to attitude changes; but without dealing with (hypothetical) motives and "forgotten causes," no genuine change will ever be brought about. Similarly, realistic corrections of unrealistic self-perceptions of future role possibilities will undoubtedly help the student in his confrontation with learning-tasks as well; at least some sort of affective "detente" is likely to help the learner concentrate on his assignments in a more objective way.

Some Unsuitable Cases

It is needless to include, in any discussion of integrating individual treatment actions with rehabilitative teaching, those cases of behavior disorders that appear in primarily retarded children with their type-conditioned basis. In some it may be indolence toward cognitive and social behavior-tasks, in others paranoid interpretation of whatever happens to them, in some followed by fears, in others by aggressive reactions. But none of these symptoms is accessible to treatment by a social worker or a therapist in a day school; these children require much more comprehensive conditioning, and even when it is available, the chances of success are limited. Only isolated cases of such disorders appear in schools or classes of secondarily retarded pupils (as a result of inadequate initial diagnosis). Much greater is the chance of primary (so-called preoedipal or oedipal[12,28] behavior disorders appearing in secondarily retarded children.

We have pointed out that externalizing life conditions, of the social and of the cultural variety, explain the two essential causal elements in such disorders: basic insecurity and earliest disappointment of the child in his parents when the latter shift their attention from him the very moment another child is born or he enters a phase in his development declared and defined to be a phase of "beginning responsibility." In these cases, the original attention was not an expression of personal feelings intentionally directed toward "the child as a person," but was the expression of a more or less patterned behavior as expected in the parents' culture. Though it did not produce security (*because* of its impersonal character), its sudden disappearance was traumatic enough to cause generalized aggressive reactions.

We have said, when dealing with the forms of heterogeneity, that these children's deep-rooted need to prove the negative character of the adult world and to fight against any form of cooperation with the adults, particularly parents and teachers, makes them unsuitable for any nontherapeutic school system. They definitely need institutional care. But unfortunately, adequate treatment facilities are rarely available, and there is practically no class of secondarily retarded children in which such behavior problems are *not* to be found.

Here, the need for full integration of social work with teaching programs becomes evident. To the extent that the teacher must continue to deal with such cases, within his class, intensive and frequent casework contacts should accompany the teacher's efforts to give them learning assignments. Maximal flexibility is of the essence. Thus, it may be necessary in one case to limit the learning assignments to one or two subject matters in which an aggressive child of this type may take a particular interest; in another case it may be advisable to give him an activity program with theoretical studies only loosely attached. Almost invariably he needs individual tutoring outside or inside the class, sometimes in cooperation with the social worker. Individual treatment-actions should be characterized by repeated attempts to relate personal experiences to cognitive material.

As a rule, such a child's intelligence is not impaired functionally; he does understand interpretations of meaning or attempts to show the relevance of facts and of principles for an analysis of human behavior. It is through such focusing of learning on human behavior that the motivation for abstract learning can be implanted in primarily aggressive pupils. If so, we understand why the social worker can, and often must, take an active part in teaching this type of child, provided, of course, he has received special training in addition to his social-work training.* But even then, he must be prepared for limited success only, though it may be the maximum attainable. It is, in any case, the only possible way of behavior modification in these most difficult cases (at least within the school's area of competence).

---

*Obviously, a social worker can never be "at home" in the various areas of knowledge represented in the curriculum; he cannot hope ever to be competent in teaching specific contents. But then, his function is essentially different: he should learn (through contacts with the teachers) enough of the contents taught in the class to refer to them as supporting or contradicting some of the child's distortions of life events or of behavior observed. The chances that such interventions by the social worker (in individual contacts with the pupil) will become meaningful and will help in modifying his behavior, or even his general outlook on life, will be better in the elementary classes and during the first junior high school year than later.

"Neurotic" Behavior Problems in Secondary Retardation

In some secondarily retarded children, symptoms of what seems to be neurotic behavior can be observed. Here, it may be the compulsiveness of repeated aggressive acts that indicates a neurotic pattern, perhaps a kind of escape from fears and anxieties. There, depressive moods may cause indolent acceptance of failure and, at the same time, be deepened by the experience of failure. Here the symptoms may be an excessive feeling of inferiority, there an irrational fearfulness.

In these and similar cases we ask: how is secondary retardation compatible with those inner tensions that we are used to holding responsible for the emergence of neurotic disorders? How can we explain the emergence of early ambivalence-conflicts (believed to be the roots of inner tensions in neurotic developments) under conditions of externalization, that is, of growing up in a climate of impersonal relationships between parents themselves and between parents and children? Are the neurotic "additions" to the secondarily retarded child's cognitive and social behavior genuinely neurotic? Or could it be that children presenting these symptoms are *not* secondarily retarded?

We suggest a number of alternative answers, each one relating to certain groups of cases. We have said several times already that any concept used in any analysis of behavior, hence also the concepts of externalization, relational impersonality, or secondary retardation, are but ideal-type constructs. In reality, underprivileged children are born into and grow up under, the externalizing conditions of "more or less" *impersonality of relationships,* "more or less" *inadequate care,* and, as a result, are, at a later stage of their development, only "more or less" *unable to differentiate,* to think in abstract terms, and to relate to their learning-tasks responsibly—more or less but not absolutely.

It follows that when the child's conditions of growth are *not* conditions of *extreme* externalization, he *does* have a chance of experiencing his "parents as persons" and not only as impersonal representatives of rigid and rationally incomprehensible patterns. This mode of experiencing the parents accounts for the child's ability to feel inner tensions, though it will not be of the so-called oedipal type.

In some cases the child may *interpret* as intentionally related to him (or her) certain negative attitudes of a father's generalized and/or culture-conditioned agressiveness, his sexually stimulating behavior in general and, particularly when directed toward the daughter, a mother's ineffectiveness, indolence, or externalized affectivity. In this way, the child not only "feels meant" by the parents' behavior, the outcome is necessarily inner tension. In order to overcome this tension, escape into some form of externalized behavior is much more effective than are openly neurotic symptom-formations. The former has the "advantage" of fulfilling two purposes, that of avoiding the feeling of being meant personally and that of identifying with the frightening, the threatening, the seducing, the frustrating, the ineffective parents, by way of imitating their behavior or, at least, some of its manifest expressions.

We should be careful not to describe or analyze these processes in terms of psychoanalytical theorizing. The conflict is not one between contradictory libidinal tendencies, not one between unconscious wishes and fears. The conflict is one between a more or less conscious insight and an equally conscious emotional need. On the one hand, there is the *knowledge* that parental behavior is *not* directed toward (or against) the child, that the feeling of being meant is an illusion (because the parents' behavior is, in fact, part of their individual or cultural patterns). On the other hand, there is the ardent *wish* in the child to be taken seriously as a person, to be meant, though not in threatening, attacking, or restricting actions. In other words: the wish to be meant as a person coexists with the wish *not* to be meant as a person as long as it would mean only to be a "personal" object of parental maltreatment.

The tensions resulting from this conscious conflict between insight and desire explain why seemingly neurotic fears or depressions accompany in these cases symptoms of externalization and secondary retardation. It is self-evident that such children need individual treatment in addition to rehabilitative teaching.

In another group we find, among pupils of a relatively high level of potential and rehabilitated intelligence, not a few who suffer from (conscious or half-conscious) guilt feelings over the fact that they have advanced far beyond the intellectual level of their parents. Such guilt feelings may then produce some sort of quasineurotic fears. It is obvious that this group is different from that analyzed before: in spite of the family's externalizing life conditions there are sufficiently strong cohesive forces at work in these cases to produce a sense of security in the children, based on truly personal relationships and identifications.* And yet, their guilt feelings may be so intense that some may use escape into regressive externalization as their "solution." (They are different from those neurotics who escape from the pressure of their symptoms into waywardness, as Aichhorn has shown,¹although they then develop many symptoms of secondary retardation, such as dependence on the illusion of knownness, inability to understand the dimension of the self, or a distorted self-perception.)

Treatment Methods in Problem Cases

In the first section of this chapter where we analyzed the social worker's functions in a school for secondarily retarded children, we tried to make it clear that, whatever treatment actions he may undertake, the main purpose of his interventions is to help rehabilitate cognitive potentials. In other words: much more than in any regular school setting, the social worker in a school in which every teaching act is geared to the task of rehabilitation should ask himself again and again what impact his interventions will have on the pupil's learning-abilities. He should ask this question even in those cases in which he may have made a highly significant contribution to improving a pupil's state of mental health. While this in itself is an important achievement and would be sufficient evidence of success in any other setting (including a regular school), the additional question, as to the significance of this achievement for the restoration of impaired cognitive abilities, is here decisive.

Much has been said and written against a predominantly in-

---

*We are *not* including in these groups those exceptionally bright children and adolescents who, in spite of their adverse life conditions, succeed in all cognitive and social assignments, owing to their integrational abilities and the intrinsic strength of their ego-structure. These children and adolescents are not to be found, as a rule, in schools or classes for secondarily retarded children; they definitely do not belong here.

tellectual orientation of the school in general and the high school in particular. "The integrated personality" is said to be a more legitimate aim of schooling. It has been argued that such a definition of purpose does not contradict a more intellectually oriented definition. But our claim is different: we claim that a child whose originally normal intelligence has been impaired by adverse social and/or cultural conditions, and who therefore is found to live far beneath his level of potentialities, *cannot* become an "integrated personality" unless his cognitive potentialities are restored. We reject as socially dangerous and morally inadmissible any attempt to define that term as meaning that man should learn how to become a well-balanced individual, irrespective of the gap between his potentials and his actualized level of functioning. We may not succeed in undoing what society has damaged, but we should at least try.

It is in this sense that the social worker's efforts in a school for secondarily retarded children fulfill a key function within the teaching team. Under no circumstances should he agree to accept "compensatory" functions, such as helping develop such a child's "social intelligence," important as the latter may be in life. The development of differentiation in emotional and relational task-contexts is undoubtedly of great human value, but the school should never consider this an equivalent or a substitute for developing differentiation in assignments that require abstract thinking.

The social worker should ask himself to what extent the development of understanding for social contexts and human relationships could protect the child in his learning-tasks against the illegitimate interference of emotions or affects with his thinking, to what extent it could help the learner overcome what we have called "contamination" of feeling and thinking (pp. 15f.). It is precisely this consideration that should determine the social worker's treatment actions, in those cases in which emotional conflicts are liable to endanger the teacher's effort fruitfully to use the methods of rehabilitative teaching (see the foregoing subsection).

The social worker may discuss with such a pupil contents and expressions of his fears, his guilt or inferiority feelings, his hopelessness, his self-perception (in the present and, more important, in an imagined future), his expectations and his dreams, his aggressiveness, whether it manifests itself in feelings of hate, resentment, being discriminated against, or being persecuted. In such discussions, the main purpose is to help the child *express* his feelings but, at the same time, in a conceptually clear form. One without the other, expression without clarity, definition without feeling, would *not* serve the social worker's purpose. And it is his neutrality and permissiveness in his individual contacts—in contrast to the teacher's orientation toward contents, methods, and values, within a group setting—that helps the child genuinely to confront his inner world of feelings.

A teacher may choose an analysis of feelings as a teaching-subject in his class, connected with a lesson in history or literature; he is likely to arrive, at a much quicker pace than a social worker, at a differential definition of the variety of feelings he may have decided to discuss in a specific lesson, though on an anonymous (not a person-related) basis only. It is doubtful whether even those among his pupils who actively participate in such a discussion will feel themselves "meant," challenged to relate the contents of such a discussion to themselves; and it is doubtful whether, in the absence of such personal involvement, a discussion of the differential meaning of feelings will have any impact even on the learner's ability to differentiate.

A personal discussion of feelings, on the other hand, as an intrinsic part of the social worker's individual treatment-contacts, may lead to attitude-changes or, at least, to increased awareness. But in order to become meaningful for more adequate thinking and learning processes, the social worker must connect these personally experienced feelings with "objective" contents of the curriculum, brought to him by the teacher and the student himself.

Whatever the predominant negative feeling may be that limits a secondarily retarded child's thinking, treatment-actions must focus on two cognitively relevant aspects: perceiving the self and the other as subjects and correctly understanding the causal connection between human behavior and its results. These two aspects are interlinked: the factors determining human behavior operate through a specifically reacting subject, the individual's ego-structure. At the same time, they are the key factors in any theory of cognition, normal or distorted: only an actively selecting subject can be responsible for adequate thinking and learning; and only to the extent that the learner understands the connection between specific behavior traits and their causes and results, can we hope to correct the distorting influence of nondifferentiated feelings and affects on the thinking and learning processes of the secondarily retarded child.

It is in this way that the social worker's individual treatment contacts with such a child (and particularly a child whose cognitive difficulties are aggravated by quasineurotic fear, aggressiveness, guilt, or despair) are essential elements in the total program of rehabilitative teaching. He must help the child see his parents as persons with their individual history and their own problems. He must help him see himself as a subject in his own right and not just as a manipulated object in the hands of his environment (and since the child's feelings are only too often justified by the behavior of his parents and teachers, the social worker must always be ready to maintain intensive treatment-contacts with the child's decisive adults). He must use as much "objective" (impersonal) material as possible taken from the child's subjects of learning, to exemplify his explanations by more neutral, in any case impersonal, contents (processes and events taken from history, images and stories taken from literature, but also data relating to animal behavior, and so on).

All these actions can be brought on the common denominator of objectivization: defining, exemplifying, classifying affective or emotional experience, seeing from a distance, as it were, neutralizing irrationalities, through dealing with them conceptually and rationally—all aim at weakening the child's dependence on his impulses, his associations, his sterotypes, in his thinking as well as in his feelings, his interpersonal relationships. Whatever successful treatment may achieve will therefore be meaningful not only for behavior modification but also for cognitive rehabilitation.

Part Two

EXAMPLES AND TRAINING

4

Patterns of Distorted Thinking

I. A GENERAL SURVEY

The second part of the present study will be devoted to exemplifying the theses included in the first, theoretical part. Some of the examples will refer to patterns of faulty thinking, such as insufficient differentiation, inadequate responsibility, weak rationality, concretistic thinking, and inability to understand the meaning of the "As-If." They will be taken from teaching records in different subject matters (mainly from age group 12 to 15 in Israeli junior high schools), that is, at the beginning of a rehabilitative teaching program which had been established several years ago.

Some repetition of what was said in the first chapter is unavoidable. Nor do we want to avoid anticipating certain method descriptions, which are to be exemplified in detail only later. But even here, where the examples serve as an introduction to the practice of rehabilitative teaching, we shall see that the various patterns of faulty thinking cannot be isolated from each other as they were in the chapter on cognitive patterns (Chapter 1, Section IV). Associative thinking is linked with concretism; in one case they may appear connected with a strong resistance to using formal operations or to accepting the category of the As-If—in another, with dependence on cultural stereotypes. Other examples may demonstrate the link between simplifying methods, such as non-differentiation or dichotomies, with other manifestations of lack of responsibility for thinking and learning, or they may be linked with signs of irrationality, e.g., identifying analogy with reality.

There will follow examples of the teaching methods employed, of noninductiveness, branching out, neutralizing affects. There again, it will be difficult, if not impossible, to find class events or lessons that could be described to demonstrate each of the three methods (or, better, elements) in isolation, as it were. Although we shall try to exemplify them separately, we shall see that the elements of rehabilitative teaching are no less interlinked with each other than the patterns of faulty thinking are.

A third group of examples will refer to individual treatment actions, accompanying rehabilitative teaching and integrated with it.

Care has been taken to choose the examples so that they will not be too dependent on intimate knowledge of the Israel setting. It is obvious, however, that not every example can be "translated" adequately into the language of American school practice.

The *first function* of rehabilitative teaching is to help the pupil think rationally. Rationality is, of course, far from being identical with absence of ego involvement. One could almost say the opposite: only to the extent that each act of thinking and learning is felt to be an expression, and an intentional activity, of the ego, can it be rational and effective.

The precondition of genuine ego involvement is relative freedom from *uncontrollable associations*. The weaker an ego, the greater will be the danger of irrational dependence on what comes to the mind without being selected. The learner is not free to approach a cognitive task as an automonous subject. Strong emotions are among the essential concomitants of irrationality, which finds an expression in associative thinking; but they do not indicate ego involvement. On the contrary, they prove its absence.

This may seem strange to those who tend to identify affectivity with individuality. But when we analyze the behavior of a person whose spontaneously emerging associations are rooted in some sort of personal experience or in some kind of culture-conditioned habits or patterns (not to speak of simple stimulus contiguity), it should be evident that this person is not *master* of his ego. Hence, it would be absurd to speak in his case of strong ego involvement only because he acts and reacts under the influence of strong emotions or affects.

Adequate intervention by the teacher means here that he must dare to refer to the possible experiences or to the possible cultural roots of those associations which may have been responsible for a faulty answer; and that he must learn how to formulate his presumptions (his "hypotheses") in general, not personal, terms. Nothing would be more dangerous than trying to counteract emotionally charged associations by direct referrals to emotionally charged personal experiences. If the pupil's thinking was indeed determined by such experiences, he needs a perception of those connections as a universal, not a personal, life expression.

This can also be seen as an attempt to translate the feeling-elements of the cognitive process into objective and abstract terms. The teacher presumes the presence of such elements and tentatively defines their operation, tries to show their generality, and to replace irrational dependence on such associations by seeing, comprehending, and accepting the laws of their possible effects.

Similarly, the teacher must try to "wean" the mind of his externalized and secondarily retarded students from their tendency to *prefer concretizations* to abstractions, to substitute examples for generalities and laws, to use specific rather than general concepts, to identify values with their concrete manifestations, feelings with their external expressions. It is by no means an easy task to prove the irrationality of such tendencies and preferences, particularly for a teacher who is himself accustomed to seeing in exemplifications indispensable auxiliaries of "good teaching." Such a teacher usually overlooks the fact that examples support laws and generalities only when the latter are internalized, whereas they tend to take the place of laws and generalities when the latter are *not* internalized or not yet accepted at all (under conditions of externalization).

Closely connected, though not identical, with the second pattern of faulty thinking is the irrational tendency of a socially or culturally retarded child or adolescent *to think in terms of concrete symbols* rather than in concepts that do not contain symbolic elements; showing them to the learner as clearly as possible is one of the means of making him understand the essence of concepts. But the ultimate aim of teaching the art of conceptualization is nevertheless to show the *advantages* of concepts over symbols when we are engaged in analytic thinking: They allow for a more exact recognition of similarities and differences (see later), and they protect against contamination of cognitive by emotional elements (which are intrinsically connected with the use of symbols), hence are much less conducive to faulty thinking than symbols; the latter can be defined as "vehicles of irrationality."

A similar expression of irrationality is the tendency to *use personifications*. Elsewhere[11] we have tried to interpret this tendency as a kind of "playing with egoity" when the ego is weakly developed as a center of selection and organization. A stronger ego, we said there, will not be as "generous" in the attribution of ego-qualities to physical or biological processes, to plants or animals, to objects of nature or of technology. But externalization, this basic condition in the impairment of intelligence, is actually identical with a "life without ego"; it means living with external manifestations only (of feelings and values, of intentions and instructions, of concepts and relationships). It is therefore easy for an individual with such a life-style and with such patterns of thinking to see ego-qualities everywhere. To the extent that rationality of thinking is strengthened, the learner will also become capable of more adequate distinction between objects and processes with and without egoity. And to the extent that the teacher can convincingly demonstrate the differences between "personality" and "personification," rationality is likely to grow.

A *second function* of rehabilitative teaching is to develop the student's ability to differentiate. Inadequate differentiation can, of course, be interpreted as an indicator of irrationality as well, since rational behavior requires differentiation. On the other hand, the aforementioned expressions of irrational cognitive behavior (associative thinking, concretization, preference of concrete symbols to concepts, personification) prove inadequate differentiation as well, since differentiation requires the ability to select facts actively and rationally and to handle them conceptually. Suffice it here to mention again the last example, the tendency to use personifications indiscriminately. It is obvious that this tendency indicates inability properly to recognize and to evaluate essential differences, in this case between the presence and the absence of ego-qualities.

The teaching methods meant to protect the learner against the danger of irrationality are different from those meant to show him how to distinguish more adequately between similarities, recognize nuances, avoid simplifications through using dichotomies or sterotypes, or do justice to the dimensions of time (instead of seeing the present and the future as extensions of the past only or every time-dimension as identical with the present).

Here again, we can show that teaching-methods aimed at developing the pupil's ability to differentiate should contribute toward that very separation of the emotional (personal) from the cognitive (formal) elements of thinking which normally prepares the ground for an adequate approach to learning assignments at a later stage of development.

Thus, all the teacher's efforts of making the learner aware of differences and similarities should be focused on the formal aspects of object recognition rather than on its contents, on apperception rather than on perception, even at the earliest stages of learning. *Overlooking differences* not only in clearly contrasting but also in seemingly similar phenomena is liable to produce a reality-image that in its very ambiguity, may arouse personal associations and in this way again reinforce the contamination of thinking by feeling. But recognizing differences as such, that is, as meaningful and as essential, is more than simply perceiving them. Even in early childhood, when perceptive contacts with reality are said to be the main instruments of cognition, differences are difficult to *perceive* as long as they are not *understood*.

Lack of differentiation that produces ambiguous reality-images is closely connected with *inability to use analogies* and keep in mind their As-If character. An adequate understanding of partial similarities, however, though an essential precondition of the use of analogies, is not enough; it must be supported by an equally adequate understanding of *which* partial similarity does, and which does *not*, justify using it for the purposes of an analogy, and which purpose the latter is supposed to serve. In secondary retardation, analogies are liable to be mistaken as statements on realities. The danger of such misinterpretation, however, is not only in that they may distort the child's reality-orientation but also, and even more so, in that they produce in the person using such analogies an overevaluation of the importance of his statement. This self-inflation is characteristic of the thinking processes and the cognitive behavior of many secondarily retarded students. Hence, the importance of teaching-methods meant to make the learner aware of the essential difference between the As-If character of an analogy and a factual statement on reality.

Let us now mention the tendency in a socially or culturally disadvantaged and therefore retarded child *to use dichotomization* as a means of organizing the multitude of knowable and learnable data. Either-or interpretation not only distorts reality, it also provides the user of such simplifying methods with a false feeling of security. This, too, is some kind of contamination of thinking by feeling, though different from the form we have discussed. When the teacher succeeds in convincing a pupil that the use of dichotomies *conceals* facts and limits reality, and that it restricts the learner's involvement in his acts of thinking and learning, the teacher thereby increases his pupil's cognitive initiative, that is, his intelligence.

One of the characteristics of the externalized mind is a tendency *to identify existence with accidental presence of a fact.* Presence in, and absence from, the field of perception are mistaken for evidence of existence or nonexistence. Such a child must come to know and to understand that he does not determine what is there and what is not there, that existence does not depend on his perception or apperception. He must learn about facts in their objective independence. It is, paradoxically, this independence of reality that allows for the emergence, in his mind, of the categories of "the possible," "the imaginable," and the "unreal."

Another paradox is that the more firmly the teacher establishes in his pupils' minds the conviction that reality does not depend on their perceiving it, the more they will come to understand that their thinking and comprehension *depends* on reality; but not only their thinking or their learning, their fantasy and imagination as well, their perception of the possible and the imaginable. This recognition is of particular importance for the rehabilitation of impaired intelligence. It protects the mind against the danger of unstructured associations and fantasies interfering with learning processes, while at the same time it helps develop fantasy and imagination.

Contamination of cognitive processes by emotional elements is clearly evident in two other characteristics of the secondarily retarded individual's thinking patterns—his tendencies to use *stereotypes* and to use *inadequate, not well-understood scientific terms.*

To eliminate distorting stereotypes through adequate teaching methods is extremely difficult because of the roots they have in cultural contents *as well as* in parental examples. It can therefore be interpreted as an attempt to set free cognitive from early experienced feeling-components in concepts and in concept formation. Similarly, the indiscriminate and inadequate use of scientific terms, which characterizes many adolescents whose cognitive functions are being rehabilitated by teaching-methods (of differentiation), is but an expression of that very contamination of cognitive by emotional elements that we have analyzed before. Insecurity is likely to persist a long time, even when the adolescent's intelligence is well on its way to recovery and rehabilitation. Stereotypes and quasiscientific terms are, then, but ways to overcome that insecurity. But it would be futile, here as in other areas of intellectual rehabilitation, for us to wait with didactic interventions until educational or psychological treatment had improved the mental health of the learner to such an extent that he could benefit from proper teaching methods. It is only through the latter that the necessary change can be brought about, that is, through teaching the art of differentiation.

One of the best known expressions of inadequate differentiation is the *narrow span of time-consciousness*; past and future are understood in the light of the present only. The concepts of continuity and of processuality are meaningless as long as the essential differences between seemingly similar events or actions are not clearly recognized. The immediacy orientation of man-in-externalization and his fixation to what he believes is known to him are responsible for a false identity-feeling which, in turn, prevents all adequate evaluation of historical development, or of history *as* development. History teaching, therefore, has rehabilitative functions far more important than that of enlarging the pupil's *massa apperceptiva*: it should strengthen his readiness and ability to differentiate and to understand relativity and, through it, eliminate personal and emotional distortions of factual learning.

Learning is more than problem *solving*, it is *"living* with problems." Normally, the child learns, precisely through solving a problem, how to recognize its objective existence, that is, the challenge it presents. The fact that a problem has been solved does not "eliminate" it; it continues to be there and requires continued concentration of the mind on its possible solutions, the one already found and remembered and others, yet unknown but discoverable. This is one of the characteristics of formal (operational) thinking, one of the manifestations of the ability to use the category of the "As-If."

The secondarily retarded child, however, is *unable and unwilling to conceive of a problem as "remaining" a problem after it has been solved.* He is not ready to waste his scarce and precious mental energy on a question already answered (by himself or by someone else). But it is precisely this perception of "problems" as expressions of the intrinsic complexity of reality, and it is precisely the perception of problem solving as being a permanent mental challenge, that makes thinking productive and autonomous. Rehabilitation of intelligence impaired by social or cultural conditions means, inter alia, presenting that challenge to the mind of the learner, time and again. He must be helped to understand that, unlike a personal problem, a cognitive problem cannot be solved by changing but only by respecting and accepting facts. A personal problem may "return" to perturb the mind after having been solved temporarily; but a cognitive problem coexists with its solution or, better, with its various, possible solutions.

It may perhaps be argued that it is too much to ask of secondarily retarded pupils that they should accept not only the objectivity of a cognitive problem but also the multitude of approaches to its solution. But then, we should bear in mind that, in teaching them and in trying to rehabilitate their intelligence, we do not expect them to *find* a solution, or even alternative solutions, to a problem, by way of induction. Teaching here always starts with an explanation of laws, or of principles, or of a possible solution, or, to refer to the presently discussed case, of alternative solutions. "Finding" laws and solutions is to be replaced, in rehabilitative teaching, by finding possible *applications* of a well-explained, well-understood law or solution. Showing the replaceability of one solution by another, however, is of the essence in the teaching of secondarily retarded children and adolescents in order to counteract their usually strong tendency to accept any answer given by the teacher as final.

This leads us to *another function* of rehabilitative teaching: to make the students feel responsible for his acts of thinking and learning. We have already said that passive *reliance on the authority of a teacher or a book*, that is, heteronomy, is *not* based on personal trust. On the contrary: absence of trust produces impersonal dependence on exchangeable authority-figures (whereas trust prepared for independence). Hence, the specific dilemma in rehabilitative teaching: the teacher must establish himself in the child's mind as a convincing image of trust; at the same time he must avoid attitudes through which he would support overdependence. Teaching and explaining laws and principles make him trustworthy; showing him how to apply those laws and principles weakens the child's tendency to be overdependent. This is also an indispensable precondition of rationality and differentiation, since both require a higher degree of ego participation and of initiative than dependence on authority ever allows for.

We have mentioned that overdependence on authority is, paradoxically, accompanied by a belief in *manipulations taking the place of causal* relationships and processes. Cognitive responsibility presupposes recognition of facts existing in their own rights. Manipulation of facts, on the other hand, indicates belief in chance and arbitrariness and in the almost magic ability of the individual to determine facts and truths by his own choice.

The teacher should try to counteract this pattern by helping his students overcome their inability to *understand the universality of laws*. But we should stress again: they will not be able to discover these laws through experimenting with facts, that is, by way of inductive thinking. The teacher must show them the law in its various possible applications, and he should explain why it does *not* apply to certain other facts. It is only through such explanations that the learner can be brought, gradually, to suggest himself other applications of the law and, in the end, understand its essence as regulator of facts and processes. The universality of a law or principle is understood only when it is accepted as limiting the learner's freedom of choice.

Practically all the patterns of faulty thinking mentioned so far could also be interpreted as expressions of the child's ability to take upon himself responsibility for his learning assignments. Their interpretation as indicators of insufficient rationality or of inadequate differentiation is, however, far from being a matter of semantics or of classification only. It means a different emphasis on this or that method of teaching.

This becomes particularly evident when we face the disadvantaged and impaired pupil's tendency *to imitate a teacher's idea or ways of argumentation*—a tendency rooted in externalization and insecurity. The teacher must learn not to accept such tendencies, flattering as they may be (especially when he is himself insecure). He must learn how to work without wearing a mask of authority and ominiscience. He must learn how to relate to a pupil as one subject to another and not as a subject to an object. These are attitudes likely to strengthen or to weaken the pupil's readiness to take upon himself full responsibility for his thinking and learning.

Finally, we refer again to the tendency to use personifications, which we have already mentioned. We have seen in this tendency proof of *irrationality*, insofar as it reflects ego weakness; we have seen in it a sign of *defective differentiation*. But we must also include in it the group of patterns indicating lack of readiness, on the part of the pupil, to take upon himself responsibility for his cognitive operations: personifications appear mostly in answers to questions about causal connections. Through personifications, responsibility for the appearance or disappearance of a phenomenon in biology, in history, for the behavior of an individual or a group, even for a mathematical relation or law, is vested in some, more or less accidental, external, "humans." Their arbitrary decisions are felt to be responsible for reality. It is the function of rehabilitative teaching in this case to *replace* personifications by detailed descriptions and, if possible, by exemplifications of the causal processes "responsible" for a specific phenomenon. It must be considered the teacher's function to present personifications as "façons de parler" only.

As regards the pupil's *inability to see different aspects of a problem, a task, or a phenomenon at one and the same time or to follow two or more directions simultaneously,* the teacher should try to explain the possible use of different criteria or viewpoints.

Accepting the coexistence, and not only the consecutiveness, of various aspects is actually whole-perception or synthesis. Whole-perception, however, can be dangerous for the development of rationality and differentiation unless it is accompanied by adequate comprehension of the component parts of the whole. But when the teacher knows how to present each aspect in its own right and in all its implications, and yet to make his students feel that diversity of aspects is compatible with unity, in fact, is one of the essential characteristics of individuality—he has indeed succeeded in rehabilitating intelligence.

Different from seeing several aspects of a problem or a phenomenon is *understanding several directions* (and not their consecutive application), which makes an adequate approach to problem solving possible. Here, the whole is the task, and it is by changing one of the directions that the whole-character of the original assignment (with its multiple directives) can be made clear and convincing. Analysis should in this case *follow* the solution of the problem according to the two or more directives given, and not precede it.

II. EXAMPLES

Insufficient Differentiation

(1) In a ninth grade (age 15) literature lesson, two stories were compared, which had one point in common: in both stories, two brothers fought against each other for the right to be recognized as owners of a piece of land inherited from their father; in both, the end of the struggle was tragic: the brothers perished after the quarrel was over, and the winners did not enjoy their land.

However, the *essential differences* were much more significant for an adequate understanding of the stories than this external similarity: in the first one, it was shown how the brothers became slaves of their hatred: even the legal success of the one did not make him happy but drove him into paranoid fears of his "beaten" brother. The latter, although becoming a most successful businessman in another country, was unable to overcome his feeling of being mishandled by justice; he translated this feeling into all kinds of aggressive, even antisocial activities against colleagues and competitors, all of whom served him as—consciously or unconsciously perceived—substitutes for his brother. (We do not want to go here into details of the story, which was loaded with psychological sophistication.)

In the other story, the one who finally won the case had been forced into the litigation by his ambitious wife. She hated her brother-in-law because he had rejected her before she became engaged to his brother. Actually, the story was more about her than about the brothers, whom she gradually destroyed. It was a story about how the two brothers, who loved each other, were driven by her into mutual estrangement and strife.

When the teacher asked the pupils to compare with each other the essentials of the two stories, and to define similarities and differences, most pointed out the similarities (a feature well-known from the reactions of underachievers in intelligence examinations): two brothers, quarreling about a piece of land, one winning in court. They all hate each other, added one, unaware of the inadequacy of the answer. They all die in the end.

The differences were overlooked, and even a repeated request by the teacher did not produce more adequate responses. Emphasis on similarities satisfies the mental needs of a basically insecure individual much more than the analysis and definition of differences. And yet, differences must be emphasized if we want to make the essentials of the stories intelligible. Understanding the essentials of any content of learning requires simultaneous perception of similarities *and* differences.

It is therefore the teacher's task to *initiate* differentiation, even by *formulating* a number of contrasts: the basic character-weakness of the brothers in the second story, where they actually love each other, but, because of their weakness, allow the woman to drive them into foolish strife; as against the basic badness of the brothers in the first story, as manifested during and after the legal strife; the difference between their reactions. To strengthen the secondarily retarded pupils' weak ability to differentiate means: to help them formulate as many contrasts as possible and to show them the meaning of similarities as external only, as against the essentiality of differences.

(2) One of the clearest manifestations of insufficient differentiation is the tendency to use *dichotomies* for the organization of varieties and to overlook nuances.

The subject of an algebra lesson was the presentation of negative numbers on a continuum "passing through" the zero. One pupil wanted to know to which side the zero belonged, to that of the negative or to that of the positive numbers. Another suggested the use of $+0$ and -0, but a third one saw the absurdity of the proposition: in this case, she said, there would be numbers between the two zeros, and they could not be defined.

At this point, the teacher offered an explanation of zero not as a number but as a point of reference, from which the numbers diverge in opposite directions and on which they converge from two directions. "Coming near" and "getting away" are not only correct descriptions of the essence of (static) numerical units, they are also categories of personal experience. And although it may be dangerous to introduce such categories into cognitive processes, we should remain aware of the fact that they help strengthen the learner's personal involvement.

The same happened when the "absolute value of numbers" was discussed. It was defined as their distance from the zero, irrespective of the direction from which the distance was measured. Some pupils found it difficult to give up dichotomization. They thought that when the absolute value of -5 is 5 ($+5$), the absolute value of $+5$ should be -5. The teacher, again, succeeded in overcoming that difficulty by using the concepts of "approaching zero" and of "getting away from zero," while counting the units.

(In all of these examples of active intervention by the teacher through his explanations, demonstrations, or interpretations, the noninductive character or rehabilitative teaching becomes clear.)

We should understand these children's need for security derived from schematic data organization. But on the other hand, they must be gradually brought to see that overcoming their rigid method of organizing their universe of facts offers the advantage of flexibility, of seeing a greater variety of aspects, of criteria. But this is a slow and long, drawn-out process, one that has to be repeated again and again.

(3) A convincing example of "nuances versus dichotomy" is the color spectrum, in which even the extreme points are *not* ultimate opposites. But it is in discussions of literature or of history that rehabilitative teaching should try to explain the futility of dichotomization: it is here that using differential criteria for the evaluation of character and behavior becomes meaningful. Using differential criteria, according to which the hero of a story or of a certain action appears in "changing value-shades" is one of the most effective means of developing differentiation in secondarily retarded pupils with their typical tendency to use dichotomies.

Inadequate Responsibility

(4) Here are a few examples of how automatic, emotion- or culture-conditioned associations, dependence on cultural stereotypes or on authority, tendencies to imitate the teacher, and so forth, are liable to distort thinking and learning processes.

In a grade nine physics class, the concept of work was demonstrated by comparing with each other lifting an object of one kilogram to a height of two meters with lifting another object weighing two kilograms first to the height of one, then to the height of two meters. Work *A* was shown to equal work *B* and to be one-half of work *C*. The unit of work (kilogram-meter) was defined.

The pupils first of all could not differentiate between "work" in the everyday sense of the word and "work" in terms of physics. How could one say that a soldier standing on guard or at attention for a long time did not "work" in spite of his extreme fatigue, while a child throwing a stone *did* perform "work"?

The difficulty could be interpreted as inability to think in operational terms, expressed in the present case as the pupils' dependence on the concretely demonstrated, everyday meaning of the term "work." When another example was given, that of pressing forcefully against a wall, and the teacher asked why we could not speak of "work" in this case, students of an ordinary class immediately answered: "Because there is no displacement of the object; the distance by which the object is moved, is zero." The children in our class, on the other hand, answered: "Because there was no height.'' It took the teacher some time to detach the pupils from their associative dependence on their first example and to make them understand what it meant to formulate rules and laws, which are only exemplified by this or that specific "case."

One didactic conclusion is evident: associative and concretistic thinking makes essential the use of different, even seemingly contradictory, examples, in order to "block" the way out into irrelevant (or falsely recalled) associations. (In our case, it was difficult to offer a variety of different examples because the pupils had not yet studied the problems of friction.)

Another difficulty was due to the intervention of an affective element: the distinction between the scientific and the practical meanings of "work" (between "work" and "working") had not been understood completely and certainly had not become part of the pupils' internalized knowledge. Secondarily retarded students take a long time to give up their resistance to formal definitions, which often contradict as it were, the common-sense meaning of a term or a phenomenon to which they are accustomed. Unless they are helped to understand the *practical* worthwhileness and the applicability of scientific definitions, they will almost be offended by them, will see in them a mere waste of energy, and consequently there will be no motivation to learn them, to understand and to accept them as legitimate.

(5) In a biology class the teacher spoke about the miracles performed by the instinct that allowed a trout born in mountain rivers to find its living thousands of kilometers away in the sea (unaccompanied by its mother, who had died immediately after leaving her eggs). Here, an *emotion-conditioned association* interfered with the thinking process, that of the "abandoned child." For a long time, it was almost impossible for the pupils to understand the main point in the teacher's explanations: the limits to our rational understanding. They suggested all kinds of rational explanations in complete disregard of the facts mentioned by the teacher. "The researchers probably have not seen the mother fish accompanying their young ones; no mother would allow her children to travel such long distances all alone," said one girl. "What is the use of in-

stincts? They can go astray, and then, the instinct won't help them," said another girl, thus proving that she had not been able to accept the essentials in the explanation of instincts.

It is of interest to compare these irrelevant emotional associations with the reactions of another, secure and well-functioning girl in the same class. "On the contrary," she said in reaction to what the others had suggested, "the instinct is a much better protection than a mother. After all, the mother would not be of any use either, unless she were guided by her own instinct. Therefore she is unnecessary."

Almost all the underprivileged and secondarily retarded children in the class, the majority, reacted to this statement with violent protest, and the lesson "blew up." The teacher saw that she had failed to achieve what she had wanted to explain. (We shall see later how such a situation could have been handled more adequately.)

(6) The process of changes in culture-conditioned patterns of behavior was discussed in a civics class of 17-year-old boys and girls. Several years of rehabilitative teaching had brought about significant positive developments in their readiness and ability to accept the demands of formal (operational) thinking in practically every subject matter.

All the more astonishing was their rigid clinging to an absolutistic perception of, and attitude toward, their cultural group's patterns of behavior and values. It expressed itself in beliefs, preferences, feelings. The concept of change, already well internalized in their understanding of historic or biological processes, proved not to be "freely available" when it came to a discussion of such values (not to speak of their application to intrafamily and interpersonal relationships; see Chapter 3).

Thus, values such as "planning ahead," rational budgeting, defining priorities were accepted and justified theoretically, but did not, as it were, require practical application; on the contrary, opposite demands of their own cultural group's value system remained the accepted norms of "what must be done." The contradiction between these two attitudes, the deep gap between cognition and behavior, between thinking and feeling, did not even enter their consciousness as such, not as a contradiction or as a challenge to find a synthesis, a unification, or a compromise.

One could speak of a deep ambivalence-conflict, not of a personal but of an existential character: on the one hand, the students were ready to reject certain patterns as "primitive"; on the other, they rejected the opposite patterns of the dominant culture as "inferior," as "less convincing," at best as "different." The question of cognitive expediency, of suitability for the advancement of abstract thinking, was not asked.

It could be observed, in a lower age group, how children who came from one ethnic background "solved" the same problem differently. Ambivalence here caused a split: some affectively rejected as "primitive" their group's behavior-patterns; others accepted them with equal affectivity as "beautiful." Both considered their attitudes as vehicles to social equality, the first ones "in the name" of the new culture, the others "in the name" of cultural pluralism. However, neither the one nor the other attitude was conducive to more effective thinking or learning.

(7) Culture-conditioned associations that are liable to distort proper thinking and learning processes include—are, in fact, identical with—*stereotypes*. True enough, stereotypes are integral parts of an ideologically oriented education, but it is nevertheless correct to see in them specifically distorting factors; ideological education as such is likely to weaken critical and responsible thinking. Here are a few examples:

In a history class, drawings from the caves in Spain and Southern France were shown, and the teacher told his pupils how they were discovered and how their beauty and the techniques employed by these ancient craftsmen who lived 30,000 years ago contradicted our concept of "primitivity." He then went on showing his pupils samples of art productions in ancient cultures, among them samples of Sumerian art with their typical rigidity of expression. It was the teacher's purpose to help the pupils compare with each other different art-styles, to teach them how to use different criteria of evaluation and how to form their individual preferences.

Most pupils spontaneously preferred the vividity of the cave drawings. Yet some remarked: "They are not beautiful. How can they be beautiful? They were, after all, primitive, savages, while the Sumerians were a nation of high culture." It was obvious that here stereotypes irrationally determined evaluative reactions.

It was necessary to discuss the complexity of the concept of "primitivity," according to various criteria and without referring to the stereotyped answers given. The purpose of this discussion was to help all pupils think without using simplifying preconceptions of an emotional nature, and to reinforce their ability to differentiate through an unprejudiced comparison of different styles of art.

(8) An almost contradictory pattern is that of the pupils' excessive reliance and dependence on their *teachers' authority*.

Pupils in a grade eight algebra class were asked to prepare their own exercises, in addition to those in the textbook. Some returned empty pages. One asked: "How can we invent exercises? Are we authors?" And when the teacher wrote on the blackboard an exercise of his own he asked: "How did you learn that? You probably have read lots and lots of textbooks."

For him, the only reliable authority was the book, and he was ready, at this stage, to accept the teacher as an authority only to the extent that he could identify him with the book. On another occasion, when the teacher wrote on the blackboard an equation to be solved by the class, that same boy wanted to know, whether the teacher had "made up" this one. He began to work only after the teacher assured him that she had found that equation in a textbook.

This boy had particularly severe problems with authority figures, for all those that he had experienced in his immediate environment "excelled" in their arbitrariness—hence his tendency to trust "the book" only. However, the teacher thought that the time had come for the boy to learn how to trust her and thus gradually acquire a reliable motivation to learn. She therefore wrote on the blackboard another equation which she had *not* taken from the textbook, an easy one. She explained that the advantage of "inventing" exercises was that she could plan some that were not so difficult to solve as those in the book.

From here, the teacher went one step further: she encouraged the boy to invent equations of his own and offered him her help to discover their inner logic. Thus, she became in his eyes a trusted adult, and he could overcome his fears of independence and responsibility.* [This boy's reaction could, of course, also be interpreted as symptoms of insufficient differentiation. But then—as we pointed out at the beginning of this chapter—didactic analysis and classification does *not* mean unambiguous diagnosis, but only serves the purpose of determining the choice of (alternative) didactic interventions.]

(9) For a time, three literature teachers were employed, each with his specific teaching-style: the first tended to emphasize the hero's motivation; the second, the central idea; the third, the moral of the story. It soon became clear that the pupils of each of the three teachers *imitated* their specific ways of interpretation; they even transferred them to other content areas where they were entirely irrelevant and unsuitable.

Thus, it happened in a history lesson that the pupils were asked about the difference between democracy and oligarchy in ancient Greece. One of the boys, who apparently was much influenced by the first teacher (the one emphasizing "motivation"), said: "How can we answer the question without knowing the motives of the leaders?" He did not understand that his present function was different: to describe, and to compare with each other, two historical phenomena and not to analyze them psychologically. This latter function apparently was more attractive to him and therefore made him apply uncritically certain principles of interpretation to areas in which they were irrelevant.

Even in an algebra lesson, one of this group of students tried to apply the same principles. When the relationships between positive and negative numbers to zero were discussed, he spoke about their "motivations" and distorted the problem through an excessive use

*In another case, externalized overdependence on authority found its expression in a girl's refusal to accept as equally justified two opposite interpretations of a story and to compare them with each other. She said: "They would not have published the first essay if it had not been correct. And if it was correct, then the other essay was not. So what is the use of comparing one with the other?" Here, absolute authority was vested in the very act of publishing, to the detriment of seeing the justification of different criteria.

of personifications. Thus, he said: "The numbers have opposite tendencies. They oppose each other. They, too, have their motivations."

The same tendency to imitate a certain teacher found its expression in another group as well. They were apparently much impressed by the literature teacher who always emphasized "the moral of the story." Thus, one of the pupils said, in a biology lesson in which plant classification was explained: "What is the purpose? What are the conclusions? What does it teach us?" The teacher at first did not understand the intention of the pupil's questions and thought she asked about the scientific as against the practical, applicative value of classification. When she started to answer in this direction, the girl interrupted her saying: "I understand all this. But there must be some meaning and value of it also for our day-to-day life."

The teacher reacted by asking, "Where did you learn asking such questions?" "In the literature lesson," answered the girl. "Well, let us, then, ask whether it is legitimate to transfer what we have learned in one subject matter to another one. What are the differences between literature and biology?" "In both we deal with life," was the answer. "I asked about differences and you answer by pointing out similarities." "The difference is that in biology we make experiments," said another pupil; "we observe and we find laws; in literature we speak about what the writer wanted to express and how he tried to convince us." "If so," summarized the teacher, "it is correct to ask in a literature lesson what we can learn from a certain writer's intentions about our own life. Or we can ask, how *we* would have reacted in a situation similar to that described in the story. Or, whether we agree with the writer or not. All this applies to literature but not to biology."

Here, it becomes evident how important it is for teachers in rehabilitative teaching to keep in close contact with each other and exchange information about their students. It may, of course, be argued that this is helpful in every class. However, when we want to help underprivileged and, therefore, retarded children to regain their original level of intelligence, it is much more important for all concerned to know what the sources of a faulty cognitive pattern are; in our case, for instance, the tendency to imitate a certain teacher's way of thinking.

Insufficient Rationality

(10) The subject of a grade nine physics lesson was "the inclined plane." It was first described by examples, and formulae were learned subsequently to calculate the power needed to raise a body on an inclined plane, by its geometrical properties and by the properties of the body to be raised.

In another lesson, the pupils were asked to define an inclined plane. One pupil mentioned height, distance, mass, form, and added "the law of gravity." Although the boy, as could be seen shortly afterward, *knew* the proper answer, it was more important for him to show off with every term he knew.

In such cases, the teacher should avoid direct criticism of the use of irrelevant scientific terms but should rather try to help the pupil differentiate more properly. It can be hoped that such a pupil will give up this doubtful pattern of externalization to the extent that he becomes more sure. The teacher must decide judicisouly what the most important issue of the moment is and concentrate on that issue, while postponing the decision on other points that may require his critical attention.

The teacher should also be able to distinguish between cases in which the use of seemingly scientific terms serves the purpose of giving the impression of knowing and cases in which showing off with such terms comes to demonstrate, in a typically externalized manner, that "I belong to your culture of science." It is obvious that in the second group of cases, more than in the first, proper thinking and learning processes are likely to be distorted by that pattern.

(It is the affective character of motivation that would allow us to put most of the preceding and the following cases as well into the here-discussed category of "insufficient rationality.")

Concretistic Thinking

(11) The best-known expression of a secondarily retarded child's

preference of the concrete to the abstract is his tendency to give *examples when asked to define* a phenomenon or a concept. Although this is an almost universal sign of cognitive negligence, and so-called regular students of various age levels manifest similar tendencies, it is easier for them to understand the essential differences between examples and definitions than it is for those children whom we have in mind here.

The origin of relgious beliefs was discussed. The teacher chose the "naturalistic" theory. One pupil said: "For instance, when there was rain, people wanted to know who made it." Another reacted by saying: "Natural phenomena made them believe in someone stronger than they." It was easy for the teacher to show the class, by using the two answers, the difference between exemplifying and generalizing, between an example and an abstraction.

But since a secondarily retarded pupil, as a rule, does not see the "advantages" of concepts and generalizations, he needs frequent demonstrations of the unreliability and the limited validity of examples. He needs help in translating examples into concepts, to learn one of the essentials of abstract thinking and, through it, the use of a differential language as a vehicle of abstraction. The teacher must insist on accuracy in the wording chosen by the pupil (which puts him, the teacher, under an obligation to be equally accurate in the choice of his words, whether he offers an example or a definition).

(12) Here is another case of *preferring the concrete* to the abstract. The subject was the ray of positive numbers, and the class discussed the function and the meaning of the zero on that ray. One of the pupils said that when we used the word "one" or "two," we could *see* an amount that was one or two. But "zero" could not be defined as an amount. If so, "zero" was an exception, was different from all other numbers.

One girl asked: "Why *can't* there be an amount called zero? When I don't have anything I can say that I have nothing, that is, zero." The first-mentioned pupil reacted to her by saying: "If so, I am right, that zero is different from every other number." Here, the teacher intervened.

"Let me suggest that we don't continue discussing what I have or what I don't have. Let us go back to our definition of the numbers on the ray. Every number on the ray represents a distance from a certain point, which is the beginning of the ray (0, 1/4, 1/2, 1, 2, 3). What is the distance of the zero from the beginning of the ray?" Pupil A: "It *is* the beginning." The teacher then indicated every number marked on the ray, always repeating his question: "What is the distance of this point from the beginning?" and received the correct answers: three units, two units, one unit, one half, one quarter. Then he pointed to ever smaller distances, *approaching the zero*, until he reached it. At this point, all answered his question of what the distance from the beginning was, by shouting, "Zero, zero units."

The pupils had become used to basing their understanding of arithmetic on quantitative examples, a "skill" that they had acquired through experience, or through the tangible examples that were given when they began to learn arithmetic in the lower classes. Now they no longer spoke about marbles or candies, but rather about "an amount that is one." However, it was obvious that they were still tied to the demonstrability of the number itself. This attachment made it difficult for them to use the abstraction required for an adequate understanding of numbers as concepts. They were ready to accept a number only when they could reconstruct the concrete representation of the number, and unwittingly lean on its concreteness. This way of thinking is typical of many pupils at the early stages of learning arithmetic, but as time goes by, after they have used numbers a lot, they usually overcome this need to rely on concrete representation; this process usually occurs when they are still in the early classes of elementary school. Our pupils, however, still had difficulties in breaking away from their dependence on concreteness in grade nine.

Our assumption is that this difficulty in understanding the abstract concept of "zero" stems, partly at least, from the fear which the zero is likely to arouse in a socially underprivileged child. (Signs of such anxiety can be discovered in other contexts as well.) The more often the child has had experiences of "not having," the more likely is the zero to become a symbol that represents something dangerous and threatening. Thus, feelings (in this case, irrational fears) can cause difficulties in the processes of conceptualization.

The following three forms of didactic interventions on the part of the teacher seem to be indicated here: (a) The teacher must accept the pupil's explanation, and at the same time help him formulate more clearly his view about the differences between numbers representing amounts and the zero. (b) He should then lead the pupil back to the level of formal definitions as they were learned in class. (c) He should try to reduce the fear of the zero as "nothingness," by approaching it in steps, and presenting it as the limit to which positive numbers can be reduced.

It may be impossible to teach arithmetic in the first school years without concrete examples of objects. But the teacher should be aware of the difficulty that may be created in socially (secondarily) retarded pupils when the time comes for them to break away from dependence on concretizations. They should be helped toward forming the concept of "number" as early as possible, before they become too rigidly dependent on concretizations. Among "regular" pupils, this kind of problem does not arise, as a rule, because they are capable of reaching the level of abstraction necessary for conceptualization without much direction from outside sources. In order to prevent a reinforcement of the socially retarded pupil's dependence on concretizations, it is very important not to use quantitative analogies when working with numbers, for example: that zero is represented as a symbol of absolute lack, or negative numbers as debts or deficits.

Here again arises a critical question, which has been discussed several times already: should the teacher deal with the emotional factors presumed to underlie faulty thinking? Is he qualified to do it, when known or unknown fears cause a pupil to avoid the abstract and to prefer the concrete? Does the very didactic attempt to detach the socially retarded child from his dependence on the concrete necessitate dealing with the experiential-emotional background?

It would seem that an emphasis on the rational approach and outlook (for example, by commenting on distances rather than on amounts) is sufficient to weaken the negative influence of emotional factors on the pupils' thinking. But, in an almost paradoxical way, we can add: if the teacher knows how to use teaching methods capable of developing formal rational thinking, he will also be able to make the pupil aware of emotional and experiential influences without thereby arousing affective reactions. A comparison between the personal plane in the child's thinking (represented by his emotional associations, and by the preference of the concrete) and the formal plane of thinking (represented by conceptualization, abstraction, formulae, laws, and so on) can weaken the influence of emotional factors, and is beneficial to formal thinking.

(13) Another manifestation of concretistic thinking is the tendency to identify reality (or existence) with what is *present and perceivable.* This means a serious handicap to the understanding of "development," which implies understanding the concept of "latent existence."

Some pupils could not see the rootlet as identical with the root at an early stage of development because its "present and perceivable" form had little in common with the fully developed root. They described the relationship between rootlet and root as one of nearness, not of—potential—identity.

In another class, a pupil said: "A positive number *is* something. But if a number is *not* positive, what is it then? Then it is nothing, and this means it is zero. So, why should we distinguish between –1, –2, –3, etc. All are nothing, all are zero." Here it was necessary to give examples of the perceivable difference between negative "quantities" (for instance, degrees of low temperature and their different results), to convince the pupils that negative numbers were far from identical with zero, and that zero did not represent nothingness, that is, nonexistence, but served as an arbitrary and alterable point of reference only.

The concepts "light-speed" and "light-year" were explained, and the teacher mentioned the fact that certain stars which long ago ceased to exist still are perceived as shining on the firmament. For most of the students, this was absolutely incomprehensible, since their concretistic way of thinking excluded acceptance of any form of past as well as of potential existence as real.

(14) The just-discussed category of distorted thinking in secondarily retarded learners is clearly linked with another one, which, we have suggested, should be called *narrow time-consciousness.* It manifests

itself in mixed-up time sequences, in anachronistic history interpretations, in transposing meaningful figures from a far away past into the present or, at least, into a "still-perceivable" past.

An extreme example of this variety of cognitive distortion—one that could have been included also among the foregoing examples—is that of a 14-year-old girl who said: "Why do we learn history? After all, it deals with the past only, and the past no longer exists. So, why bother about what once was and no longer is?"

It sounded almost like a philosophical remark. But from the teacher's point of view, it revealed a source of dangerous misinterpretations of factual contexts that require causal understanding, hence recognition of the past as "still existing." Didactically, it requires repeated attempts to demonstrate and to exemplify the reality of coexisting time dimensions.

A more specific example can be found in a lesson that dealt with Cromwell's rebellion against the tyrannical kings. It was shown how he himself became a tyrannical ruler, in contrast to the principles that had guided him before. The teacher asked how this change could be explained.

One of the pupils answered that Cromwell had to use force in order to achieve his aim, that he had to suppress his enemies forcefully. She disregarded what the teacher had said namely, that Cromwell became tyrannical *after* he had achieved his aim. She did not think in terms of what *caused* the change in Cromwell's attitude, or of what he *wanted to attain* by such a change, but simply failed to keep in mind the category of time as a "sequence of times." All that happened in the past, happened, in her mind, at the same time, "*the* past." She could not see it as divided into a past that *preceded* a (past) present, which, in turn, was followed by a (past) future.

She mixed up the periods in Cromwell's life, periods that had not been very far from each other, but which were both rather far removed from "her" present. Seen from the vantage point of this present, the various periods of the past merged into one undifferentiated period of times, *the* past. What may have caused this limited time-consciousness in the pupil?

One of the emotional factors explaining the lack of differentiation between the temporal components of a historical period is the pupil's lack of involvement in what does not belong to the immediate present, his inability to imagine the past as a reality, as a present in the past. To create such an involvement, the teacher should try two actions: to connect that past as a direct or indirect causal factor with some present, some "convincing" reality;* and to help the learner see himself as a developing, that is, a "historical," individual, having his own past, present, and future.

It is true: such causal connections require a considerable amount of branching out from the topic dealt with in a specific lesson (see pp. 34f). But faulty thinking due to limitations of the time-consciousness cannot be corrected unless the teacher shows as many connections as possible between a historical past and an actual present, and thus evokes and strengthens personal involvement in the past.

Growing awareness of autobiographic processes has little direct bearing on the understanding of historic sequences; and we certainly should remain aware of the dangers implied in too much psychological actualization, which may lead to all sorts of misinterpretations. But in order to learn in which way a historic personality (in our case, Cromwell) developed and changed in his own life (and thereby may have changed the course of events)—in other words, in which way the past was once a present—a secondarily retarded pupil must be taught to see the parallel between historical and individual developments: the changes that have taken place in the course of the pupil's life throw light on the changes that may have taken place, centuries ago, in individuals then alive.

(15) To make clear the meaning of a "universal law" an arithmetic teacher said: "It is a law that the absolute value of both a positive and a negative number increases with its distance from the zero." But when he asked how we know that $(-8) + (-5) = -13$, the answer was, "Everybody knows that." The teacher tried to make them formulate their answer in accordance with the law he had just defined, but to no avail. He then offered examples such as: "Every number

---

*In this respect, the didactical intervention is identical with the one indicated in the case of the before-mentioned pattern: rehabilitative teaching must bring the secondarily retarded child to see that the present is not the only valid, that is, committing, reality.

can be divided by 2.'' ''Every number whose aggregate sum is 3, 6, or 9, can be divided by 3.'' The reaction was, ''What is the use of such laws? We can try; it will not take more time.''

One boy went even further and suggested: ''It is better not to rely on laws. The law may be wrong, and then all the results will be wrong, too.'' Here we see a strange perversion of what may seem an expression of personal responsibility, but is, in fact, an expression of concretistic thinking. The boy saw in the law an anonymous force trying to take the place of his trial-and-error contacts with the concrete givens of reality and therefore rejected it.

(We shall come back to the problem of rejecting laws in favor of reliance on the concrete givens of reality when we deal with the secondarily retarded pupils' difficulty in thinking in operational terms.)

(16) We mentioned in the Chapter 1, when dealing with the cognitive patterns of secondary retardation, that *manipulative thinking* replaces causal thinking in terms of processes taking place to connect cause and effect. We have also pointed out that processuality is less likely to provoke strong affects, particularly of an aggressive character, than manipulative thinking in which the result depends on the arbitrary decision and the forcefulness of purpose of the ''manipulator.''

A good example (previously mentioned on p. 52) is the following: In a ninth grade biology class the teacher explained the process of phototropism, using as much as possible concepts taken from the field of organic chemistry. His purpose was to teach his pupils how to think in terms of cause and effect and how to avoid personifications.

When he came to summarize a number of lessons devoted to that problem and asked how we can explain the fact that leaves tend to turn to the light, one boy, a typical representative of secondary retardation, said: ''The sun (he did not say: the light!) is much stronger than the poor plant (sic!) and therefore forces the leaves to turn to it. Perhaps they don't want it. I think we should give the plants an injection to strengthen them, so that they could resist it.'' The teacher was more than surprised by this interpretation, which proved that whatever he had tried to explain had remained without any effect.

The boy completely identified with the principles of his manipulative thinking. He apparently interpreted a natural process as a pathology, a clear case of projection of personal aggressiveness (which in our case was evident in every detail of the boy's behavior) onto his facts and acts of learning.

This is one of the patterns of faulty thinking in which the value of purely cognitive interventions (through the methods of rehabilitative teaching) is doubtful unless they are accompanied by individual treatment actions whose purpose it is to strengthen the learner's security, so that his need for aggressive reactions will gradually weaken.

(17) In another example *manipulative thinking* is almost identical with that pattern of faulty thinking which we have defined as identifying reality with what is "present and perceivable" (see p. 45).

The class was discussing rational numbers. The student found it difficult to understand that between any two rational numbers lie infinitely many other rational numbers. The teacher explained that by multiplying the denominator of a fraction, for instance, we can enumerate as many intermediate numbers as we want. The students were successful in applying the principle and gave examples of what they called "in-between fractions" or "in between decimal values."

However, they insisted that these "in-between values" did not exist as long as we did not discover, or better, create, them by our manipulation. Hence, the importance of the noninductive teaching method, which starts out from the definition of a specific principle and requires from the students exemplifications only. (A "regular" student, on the other hand, understands well that and how a priori laws *limit* applicability.)

(18) Concretistic thinking may also find its expression in another pattern, the learner's inability to carry out a cognitive assignment *in accordance with different directives simultaneously* instead of acting according to each directive consecutively and thus distorting the assignment.

"In which case," asked the teacher, "have the two rays of an angle more than one point in common?" The correct answer was, of course, "an angle of zero degrees." One of the boys drew on the blackboard first one line, then another line exactly covering the first one. It seemed he had understood the assignment with its two directives ("angle" and "more than one point in common"). But when he had reached the end of his line, he added another one at an acute angle. It was obvious that the concrete image of an angle was a much stronger determinant in his mind than the abstraction of a line being an angle of zero (or 180) degrees. (And it was equally obvious that the boy could not follow two directives simultaneously.)

Inability to Understand the Meaning of the As-If

We have emphasized several times already in the course of our study that secondary retardation is characterized primarily by the learner's inability to think formally or operationally (to use Piaget's terminology). We have mentioned that this inability can be demonstrated by the pupil's difficulties in understanding the difference between analogy and reality, between personification and meaning, between symbol and concept, between the scientific and the personal meaning of a "problem to be solved." Practically every other pattern of faulty thinking can be brought onto the same common denominator of inability to think operationally, which can also be called the "inability to understand the meaning of the As-If." For, in every act of formal thinking is implied a kind of substitution of reality through an illusion, the illusion that conceptuality can ever do justice to reality. And yet, adequate thinking and learning are based, depend, exactly on that "illusion."

(19) Our first example is taken from the field of *analogies*. In which respect are the two phenomena linked to each other in an analogy different, and in which respect are they similar? What is the difference of purpose between a simple comparison and an analogy? What should the teacher do to prevent misinterpreting analogy as reality? Such and similar questions were asked in a small textbook devoted to the teaching of analogies.

A picture was shown in which a present-day soldier appeared against a background of (imaginery) soldiers from a glorious past. Before the teacher could ask his well-prepared questions, a 13-year-old boy reacted affectively: "What nonsense! How can they show soldiers dead so long together with a soldier of today? How do they know what they looked like?'' For him, the (symbolic) background figures were as real as the picture of the present-day soldier.

Similar reactions could be observed when fables were discussed, built on the principle of intensifying a moral or social message by using analogies. It was obvious that for many of the secondarily retarded children it was difficult to accept the teacher's explanations and to see in the pictures or stories challenges to their imagination and to define the essentials of the message conveyed by them. In other words: they could not think in terms of the As-If.

(20) Taking *personifications* literally is another form of that same inability to think in terms of the As-If. The lower the pupil's age, the more absurd are the misunderstandings likely to be that result from this inability.

In a class of 11–12-year-old pupils an experiment was conducted to observe plant seeds sprouting. In order to make it easier for the pupils to see the process, the teacher placed the seeds on the surface of black paper. When the pupils were asked why they thought the teacher used black paper, one of them replied: "The seeds need darkness so that they can rest before sprouting." When the teacher asked why this answer was incorrect, one answer was that the black paper was not enough to give the required darkness. Another one: that the seeds needed light in order to see where they should go during the process of sprouting. Another pupil continued that idea and said that growth was impossible without light.

The teacher said: "It is true that human beings need sleep, if possible, in a quiet and dark room in order to gather strength for their next day's work. But do plant seeds really resemble humans?'' From here, he passed on to a direct explanation of the differences between different forms of life, human beings, animals, and plants. In the end, he explained the concept of personification and pointed out the danger of distortions arising from this kind of thinking.

Finally, he received a correct answer from one of the pupils. However, it was obvious that the majority showed no interest in such explanations, but preferred their mode of thinking *with* personifications.

In other age groups, the use of personfication often leads to empty phraseologies. Thus, in a literature class, the teacher compared with each other the different forms of poetic creation, and the changes that had taken place in some of these forms were discussed and demonstrated. Here, the teacher made a mistake when he used an anthropomorphism in his question: "What was the fate of the ballad?" One girl, probably stimulated by the word "fate", answered: "The ballad experienced many trials and tribulations, until it reached its present-day form." It was relatively easy for the teacher to make that girl understand the inadequacy of her formulations: "Sometimes we refer to an object, *as if* it were alive. Children's stories are full of such personifications. Many like them and take these imaginary comparisons seriously or, as we say, literally. But we should not use them in a theoretical or scientific analysis, such as the one in which we are engaged at present. There we must use exact accurate terms as much as possible and avoid imaginary speech-forms."

It is precisely the secondarily retarded child's weakness as a subject that explains his tendency "generously" to distribute human qualities to nonhuman objects. This faulty pattern of thinking limits his expressive and abstractive abilities. It can be corrected only by frequently repeated demonstrations of the essential differences between the various categories of beings. Personifications should be "translated" as much as possible into the language of abstractions and exact descriptions or definitions. Causal and processual categories must take the place of personifications (which a teacher of secondarily retarded children should be careful not to use).

(21) A much more effective "vehicle of meaning" than analogy or personification is the *symbol*, provided, of course, it is not misinterpreted concretistically—which, however, usually is a problem with secondarily retarded children.

During a history lesson the teacher asked: What happened to the freedom-fighters of a certain underground movement after they achieved victory? What are the difficulties implied in the transition from the heroic and adventurous life-style of lawlessness for the sake of a patriotic cause to the monotonous routine of civic order?

The most impressive part of the story was the description of the freedom-fighters' life "underground," in caves and mountain hideouts, where it was almost impossible to detect and catch them. "The cave" became in the pupils' mind a symbol of freedom. Therefore, it seemed logical to them that the fighters, after having achieved victory, "were free to return to their caves and no one would persecute them." The cave as a symbol of security now became a symbol of freedom, though freedom no longer meant freedom from the oppressor but freedom to live without restraint, without commitment—a typically externalized ideal.

It is the function of rehabilitative teaching to weaken the affective elements in the pupils' concretistic perception of the symbol and in this way to prepare them for a more adequate, less personally tinged comprehension of historical processes.

Another form of concretistic misinterpretation of symbols, well-known from the field of observable behavior, is an affective reaction to some concrete givens symbolizing a rejected person or institution. Violent aggression against that symbolic object is known to be a favored expression of projection or substitution of irrational feelings. We find it in normally functioning, often highly intelligent children not less, perhaps even more, frequently than in the secondarily retarded. It is the impact of this "mechanism" on the latter's cognitive pattern that makes it different in the two types of learners. As a rule, it does *not* distort the thinking processes of the intelligent child but acts as a defense mechanism against unconscious complexes and fixations. In the secondarily retarded child, on the other hand, it determines, and distorts, the conception of causal connections through replacing the factors of actual determination by their external symbols.

(22) It is difficult for a secondarily retarded pupil to understand the objective "impersonal" nature of a *scientific problem* to be solved. He tends to interpret each problem as one of personal concern, not one of general validity—it ceases to be a problem once it has been solved, and all we need is someone to give us the answer, the solution. It takes time and requires frequently repeated explanation to make him understand that a scientific problem always remains one, "as if" it had not yet been solved, "as if" it waited for him only to discover its solution.

To give an example: In a discussion of Galileo's discovery, the class answered the teacher's question about what his problem had been, by saying: "how to evade the Inquisition," or: "how to convince the others." No one mentioned the *scientific* issue that Galileo had investigated, that of the earth revolving around the sun or the sun around the earth. The personal, biographic parts of the "story" were much more attractive than the scientific side.

Here we understand why all the patterns of faulty thinking discussed and exemplified in the present chapter can be brought onto one common denominator: the secondarily retarded pupil's difficulties with formal, operational thinking, in which readiness to accept the As-If is essential. Operational thinking means: thinking in abstract terms, *as if* concepts could "replace" reality; *as if* meanings, laws, principles, solutions "existed", *as if* understanding them was the learner's primary responsibility, or—more—his raison d'être.

5

Definitions In Rehabilitative Teaching

I. INTRODUCTORY REMARKS

In Chapter 2 we have defined the first element of rehabilitative teaching as "noninductiveness." In contrast to the ideals of "inductive" teaching and particularly of the discovery method, it is the teacher himself who, after raising a question and receiving his pupils' reactions, should *give* the correct answer without hesitating to interrupt the often diffuse "question-and-answer period." Only after the basically insecure (secondarily retarded) pupil's reliability-needs are satisfied through experiencing reality as explicable, as understandable, as "logical," will he be ready to respond to the next step: the teacher can now set in motion processes of differential thinking by questioning the validity of his own answer. But in both phases the teacher must be prepared to define clearly every concept and every phenomenon he mentions.

On the other hand, a didactically relevant definition differs from a scientifically adequate one. The latter serves the purpose of formulating the essential characteristics (elements) of a given phenomenon, process, property, concept, or method, while distinguishing between necessary and possible attributes. Scientific definitions prepare the ground for adequate differentiation, particularly between partially similar and partially dissimilar givens. In this sense, defining helps the learner, the scientist, or the active person toward a better orientation in the multitude of phenomena he may encounter in his studies or actions. Such orientation (understanding), in turn, prepares the ground for deeper penetration into the essence of its objects.

The alternative is adducing as many examples as possible to illustrate the multitude of learnable contents. Actually, it is in this way that most learners at every age level acquire their reality-orientation without relying on definitions. Their effectiveness, even in theoretical transactions, does not suffer as a result of their avoidance of definitions. In this respect, the teacher is no exception. He may know definitions, he may have learned how to use them properly, and yet he teaches without them. Examples produce closer ties, he claims, between the learner and his facts of learning, between these facts and their understandability. Definitions, he feels, can never replace explanations with the help of examples, although they may help develop accuracy in expression and avoidance of ambiguity and distortions.

These functions are of particular importance in rehabilitative teaching, in each of its phases: in the presentation of the problem, in giving the "correct" answer, in formulating laws or principles, in comparing different answers with each other according to their "quality," in referring to presumed sources of an incorrect answer, in summing up the results of a learning process. *But in each, definitions do not precede explanations, but are accompanied by them and take shape gradually, through constantly referring to the pupils' reactions.*

In contrast to definitions in scientific endeavors, definitions in teaching are primarily concerned with the learner; they are meant to help him organize his universe of learnable facts and orient himself in a basically "foreign" world of universal laws, of which realities are but examples.

It is the purpose of the following examples to show how the here-suggested functions of defining are intrinsic elements of rehabilitative teaching, in that they increase the secondarily retarded pupil's trust in a reliable universe of facts. The examples are not meant to be "models," which would only limit the teacher's initiative and imagination. Models, sure enough, may help him build up a lesson, but on one condition only: he must not try to "transform" them into lessons (directly); he should only "use" them to enrich his associations.

One more preliminary remark: a definition becomes didactically significant in comparative contexts only. To the extent that the learner sees in definitions means for distinguishing between different phenomena, he will begin to take a simultaneous interest in them as well. Thus, they will contribute to the gradual growth of his *massa apperceptiva*, in addition to developing his sense of trust in the regularity of the world. Only after his cognitive abilities are rehabilitated, will definition become part of operational thinking.

II. BELIEF AND SUPERSTITION

The Problem

In religious belief, the absolute trust of the believer in some superior, creating and directing, power finds its expression. Sometimes, it is "defined" as belief in the existence of justice and meaning, precisely when reality does not seem to confirm them rationally. Or it is "defined" as belief in the "self-revelation of God" in miracles or prophecies. Implied is the acceptance of a reality not governed by the laws of causality, in temporal or spatial relationships, laws that could be understood by way of rational analyses.

Religious belief should not seek evidence to justify itself. It can even be said that an inner need for evidence *contradicts* belief, and the many attempts of rationalists to discover logic in the contents of belief or to translate belief into terms of rational and ethical behavior only come to prove this point.

Here, then, would be the place to define "belief" as against "opinion" or "hypothesis," which are characterized by the absence of certainty and by an urgent need for evidence. (It is precisely because of the ambiguity in a secondarily retarded child's concepts of "certainty," "trust," and "need for certainty" that we have chosen "belief" as our first example. A second reason is the affinity, in his mentality, between belief and superstition, as we shall try to show later.)

In most languages the word "belief" has other meanings as well. It means the opposite of certainty, man's cognitive attitude toward something not yet proven: he believes that one day he will be able to know what today can "only" be believed. Here the meaning of the word is the exact opposite of its original, religious, meaning.

For the teacher, the second meaning is of particular importance because of its ambiguity. Here, belief may either become the driving force toward research and discovery and thus help in the development of responsibility, or it may lead to an opposite attitude, particularly in the mentality of externalized man, that is, to the conviction that others, men of learning, scientists, will one day present evidence of the truth of what today is only a matter of belief. He gives up all personal initiative and responsibility; he passively anticipates future certainty.

A similar attitude may (but must not) result from a nonreligious interpretation of the concept when we consider the area of personal and interpersonal behavior. One man may "believe" blindly in a political leader, another in a better future, a third in the fundamental goodness of man. When such belief is based on inner certainty of a religious or quasireligious kind, it does *not* affect the believer's sense of personal responsibility ("in the service of his belief," as it were). But when it is the conscious or unconscious expression of man's reluctance to take personal responsibility, this form of "optimistic belief" becomes dangerous because it is bound further to support his reluctance, further to weaken his initiative, his willingness to make an effort. There is no need to add that this is one of the characteristics of the externalized and the secondarily retarded child.

In addition to the forms of belief, both positive and negative, mentioned so far, we should mention antireligious belief (usually disguised as atheistic knowledge or proof), stereotypes or prejudices, and belief in "bad luck" (often of a markedly paranoid character). All these varieties of belief are clearly distinguished from each other by their relatedness to outside factors of determination as against exclusive ego-relatedness.

Superstitions are defined as belief in the magic power of certain words or actions or avoidance of certain words or actions to bring about something or to prevent something from happening. They are known to appear as frequently in the behavior of externalized and nondifferentiated persons as in that of highly differentiated and developed individuals. The latter may feel ashamed of what they consider their weakness and try to explain superstitions as "residues of man's irrationality." But the fact remains that all are their equally helpless victims.

In the context of our present discussion, it is sufficient to sum up the teacher's task as one of making his pupils aware of the essential difference between genuine belief and superstition on the one hand, and between superstition and rational understanding on the other. (Scientific questions about the origins and the essence of compulsive dependence as indicative of individual pathologies and unconscious fears or a transpersonal, culture-conditioned reality of symbols are of no concern to the teacher in his functions.)

These brief remarks are meant to point out some of the difficulties for which the teacher should prepare himself before he tries to define certain concepts. We have chosen those of belief and superstition because of their implications in the thinking, learning, and behavior of secondarily retarded children, most of whom come from a social or cultural background of which externalized beliefs and superstitions are characteristic. We must, of course, distinguish between the ways in which a teacher should *organize his thinking* about a certain concept (and thus prepare himself for definitions that may become necessary in this or that teaching context) and ways of *using the material* he may have prepared.

Here are a few guidelines for the teacher in the use of definitions:

The concept or the phenomenon to be defined should be reduced, if possible, to one area of meaning, depending, of course, on the context and content of the specific lesson (for instance, the concept of "belief" in its religious meaning only). Such reduction, or simplification, has the advantage of making room for questions meant to stimulate the pupils' cognitive activity.

Should the pupils ask about different meanings of the concept defined (for instance, about one of the nonreligious meanings of the concept of belief), the teacher should be prepared to deal with their questions by branching out into other fields of learning.

In this way, the originally offered definition is enlarged gradually (in reaction to the pupils' remarks to the extent that they are relevant). It is up to the teacher to decide when to prefer such concept enlargement to dealing with his initial subject matter, and when to postpone this exercise in conceptualization in order to return as quickly as possible to his teaching subject.

The teacher should make it clear to his pupils that every definition can be formulated in different words, and that the formulation chosen by him is not final.

The teacher should accompany his (partial) definition by examples, unlike the scientist, for whom defining is a formal operation. On the other hand, the teacher should be careful in choosing his examples, which should not be ambiguous and thereby set in motion processes of uncontrolled and uncontrollable discussions.

Belief

In Israel, the Bible is an important teaching subject in every secular school. Some teachers see in the book an example of the great works of world literature, others emphasize historical aspects, and all include philosophical discussions of the often conflicting ideas that emerge from its stories, laws, poetry, and oratories.

In one junior high school, the story of how God promised Abraham to give the land of Canaan into the hands of his descendants was read and discussed. "Abraham believed in God's words," said the teacher. "We can learn from the story something about what real belief means: *Abraham was convinced that he had heard God speaking to him and that these words were reliable, even though he had no way of seeing in his lifetime the fulfillment of the promise.*" "Abraham knew that God loved him," said a 13-year-old girl, with deep feeling (undoubtedly revealing her own need for reliable love). A boy added, "Also when God asked him to sacrifice his son, he knew that God would not allow such a horrible thing to happen."

The strong affects of fear underlying these remarks showed the teacher that her pupils were not ready, at this stage, to accept the philosophical (theological) definition of belief in God as "unconditional acceptance," since they could not face the cruel implications of absolute obedience. (In other words, they were not ready for purely formal operations with hypothetical realities.) On the other hand, she felt that the tradition-directed education they had received at home would make a psychological interpretation useless and ineffective. She therefore offered the following, slightly enlarged, version of her original definition by saying: *"Belief means feeling protected by God."*

Here, one of the girls wanted to know whether people who did *not* believe in God necessarily feel unprotected. Another one immediately suggested, "There is the Police and there is the Army to protect them." After a number of critical and affirmative remarks made by the others, the teacher enlarged her preceding definition by saying: *"Belief can be religious belief, in God, while others may believe in a good and reliable person or institution, like the Police or the Army. But all of them feel protected."*

Science-oriented teachers would have tried to compare these "sets" of belief and their similarities and dissimilarities. But the discussion had not yet come to an end. One of the boys said, "If they fail to keep their promises, every belief is liable to collapse, belief in God or belief in persons." (The fact that this pupil was able to generalize, proved he was *not* a typical secondarily retarded pupil.)

The teacher referred to the last remark: "What you say, does not contradict our initial definition. But you have added an important element: You have pointed our that *there are people whose belief is very strong and they continue to believe and to feel protected, even when some adversity happens. Others whose belief is weak, despair immediately when they feel disappointed.* But this does not mean that our definition was wrong."

Some Conclusions

This was an example of "gradually expanding" definitions in rehabilitative teaching. Its phases are determined by the pupils' reactions and particularly by those of an emotional or aggressive character. It follows that, in teaching, definitions serve a double pupose: to help the learner think differentially and to weaken the negative impact of affective elements through the very aid of defining and thus bringing the affects to the surface of consciousness.

The essential difference between didactical and scientific or philosophical definitions is evident: we have already mentioned that, when defining "religious belief," the teacher will prefer consideration for the child's needs to philosophically more comprehensive and more exact definitions when the latter may arouse in the child fears or similarly threatening feelings.

In rehabilitative teaching an assignment should be delayed in which confrontation with the tragic elements or the irrational threats of human existence is implied; they should be delayed until the child's security needs are satisfied to such an extent that he is ready to face "negative truth."

In the last instance, this readiness is a symptom of formal (operational) thinking, that is, of full cognitive rehabilitation. Only when what we have called "contamination" between feeling and thinking is eliminated, will the pupil be able to tolerate alternative solutions, even when they are frightening him personally.

Superstition

In one of the following lessons the teacher asked about the meaning of the concept of "superstition." One of the few regular pupils in the class reacted by saying, "All sorts of nonsense." For most of the others (who came from underprivileged families) it had a surprisingly differnt connotation. One boy suggested, "It is belief in something wrong." For instance: "I believe that it will rain tomorrow and it does not. Then it was a superstition." This strange "definition" elicited similar examples from the rest of the class, by way of association.

The teacher decided not to refer to the definitions so far suggested,* but to take the initiative in her own hands (in a noninductive way). "Let me give you first a few examples," she said. "There are people who believe that something bad will happen to them, when a black cat crosses their path or when they walk underneath a ladder that leans against the wall of a house. Or they hang over the entrance door of their house a horseshoe or a copperhand [known in Islamic countries as Khamssa, five fingers], 'against the evil eye, as they say. Or they knock on wood three times, after having said something good, since otherwise something bad will happen. Or they simply say 'Touch wood,' or something else. Or they put a talisman on their

---

*She interpreted them as an attempt to avoid any form of rejecting the legitimacy of their deep convictions by calling them superstitions and thus denying their reality character.

heart before they go to the hospital for an operation and are convinced that it will protect them. These are superstitions, and they exist everywhere in difference forms."

"Well, some of these things are really nonsense, as Mike has said," interjected one of the secondarily retarded pupils, "but not the evil eye or the camea [the talisman]. They really bring bad luck or good luck."

"It seems you all agree that there are some customs that make no sense, as Mike has said." (At this stage the teacher refrained from differentiating between different kinds of beliefs and superstitions.) *We call them superstitions. They are beliefs in our ability to prevent something bad from happening by doing something or by avoiding doing something.* Everybody who uses his brains can see easily that there is no connection whatsoever [she meant, no *causal* connection] between something bad that may happen and the ladder leaning against the wall, or between the operation and a talisman."

"But how is it possible that so many intelligent people, even doctors and lawyers, believe in these things?" asked one of the boys. "I do not know," answered the teacher; "but I do know that all these intelligent people go to see a doctor when they are seriously ill and do *not* rely on a camea." "In our neighborhood everybody uses talismans, even when they go to the clinic," interjected a girl. "This means", said the teacher, "that they use medicines because they trust the doctor. And they put on the talisman, without knowing how it works, because their grandmother's grandmother may have done so, and also because they are afraid of what might happen, if they cease to keep the tradition. *This is called superstition: continuing to believe in a custom because generations have kept it and because we are afraid of breaking the tradition.*"

We have presented this example in some detail to show again the difference between the educational intention of didactic, as against the organizational function of scientific, definitions. This educational intention, particularly in rehabilitative teaching, is twofold: to help the secondarily retarded pupil differentiate more clearly between the concepts he uses, and to weaken the attractive force of strongly affect-laden concepts, in our case "superstition." It would seem that our teacher failed in the second task. The cultural pattern that manifests itself in superstitious beliefs is much stronger than any rational explanation. The often used method of explaining superstitions as petrified residues of a theory once accepted as "valid" or attempts made to depreciate superstitions by contrasting them with "modern rationalism" are of little use for affect-correction, in fact, are little more than superstitions.

Following her failure until then, our teacher tried another way, based on the same rationalistic prejudices (we shall soon give an example of a different, almost opposite, approach): She spoke of the belief in the healing power of sacred springs or of holy stones or statues. As long as she referred to believers belonging to other religions, the pupils were ready to ridicule their beliefs as nonsense and as "silly superstitions," thereby giving expression to their deep-rooted cultural superiority complexes and their aggressiveness. But when examples were taken from their own cultural background,* they were again unable to recognize the common element of irrationality. *It was a serious mistake on the part of the teacher to identify superstition with irrationality, without distinguishing between legitimate and illegitimate varieties of irrationality.*

Instead, she tried (unsuccessfully again) to appeal once more to her pupils' rationality by adding: "You see, everyone now knows what 'superstitious belief' means. But you see it only in the beliefs of other groups, not of your own. Yours are truth; theirs are nonsense. The others feel, of course, the same when they hear about your beliefs."

Since the class did not react to this last distinction, the teacher summed up the discussion: *"Genuine belief, we have said, is based on trust; superstitious beliefs are based on all sorts of fears of unknown dangers. When you have trust you know how to protect yourself or you pray.* When you are superstitious you do all sorts of silly things." And continuing in that same rationalistic vein she added: "It is true that sometimes things happen to us which we cannot explain. We then say that they happened by chance. Or we speak of luck, good luck or bad luck. I think it is much better to say 'bad luck' than 'evil eye.' It is less frightening than to think of little

---

*One girl, for instance, defended her belief in the evil eye: "It is very simple, my parents have explained to me that there are little devils all around, and when we say something nice about someone, they look and envy him and then they cause him injuries."

demons all around us.'' (She thought that in this way she could neutralize her pupils' affects.)

"But what causes bad luck and good luck?" asked one of the intelligent boys. The teacher replied: "It is a good question, but very difficult to answer. Think, for instance, about two brothers, living under the same conditions, eating the same food; and suddenly the one falls ill and the other remains strong and helathy." "The one was weaker than the other," suggested another pupil; "perhaps he was born weak." "Like one who is more clever than the other," was the next comment. Here the teacher added: "Some grow up under good conditions, others under bad conditions, and *they then tend to say that they have no luck, or bad luck. Those that are superstitious prefer to say that someone has put the evil eye on them.*"

Another Example

In another group of secondarily retarded pupils, age 14, the teacher based her attempts to define the concept of "superstition" on the presumption that superstition, too, is a form of belief. It has in common with genuine belief, so she explained, its effectiveness, its strong, though irrational, impact on the believer's soul and body, his achievements, and his physical condition. "Many people," she said, "take the same medicine when they suffer from the same illness, but not all are helped by it. Some believe very strongly in what the doctor prescribes and are also very careful to follow his prescriptions to the letter; others do not believe in the doctor, they are convinced that nothing will help them, and they are indeed *not* helped." At this point, a lively discussion developed:

"Yes, the one believes in medicines, and the other says, it's all nonsense, superstition," said one of the relatively successful pupils.

"But everyone takes medicines when he is ill," reacted another one; "it is not superstition, like knocking on wood three times or not walking underneath a ladder."

"And when they don't help, the doctor gives you something else," added a third one, "and then, we believe in the second medicine, the one that has helped." Here, the teacher reacted by saying, "I had said: medicines often help when you *believe* they will help, and you say: we believe in them *when* they help" (a clear case of strengthening the ability to think differentially).

"Yes, and also that medicines are not superstition."

"But what about believing in the evil eye which may cause harm?" continued the teacher. "And what about believing in a talisman which may prevent bad things from happening? Are *these* superstitions?"

"That is something different," was the reply. "Medicines cure a sick person, and the talisman protects him."

"And what about the evil eye?"

"This also exists, and you must protect yourself against the evil eye."

Here, the teacher summarized the discussion by saying: "So, what you say, is the following: the doctors claim that a certain illness is the result of an infection, and he tries to learn all about how the infection works, how to prevent it, and how to cure its results. And you agree that he is right, because he has studied and knows all about illnesses. But you add: Not everyone reacts to the same infection in the same way; this depends on the evil eye that someone may have put on him or not. And not everyone reacts to the same medicine in the same way; so you put on a charm, and you believe it will help."*

"Yes, that is correct", said the pupil; "you yourself have said before, all depends on how strongly you believe in the medicines."

Here one of the more adequately functioning boys in the class got up: "And if you do *not* believe in the evil eye, then it will not *harm* you. And the same with talismans. I don't believe in them."

"And why is it that one falls ill and another remains in good health? And that one and the same medicine helps the one and not the other?"

"People are different. One is stronger than the other. We have learned something about that in biology. But all you have said about the evil eye and the talisman, is superstition."

The teacher decided to continue with his generalizations: "We can see from the discussion that our beliefs differ from each other. The one tries to explain everything by factors in nature, in the body, and

---

*This is an example of noninductiveness: the teacher used the summary for the purpose of formulating the pupils' statements more precisely and as more generally valid principles.

in the environment; the other may agree with him, in part, but he also believes in something that he may have learned at home, from his parents and grandparents who also may have learned it from their parents and grandparents.''

"So there is no difference between belief and superstition?'' asked the first boy.

"Well, there *is* a difference,'' replied the teacher. "You remember that we have already made one distinction previously: between true belief which gives us a feeling of being secure and protected, and superstition which is always accompanied by fear of something threatening. Another difference is in the effort we make and in how much we think about what we are doing. When belief is genuine, we never cease to feel that the outcome depends on us, that we are responsible for it, that belief is not enough. In superstition, on the other hand, we are convinced that all we have to do is to say a word or to do a thing as prescribed, and the result will come of itself, automatically, as we say. But in one respect the two are *similar*: the stronger we believe in what we do, the better are the chances of success.''

In the second lesson, the teacher did not see his primary aim in defining superstition, but emphasized much more the importance of *comparing* superstition with other forms of belief. Even when explaining the difference between people who relate themselves to their doings in a responsible way and those who do it in an "automatic'' way, she refrained from all value judgments that could be interpreted as disparaging, as disapproving of the family-culture in which the superstitions are rooted.

III. DEFINITIONS IN LITERATURE-TEACHING (Examples)

The Hero of a Story

The next example is taken from the field of literature-teaching in a class of 14-year-old boys and girls, practically all from underprivileged families and all in need of rehabilitative teaching. It is *not* the intention of the following class discussion to illustrate again the gradual "growth'' (expansion) of a definition. Rather, we want to show this time some of the difficulties that these children's cognitive patterns are likely to create for the teacher who wants to define a certain concept. Often, it is precisely through encountering such unforeseen difficulties that the teacher becomes aware of how to offer his pupils unambiguous definitions and thereby to strengthen their ability to differentiate and to think abstractly.

"Whom do we call a hero?" was the first question. The answers were: he should be brave, daring, ready for self-sacrifice and . . . successful (mostly, war or warlike actions, implying violence, were mentioned); he should be superior, able to beat his adversaries, even when outnumbered by them; he would earn the admiration of others, without, however, inviting it. Obviously, the hero's qualities mentioned bore the character of externalization and of over-compensation for the pupils' own inferiorities.

No one agreed that a hero could also be someone defeated in his struggle or someone who was simply human, an unselfish and honest adherent to an idea or an ideal he considered important (or even a mere introvert). Representatives of such attitudes were considered simply to be "good people," a bit silly, but certainly not "heroes"—provided they had not protested and fought against the establishment.

The teacher tried in vain to enlarge their conception of heroism: his many examples were much too far removed from his externalized pupils' day-to-day reality to convince them. He therefore began to deal with his actual topic: the meaning of the concept of *"the hero of a story."*

In literature, he explained and defined, the hero is "the central figure" of a story, a ballad, an epic, a drama. Often there are several heroes, different from each other in character, deeds, and fate. He asked for examples from pieces of literature that they had learned (and which he mentioned). But when one of the figures was weak or was shown to be defeated, the children could not understand why he should be called a "hero" (of the story), still less when he was shown as a "bad character." Externalization,* particularly in children,

---

*A convincing example of such externalization and aggressiveness and of such absence of genuine moral differentiation can be seen in the words of a boy who was enthusiastic about a film he had seen. "It's a wonderful film," he said, "with two heroes. In the first part they show a thief, what a thief, he is so clever that no one can ever catch him; and in the second part, there is a policeman, he is so clever that no thief can escape him."

finds one of its typical expressions in their stereotyped, phraseological moralism (often definitely in contrast to their actual behavior!). It seems that they fear negative identification no less than they fear punishment (unless they belong to the group of primary behavior disorders and primary aggressiveness,[12] that is, to the group of those who reject the world of the adults and their demands after having experienced, in early childhood, severe disappointments in their parents).

How can the teacher help secondarily retarded children overcome their resistance to accepting formal definitions, such as that of the "hero of a story" as the central figure, irrespective of the quality of his behavior and his actions? In our case, the teacher tried to explain first the difference between reality and the intention of an author who writes a story. He may use facts of history or facts that have occurred to him or facts about which he may have read in an old book or in newspapers. He selects from these facts what suits his purpose, his intentions. For, every author has an intention: the one wants to show the development of a person, the other the development of a group; a third one may simply want to say what he has to say, in an interesting way, or in beautiful words. But everyone has an intention and, accordingly, selects from among all the facts of his fantasy or his reality those that suit his purpose. Even the one who *invents* his facts, selects them. This is the definition of a literary creation: using reality, using so-called facts as new material for the author's composition, for what he considers a convincing picture of a person or an idea. Why is it justified, asked the teacher, to use the same word ("hero") to designate the central figure in a story irrespective of whether it is a positive or a negative figure *and* an important figure in a sequence of reality events? After a short and rather diffuse class discussion the teacher gave the answer: exactly as in the reality of past and present occurrences, so in literature we call "hero" not only the brave, daring, and successful actor but also the one who *determines the outcome* of events, changes, of the fate of his own life or that of others, individuals or groups, some through daring decisions and energetically, others through hesitation and indolence.

It took a long time and required many examples to make the distinction between these two types of determination clear and convincing. The weak and hesitant, the selfish and arrogant, the impulsive and inconsistent—all may determine the development of their own life and that of *others* even more strongly than their positive counterparts. Their description in a story often shows us the essence of their (negative) character traits and the causal importance more convincingly than does their appearance in reality.

"This means," said one of the pupils, "that in a story, everybody can be a hero?" "No, not everybody," answered another one; "for instance in . . . [and here he mentioned one of the stories they had just read] R. and P. and F. are *not* heroes, they are unimportant." "So, why are they mentioned at all?" the first one wanted to know. A number of answers were suggested: "There must be others, too." "Because the hero cannot do everything." "The story would be boring." Here, the teacher decided to intervene ("noninductively") by formulating a more precise answer. "It seems, what you want to say is the following: Every story, even one completely invented by the author, is based on some facts taken from reality. And even if he does not want to *describe* what has happened, reality, but *uses* the facts to give expression to his intentions, as we have said, his story wants to give the *impression* of reality. And just as in reality there must always be many people and many facts, in order that something may happen, so also in a story written by an author."

"The same as in films," interjected a boy, "and the hero is always a famous actor." "You are right," continued the teacher, "the hero in the film, the central figure, is also called the main role, and the main role is always played by a particularly good actor. And now you also understand why a hero can also be a bad character. You certainly remember films you have seen in which the main role was someone bad."

The Plot

A similar problem presented itself to a teacher in another literature class, when he defined the concept of "plot." "The plot of a novel or a drama," he said, "is the sequence of events, selected, put together and narrated by the writer according to a plan and a purpose he has had in mind." One of the pupils wanted to know why the same word is used when someone slanders another one whom he hates.

"Because both are liars," answered one of the aggressive boys. "Every writer is a liar. You have said yourself: he invents his stories."

"But that is different," answered the teacher; "he does not want to harm anyone, like the person who slanders another one and distorts everything just to offend him or to cause him harm."

"Then, why don't they write only what has really happened?" "Like a reporter who writes for a newspaper?" "Or like a policeman who makes a report?"

"Well," said the teacher, "you certainly know that many times the same event is reported quite differently by two different reporters, not because the one lies and the other writes the truth, but because each of them describes the same event according to what seems to him most important. And even a policeman often makes mistakes when reporting an incident, but he does not lie."

"But with a writer, it is nevertheless different," insisted the first boy. "As you have said, he chooses what suits him and does not mention the rest. Is this not lying?"

"I don't think so," replied the teacher, "lying means not saying the truth, because the liar either wants to harm someone whom he does not like or wants to protect someone who is important for him, and he expects some benefit as the result of his lies. A writer selects the facts he needs for his story, because he believes that his story will become better and more convincing in this way. He uses his fantasy, his imagination."

The class did not pay attention to this last remark, because all were still too preoccupied with the affect-laden word "lying." One girl wanted to know why one said that the story had a plot when we also say that someone is plotting against another one by telling all sorts of lies about him.

The teacher answered: "Because the word means planning or construing something and this is, indeed, common to the lie and the story. Both are planned, so that the true intention of the plot is not clear immediately, is something hidden that becomes evident only after a while, in the end. But the lie is planned to cause harm or, in another case, to evade justice, while in the planning and the writing of a story and its plot the writer uses his fantasy or imagination, in order to show his readers something as a reality. What does this mean?"

"Fantasy is what is not true." "Fantasy is when I remember something." "Fantasy is when I don't know something and simply say something" (guess). "I have seen a film with all sorts of animals in it that do not exist and something about stars which no one has seen; that was fantasy." It was evident that the pupils had not followed their teacher.

"We can use our imagination for good purposes and for bad purposes," said one of the bright girls in the class. Although it was more or less a repetition of what the teacher had said, he based his following explanations on her remarks, leaving aside all that had been said by the others, rather inadequately, about fantasy.

"This is exactly the point I wanted to make," he said. "It is important to understand why the same word is used for plotting against a person to cause him harm and for writing the plot of a story. But it is still more important to know, in which respect what we are doing is good and in which respect it is bad."

Here, the teacher branched out into explaining the meaning of the word "criteria," using different examples taken from a variety of fields. His main purpose was to make his pupils understand the difference between judging an action or an attitude or a person from a moral point of view (in life-practice) and from an aesthetic point of view (in literature or, for that matter, in any other art).

It was evident that not all of his pupils could follow his explanations. He nevertheless enlarged and elaborated on what had been said, as follows: "The plot of a story can be well planned and written or can be badly written, irrespective of whether it is about a morally good or bad person, about a strong man or a weakling. It is important to distinguish between the two aspects: good or bad in writing, or, for that matter, in any art, in any creation, and good or bad in life, in behavior, in society. Here again: you have the same words 'good' and 'bad', but with different meanings. Can you think of another example of something good or bad, not in behavior, not in art,* but. . . ?"

---

*In rehabilitative thinking, it is important to exclude areas already mentioned when asking for "other" examples. It helps to prevent associative repetitions, which would be meaningless.

The pupils brought examples from the fields of food ("good" meaning tasty, "bad" meaning spoiled food), medicine ("good" meaning effective, "bad" meaning not bringing relief), road building ("good" meaning well-maintained, "bad" meaning in need of repair). By branching out into different fields he helped develop his pupils' readiness to use one word in different meanings.

One of the more intelligent pupils surprised the teacher by saying: "If there are good and bad plots in literature, there are also good and bad plottings against another person, clever and stupid ones." "But both are bad morally," added another one.

The original purpose of the lesson was to use definition, in a noninductive way, in order to help secondarily retarded pupils reach a higher degree of differentiation. The lesson also came to show the close connection between at least two of the basic principles of rehabilitative teaching, noninductiveness (in formulating correct definitions) and branching out (into the differential meaning of a concept in various fields of application). The lesson was fairly successful, though probably not to the same extent for all pupils. The final remarks revealed full understanding of the different meanings of concepts such as "good" and "bad" (which tend to be sterotyped and absolutistic, particularly in secondarily retarded pupils, whereas here at least some of the children were able to use their differential meaning even in the field of morally condemnable behavior: effective versus noneffective).

Forms of Literature

One of the main criteria in selecting literary creations for the composition of textbooks is representation of the different forms, for instance, poetry or drama. It is therefore understandable why so many teachers, particularly in regular junior or senior high school classes, consider *defining* these different forms an intrinsic part of their teaching function. And yet, experience shows, again and again, not only the unattractiveness but also the ineffectiveness of this element of literature-teaching. Moreover, scientific definitions (for instance, of the different forms of poetry, such as "ballad," "lyric," "elegy") do not always suit the examples included in the textbook.

Defining becomes meaningful, if it does at all, only as part of *comparing* with each other different forms of literature. And such comparison, in turn becomes meaningful only if the form is shown to be an integral part of the content of the creation and of the writer's manifest or reconstructible *intentions*.* Sometimes, the latter can be made convincingly clear in case one author has expressed the same idea in two forms, for instance, as a novel and a drama, or as a poem and a philosophical reflection. It is obvious that if this is the way we understand the function of defining, formal considerations lose their meaning.

On the other hand, concentration on contents and intentions, particularly in rehabilitative teaching, does not contradict the inclusion of certain elements of formal definition. To give a few examples:

In every definition of a ballad, a distinction is made between anonymous, "transmitted" collective creations and others known to be written by an individually identifiable author. Differentiation between the two is more than an element of formal definition; it requires posing questions about the essential differences between personal intentions and historical processes.

In scientific analyses, a lyric (a "Lied") may be defined as a short poem accompanied (actually or possibly) by music; a drama as an attempt to re-create an As-If reality through monologues, dialogues, and talks between persons ("characters"), reflecting imagined sequences of events; and similarly a ballad, an epic, an elegy, a novel, and so on. *Didactically, it is more important to define concepts such as "lyrical," "dramatic," "tragic," "comical," and "elegiac" than to classify literary creations accordingly.*

In rehabilitative teaching, however, this cannot be done "inductively," by way of drawing the proper conclusions from "case material." The teacher must offer the definitions and accompany them by examples taken not only, and not even primarily, from the field of literature but rather from that of the pupils' personal experiences. In other words, defining concepts as part of noninductiveness in rehabilitative teaching is a psychological means to help form the externalized and secondarily retarded child's personality, to help him discover the dimension of "a life from within."

---

*When we speak of the author's intentions, we have in mind, of course, *not* his associatively emerging but only his logically elaborated, his *systematized* ideas.

The same applies to defining, as exactly and as differentially as possible, the *contents* of a literary work: moods and feelings, changes, processes, conflicts and crises, and, in the end, allusions and ambiguities. (Here, the second and more important phase of noninductiveness can be demonstrated, the phase of application: When translating the described or narrated contents into concepts, many questions of the "What-if-not" type should be asked. How would you define the mood if the author had chosen the word——instead of the word he has used? What is the difference between (two words of similar connotation)? Could the story end differently, and what would you then call it?)

The Category of the As-If

We have tried to show in the preceding paragraphs various functions of defining several frequently recurring concepts in literature-teaching as a part of noninductive teaching. Its importance and complexity become nowhere more evident than in dealing with the category of the As-If. We have already tried to explain why secondarily retarded pupils tend to reject the nonrealistic "play" character of the As-If. But it is precisely the ability to "play" with it (in conceptualization, in reaching the dimension of meaning as something no less real than the forefront of concrete givens and facts, in accepting forms of expressing feelings and ideas, through analogies, metaphors, symbols and so on) that proves intellectual security and competence.

In rehabilitative teaching, however, the teacher must start with clearly worded definitions to make applications and exemplifications meaningful for the development of cognitive functions such as differentiation or seeing various aspects of a problem at one and the same time. Neither conveying knowledge nor causing aesthetic pleasures should be considered legitimate aims of literature-teaching. Emphasis should be placed on the discovery of meaning.

It is often claimed that fairy tales, fables, and proverbs are the most suitable means for producing in secondarily retarded children the amount of imagination required to develop in them readiness and ability to recognize the dimension of meaning, to venture, as it were, into the uncertainty of presumptions. But the reactions of many such pupils to those materials teach us something different.

The fairy tale shows a reality from which logics and natural causality are excluded. The coexistence of a natural and a supra- (or extra-) natural reality makes a stronger impression on the minds of many retarded children than the so-called moral of the story (which is often very simple to formulate and define). Intellectually well-functioning pupils have no difficulty in conceiving of that contradiction between the supranatural and natural reality as a symbol, or, better, as *Jung* would say, as an attempt to concretize archetypical truth. The secondarily retarded, on the other hand, often reacts to that very contradiction either by rejecting the fairy tale as childish nonsense or by sinking too deeply into the sea of the supernatural as replacement of reality. In both cases, he shows inability to accept the dimension of the As-If. In both cases, he is, to put it paradoxically, "too much of a realist."

We find similar limitations in the way he relates to fables. It is easy to define the fable as a short story using nonhuman beings (such as animals or plants) to express an often complex and/or unpleasant truth in a simple, interesting, and pleasant way.*

On the other hand, much more active involvement was produced in the class when the teacher defined the fable as a way of expressing what he wanted to say in a symbolic way. What does this latter concept mean, he asked, and immediately offered the definition: "It is a sign or the image of a person, an animal, an object which has a specific meaning. Not everyone knows that meaning; then he does not understand the symbol."

"Why don't they say in clear and plain words what they mean?" one of the pupils wanted to know.

"There are two answers to your question," said the teacher, "one taken from history, the other from literature. In history, we often find people or groups of people who are opposed to the ruling authorites. Mostly they must live in hiding, 'underground,' as we say, in order not to be caught by the government. Then they use

---

*It may be relevant to quote here what was said in a class after the teacher had defined the fable in this way and then added a few examples. They said, "We are no longer small kids when the parents feed us with all sorts of silly stories." And: "If something is difficult to understand, it should not be said so that it *seems* to be easy. That does not help, and it is lying." And: "Fables are not interesting at all."

secret signs known only to them, a kind of identity card. These, for instance, are symbols, perhaps of their idea, their belief, the movement.''

"But sometimes, everyone knows that sign and what it means. Then, there is no secret anymore, and it is no longer a symbol,'' "Yes,'' added another one, "like the signs of a football team: everyone knows them, and everyone recognizes the team by the shirts.''

It was obvious the teacher's intention to make his pupils understand the categories of the As-If and of meaning was going to get lost in a flood of inadequate associations. He therefore decided to bring them back to discussing symbols within literature:

"When you asked why a writer uses symbols instead of saying directly what he wanted to say, I answered that I could give you also an answer as a teacher of literature. Take any one of the fables you have learned such as [here he gave two examples] and ask yourself: why did the author choose these animals and not others? Which human qualities do they illustrate? What would be the teaching of the fable, if we changed this or that detail of the story [examples followed]? In other words: The fable wants to make us *think* about the meaning of each of its details and about the meaning of the whole story.''

"But why not write a story where *humans* speak and not animals?'' asked one of the girls. "It would not be such a lie. Everyone knows that animals do not speak.''

"I agree with you,'' replied the teacher. "And you know, of course, that there are plenty of such stories, some of which we have already learned.* How would you define the difference between the intentions of a fable and those of a simple story?''

"The fable is a lie, and the story is 'true','' suggested one. "No, that is not correct,'' said another one, "because *every* story is a lie.'' "I think you remember what we have said already: a writer is not a liar because he does not want to cheat someone else when he *invents* his story and when he wants to make us believe what he describes in his invented story as reality. We have spoken of the writer's

---

*The teacher refrained on purpose from referring to symbolic stories (which, in any case, were unknown to his pupils).

imagination and fantasy. And the result is his invented story. But I asked you about the *difference* between a fable and a simple story."

"Now I understand," shouted one of the pupils happily, "when he writes a fable, he does not *want* us to believe that it is real, like when he writes a story."

"I think, you have said something very important," said the teacher. "When we read a fable, or, for that matter, a fairy tale, no one believes that it is something real. Therefore, we concentrate immediately on thinking about what it means. When we read a story, which is written so that it *could* be real, we concentrate first on the story and only later, when we discuss the story, we may ask what it means, and why these or those details have been said by the author."

In a regular class, in which a similar discussion had taken place, one of the pupils asked whether the meaning was part of the story or was something separate, something added to it by the reader when he wanted to find it. And he added the answer himself: that if the meaning was an inseparable part of the story and of the author's intention, it would be wrong to speak of different, equally correct and possible interpretations. Only one could be correct, namely, the one meant by the author, and all the rest would be pure fantasies of the readers.

In our class, the question turned up in a different way. One of the pupils said categorically: "There is only one story, that of the writer. And it certainly has only one meaning, the one the writer had in mind. And I think that, when we study literature, the teacher must tell us what the correct meaning is, of a fable or of a story."

At this point, the lesson came to an end. It was evident that the class had indeed come to understand that every story had a meaning and that this depended, at least in part, on the author's intention. But they had *not* come to understand that the *discovery* of the meaning was the function of the reader's (or the learner's) cognitive activity, or that the reality-character of meaning was fundamentally different from the reality character of an (invented) story or what we have called the dimension of the As-If.

Another teacher used a different method to make the category of the As-If meaningful. He chose a little poem by the Hebrew poet Dan Pagi which, in its English translation, reads as follows:

In marmor blocks a graven image waits.
The good jar still sleeps in the womb of clay.
The melody has lost its way
It seeks its flute between the reeds.
The building stone is still imprisoned in
The rock. Bread is still hidden in the winter-wheat.

Man reigning free in failure and in trust
Transforms wheat, rock, reed, clay and marmor blocks.

To the question about the meaning of the various verses of the poem some of the pupils answered that they made no sense because neither a sculpture nor a jar, neither a melody nor a stone nor the bread had a soul, and in the poem they appeared like human beings. Others simply said that they did not understand what it was all about, and what had man to do with it? The last lines had nothing to do with the rest of the poem, they claimed. No one understood its intention.

The teacher decided to offer his explanation and definition according to the principles of noninductiveness. He said: "We know a graven image, that is, a sculpture, only after the sculptor has hewn it out of a marmor block (you probably remember the film we have seen recently about the way a sculptor works). In the poem it is said that it waits, as if it already existed in the marmor block and the artist had only to take it out of it. The jar is shown *as if* it was a foetus in the mother's womb waiting to be born, and the clay, *as if* it was the jar's mother. The same with the bread: *as if* it existed already in the wheat, or the building stone, *as if* it was a prisoner in the rock waiting for the stone-cutter to open its prison and to liberate it."

"And what about the melody?" asked one of the girls. "How can a melody lose its way? Where does it go? And how can a melody find a flute? This is absurd."

"Well, you probably agree," said the teacher, "that a melody must be played, for instance on a flute or on any other instrument, or that it must be sung by someone, to be heard; and only when it is heard it is really a melody. And a flute is made by an expert out of a certain kind of reeds. So, the author wanted to say: a melody which is not heard, is helpless, it needs the instrument and it wants it very much, like someone who has lost his way in a forest wants to get out of it. Of course, these are only comparisons, but aren't they lovely comparisons?''

"Perhaps," reacted one boy, "but why do we need poems? All this can be said also in simple words."

"That is correct," agreed the teacher, "we can say everything we want to say also in simple words. Only then we would not have to *think* so much about the meaning. How would you say in simple words what has been said here by way of allusions and comparisons?''

No one reacted. The teacher continued: "What about the end, the last two lines? What did the author want to say? It is like the solution of a riddle." "That a clever man can make all sorts of useful things with his hands," was one answer. And another pupil added, "And sometimes he does not succeed—he is a bad worker; we can't trust him."

"Perhaps the author wanted to say that materials are there to be used by man in his creative ability, but in order to be creative, *he* must have trust in himself, although he may sometimes fail to achieve what he *wants* to achieve. Then he tries again." The teacher thus corrected certain misunderstandings of his pupils without expressly referring to their mistakes. It was doubtful to what extent the pupils had come not only to understand the dimension of the As-If, but also to accept the value of analogues as legitimate means of intensifying active imagination and thinking.

IV. DEFINITIONS IN CIVICS-TEACHING

The aims of civics-teaching are usually defined as transmission of knowledge (as if it had been proved that knowledge, in this field, is a precondition of good civic behavior) and direct or indirect development of good citizenship habits. In the following discussion some definitional material is put together with the intention of making the teacher in general, but particularly the teacher of secondarily retarded pupils, aware of the particular difficulties which he must face in teaching civics, difficulties that are rooted more in the affective than in the cognitive aspects of the subject matter.

It is doubtful whether the question of how to define democracy can be answered satisfactorily in a class of regular students by informing them about the government structure with its essential separation of the legislative from the courts and the executive authorities. It is certainly a most ineffective method in rehabilitative teaching. Nor is it adequate there to define democratic rule by emphasizing the citizens' right freely to criticize the authorities, either individually or through the communications media or the political parties. The relevant question that must be added refers to the *genuineness* of this right, freely to express citicism, and part of such genuineness is the government's readiness not only to permit criticism but also to consider it, to heed it, to change decisions accordingly. This distinction between a formal and a practical, one could almost say an existential, definition of democracy is of particular importance for secondarily retarded students: while regular pupils are ready to accept the formal definition as sufficient, since they have learned it from their parents, who, half cynically, accept the quasi-reality of democracy; secondarily retarded pupils are much more concerned with the objective meaning, the reality character of the democratic order—they are much more directly affected victims of its artificiality. The latter, therefore, make a clear distinction between phraseology and meaning, not so much based on sophisticated arguments and counterarguments as on practical experience (for instance, of the discrepancy between the principles and the reality, or irreality, of equality). Their often aggressive, anti-establishment affects make "neutral" discussions of the topic almost impossible. (Here we see the close connection between offering the pupils definitions, in a noninductive way, and the third component of rehabilitative teaching, that of neutralizing affects, without which definitions would remain meaningless.

In most textbooks of civics, "government" is defined as the organization that tries to regulate each individual citizen's behavior through laws meant to determine his duties and his rights, and to enforce obedience to these laws through the power of police and other "law-enforcing" bodies. Being coerced as an intrinsic part of the citizen's life finds an essential expression in the fact that he has no right to renounce his "membership" in the society called "state," whereas he is free to renounce membership in any other society (association) to which he may belong. We well know that the underprivileged person often affectively negates his membership in that society called state (for instance in delinquent acts or as an anarchist) without, on the other hand, giving it up; that he feels discriminated against precisely because he feels that he "belongs" (externally at least).

Here, simulation games as part of civic education will not help very much. They are much too technical and not realistic enough. They may help one acquire information (which, by definition, is valid for a limited period of time only). They certainly do *not* help develop involvement, which depends on reality situations. Nor will the underprivileged and secondarily retarded child accept as meaningful the claim that the state is there to protect the individual against the dangers of disorders and anarchy; the frequent experience of injustice and inequality makes such educational efforts futile.

The right to criticize the ways in which public affairs are conducted and to change them through participation in elections, is for the underprivileged more of an opportunity to express his affects than a challenge to exercise his legitimate rights as a citizen. For, this right is, as a rule, channeled through political parties that not only excel, usually, in demagogic phraseology but also do not recognize the legitimacy of individual decisions.

Moreover, almost never do textbooks raise the question of how to distinguish between genuine and false democracy. Seldom, if ever, are Western, communist, and Asian forms of democracy compared with each other in their essential tenets, philosophies, and practices. How is the individual seen in each of these various democratic regimes, and why do we call some of them totalitarian regimes? Why is true democracy almost a contradiction in terms?

Here appears the critical question of the limits of civil obedience. What are the intrinsic conflicts of man between his obligations as a citizen and the demands of his conscience? Where and when do they clash? Does obedience to the imperatives of personal conscience perforce produce bad citizenship? What, then, is a "good citizen"?

The simplest answer is: good citizenship expresses itself in *the individual's readiness to fulfill the small daily duties demanded by laws, customs and ideologies in anonymous settings*, without consideration of personal contacts or benefits and not necessarily on the basis of previous examination of the rationale of these laws, customs, and ideologies. Good citizenship expresses itself in the individual's readiness *to take into consideration the interests of the other person, without "personal accounts,"* to subordinate personal interests to those of the group, *to volunteer,* if it is necessary or desirable for the group, *to defend justice* after examination of the objective conditions of each specific case or constellation. Good citizenship expresses itself in the individual's readiness *to act on his own only within the limits of the existing laws* or, if necessary, through activation of the responsible authorities. It expresses itself in the individual's readiness to fight against expression of public injustice, by way of demonstration or otherwise (on condition that this readiness does not come instead of conscious or unconscious aggressiveness but is controlled by rational considerations).

Bad (or weak) citizenship is not defined as the opposite of good citizenship. Its most important characteristic traits are: a tendency to limit to its possible minimum the fulfillment of legal obligations, and to fulfill even these only if there is no alternative left, in other words, under the stress of outside control, of either the police or strong public opinion; a tendency to act only within the narrow and limited circle of what is "known" and "near," and even within these limits only in order to take care of personal interests. Bad citizens see in citizenship-demands undesirable and even illegitimate interferences of "anonymous" outside agents, which it is only natural to reject affectively. A bad (or weak) citizen is defined as one who wants to receive what he claims is due to him according to the law, without feeling bound by any obligation of reciprocal service.

When the teacher in a class of 15-year-old pupils tried to make them see the difference between good and bad citizenship, one of them asked: "Why do we say that they are good *citizens*? They simply are good people. And the others are bad." "They are not so bad," reacted another one; "they only take care of themselves because no one takes care of them. Why should they think of others, when the others do not think of them?" "Not true," said a third; "when they are sick, they go to the Sick Fund." "Yes, and my father works at———and they are on strike, and the Union pays him." "But that's different," replied the first one; "they pay for it" (meaning that this is not a case to the point made here).

The teacher welcomed this digression, this branching out into an affect-laden problem area, because it helped him enlarge his original definition of good and bad citizenship. He first summarized by saying that good citizenship is characterized by readiness to do faithfully what everyone is supposed to do, to lead an orderly life, to think of others and not only of oneself, to volunteer, when necessary, without asking what one's personal reward is, to fight for justice but only within the limits of the law. And he defined bad citizenship by referring to the examples he had given before, of people who do their duty only when threatened, and even then only at a minimum, or who take care of others, if at all, only when they know them well and who always think: What do I get out of it?

"Now you have added two questions: What is the difference between a good citizen and a man who is simply good? And: Are those whom we call bad citizens really bad? What do you think? Can a person be good and nevertheless a bad citizen? And can someone be bad and a good citizen?"

One boy suggested: "I have seen a film about Robin Hood. He was a good man because he wanted to help the poor. But he was a robber, and the police were after him. He certainly was not a good citizen." "You are right," said the teacher; "you remember that we have mentioned readiness to fulfill the little duties demanded by the law as one of the signs of good citizenship. And Robin Hood certainly did not do this." "He did not pay income tax," said another boy jokingly. "And I want to remind you," added the teacher, "that good citizenship manifests itself in man's readiness to fight against injustice in lawful, legally recognized ways only. And Robin Hood broke almost every law, although he had good intentions." "But most people are not courageous enough to do what Robin Hood did, and many are good nevertheless," was one girl's reaction, "good people *and* good citizens. I don't believe that someone can be good and a bad citizen." "Why not?" remarked another pupil, who continued, "They may be very good with their children, but they don't care about those things you have mentioned." "What, for instance?" "For instance, keeping the street clean or serving in the Army or paying taxes."

"And what about the opposite case? That of bad people who are good citizens?" Since no one reacted, the teacher continued: "There are people who give much money to charity, pay their taxes, and even volunteer for all sorts of functions, but only in order to show how good they are. In other words, people who behave *as if* they were excellent citizens, but in their hearts think only of themselves, of the impression they may make. They are *not* good in their hearts, in spite of all they do.''

6

Explosive Issues and Neutralization

I. INTRODUCTORY REMARKS

The need for neutralizing affective elements in faulty thinking processes may arise in any lesson, sometimes in the most unexpected contexts. But it is obvious that it becomes particularly urgent when the issues dealt with are of an explosive nature, as they more frequently are in civics, history, or literature than in physics, chemistry, and mathematics (biology taking an intermediate position). Affective reactions to the underprivileged pupil's and his parents' experiences of failure, discrimination, and frustration, of social injustice and inequality, with want and the havable, are liable to distort his thinking processes.

Neutralizing these affective elements, we have said, means translating them into their rational, conceptual equivalents. The following examples will serve a double purpose: they are meant to illustrate the ways in which explosive issues are liable to distort our conceptions, as well as the didactic interventions through which the teacher should try to counteract their distorting impact.

II. EXAMPLES

Loss of Freedom

The human aspects of loss of freedom were discussed in a literature lesson on three levels simultaneously, by analyzing a certain story, and by branching out into discussing certain recent political events and decisions, and into discussing the outcome of what had happened in many parts of Europe after World War II. (The pupils' age was 15.)

The story was about an influential man, a nouveau riche, who tried to persuade the owner of a piece of land to sell it to him, since he needed it, so he claimed, for "rounding up" his estate. The landowner refused, because he did not want to leave the property, which had been in the hands of his family for generations. He continued to refuse although he was offered a good price and full compensation, claiming that his feeling of belonging to his family property was irrational and therefore not "marketable." (In the end, he was manipulated by the rich estate-owner into all kinds of financial troubles until he committed an offense for which he was convicted, and he had to give up his property.)

One of the main topics discussed was the meaning of the man's strong attachment to his forefathers' land. What is the difference, it was asked, between a piece of land on which a person has grown up, where every corner is known to him, and about which his father and his grandfather have told many interesting stories, and owning money, which you can spend when you want to buy some of the necessities of life? For urban slum children this distinction is difficult to understand, since the experience of continuity and belonging is almost totally foreign to them, and the value of easily disposable money is so much more convincing, particularly since they know how often it is scarce.

Most of the pupils failed to see the injustice done by the rich man, but, on the contrary, found the poor landowner was rather stupid in his stubbornness. Thus, they misinterpreted the central idea of the story. One of the boys even went so far as to reject the landowner and found in his later offense confirmation of his own negative opinion about him. Here, again, the pupil's affects distorted his causal thinking and his understanding of the story's intention. And even the few among the pupils who protested indignantly against the rich man's ruthlessness failed to understand the essence of the story.

The teacher concentrated his efforts on developing the children's awareness of the feeling of attachment to a place where we have spent all our life (a rather hypothetical experience for town children). The explosive nature of their aggressive rejection of every kind of attachment to land property was much more evident in their relationship to the poor and honest, tradition-oriented landowner than in their relationship to the rich man. This is one of the intrinsic paradoxes of externalization due to poverty:[10] while the rich man, when confronted with a poor landowner, satisfies aggressive needs and evokes admiration for his success-through-ruthlessness, the latter's image is likely to set in motion feelings of fear (of failure) or even feelings of contempt.

Here the teacher saw his main function in correcting the externalized and therefore distorted conception of strength owing to material success. He tried to bring his secondarily retarded pupils to seeing the legitimacy of personal attachment and belonging as inner values. He turned to one of the children:

"Didn't you tell me once about the watch your father inherited from his grandfather who died abroad? And how he was wearing it and taking good care of it every day? And that he would never sell it, even when he needed money very badly? And that it was made of gold, so it certainly was worth quite a lot."

"Yes, but a watch is not like a house. We could live somewhere else."

"That is correct. But so could your father live with a good and much cheaper watch, and he could sell the gold watch for much money. He did *not* do so because he felt attached, through the watch, to his grandfather whom he loved. So was the poor landowner. He felt attached, through the land, to his grandfather who already had been born there and had lived there."

"This means," remarked one of the boys who before had blamed the poor man for being stupid, "that there are people who don't know what it means to feel attached to their grandparents, perhaps because they have never known them" (a typically externalized distortion of the idea of loyalty to one's past culture or tradition, which is not *identical* with, but is only *represented* by "grandfathers"). "Not only because they did not know them," corrected the teacher, "but also because they don't *think* about the past."

"Like the rich man in the story," reacted another pupil, "he did not think of the past, only of the future, how to make more money."

Although this reaction was not quite adequate because of its dichotomous character, the teacher decided to accept it at this point in order to replace the distorting identification with external strength by a more internalized and a more rational identification with the ideal of justice. He said, "You have touched at the main point of the story: because he did not know or understand the poor man's feelings, he was ready to be unjust and cruel to him." "Even criminal," said one of the pupils, "the way he forced him into making debts in order to ruin him, only to get his land."

"But this is very similar to the story that was in the papers the other day—about expelling people from their houses and blowing up those houses because some of them had been terrorists," said one girl. Most of the others immediately rejected this comparison affectively and categorically. They did not understand the point that the girl had wanted to make. Again, an affective element had to be neutralized to make rational understanding possible.

Neutralization, however, required, in this context, first that the teacher "remove the issue" from the much too explosive area of actualities to an area less explosive, though similar in content, that of certain events in history. The teacher chose a topic that had been discussed in a recent geography lesson: he mentioned the many population transfers after World War II, when territories were annexed by Russia, Poland, France, and other countries.

"Try to think of the feelings of those who had to leave their lands," said the teacher. "In history, we cannot always give a clear answer, as we can in our story, to the question who was right and who was wrong, where was justice, where injustice. But I brought up this problem in order to help you understand our story. You must use your judgment or, as we say, form your opinion about justice and injustice."

"But, why should we?" asked a girl. "No one will ever ask us about our opinion. *You* tell us. It's much better" (a clear expression of dependence on authority, indicating fear of making decisions, of taking sides, particularly in cases in which every yes and every no is liable to imply aggressive rejection of what may be the proper, the expected answer).

Neutralization of affects can be achieved here only by explaining the need to use different criteria, different points of view, whenever we judge historical events, political decisions, or the behavior of man in reality or in literature. This is perhaps the most difficult part of rehabilitative teaching: the teacher must know not only how to use different judgment-criteria but also how to keep the balance between such an objective (differential) attitude and the children's legitimate needs for identification with their own and their country's position.

When the teacher in our class used this method while discussing different viewpoints in the evaluation of political or individual decisions, his success became most clearly evident when one of the girls (and, incidentally, one who so far had shown much more aggressiveness than constructive initiative) made the following comment:

"We say that the rich man was bad, because he used all sorts of dirty tricks to get hold of the poor man's land. But what do you say (she said "you" and not "we"!) when a country annexes territories after a war victory, as the Russians did it, or the Poles, or the French? They [she meant, the decision-making authorities] also claim that they need it to round up the country's territory or to protect the frontiers."

"This is an excellent question," reacted the teacher, "because it proves that you have learned how to compare with each other two different fields, a story and a political decision. This is what we call applying what we have learned in our lesson to another topic. Besides that, it is a good question, because it shows that you are able to think critically and objectively, even when it comes to such a difficult problem: whether our own country, our own government can be wrong and our enemies can be right. The answer is that all we decide and do (for instance: annexation of territories after a war) can be good or bad morally *or* politically (that is, for the country), and it can also be good or bad morally *and* politically."

At this point, a lively discussion followed, in which almost all took part. The focus was on using different criteria and seeing different viewpoints. And yet, the teacher was not sure whether he had done the right thing to bring up explosive issues, which, he claimed, might harm "these" (meaning the secondarily retarded) pupils emotionally.

This contradiction between what seems to be a quite adequate ability to conduct lessons according to the principles of rehabilitative thinking and a basically wrong conception of the nature of affects and emotions could be found frequently among our teachers. It certainly confirms what we have said above (see p. 38) about the need for continuous guidance services to be made available to all engaged in this kind of teaching, particularly when it comes to the "third principle," that of neutralizing affects.

Social Differences and Clashes

One of the most explosive issues and one likely to provoke distorting and even destructive affects, particularly in a heterogeneous class, is the complex issue of social differences and clashes. The following is a brief summary of parts of a lesson in which the essential differences between collective and individual life-styles were discussed. The obvious representative of the collective life-style in Israel is the Kibbutz.

A class of 15-year-old pupils was composed of less than one-third "regular" and more than two-thirds secondarily retarded children (practically all of whom came from underprivileged areas and families). The information that the second group had on the ideology and the organization of the Kibbutz was astonishingly scanty. For them, it was little more than an institution in which social problem cases from urban areas were placed, and everyone, indeed, knew at least one or two children from his neighborhood who had been placed in one of the Kibbutzim.* Another generally known detail was the fact that all needs of the individual member and his family were met by the collective. Life in the Kibbutz was said to be particularly attractive for children because games, a variety of activities, and pleasant learning facilities were available there, in addition to physical care and group-life. And yet, not everything was so good there, said one of the boys, because they were also put to work, and "making children work" was associated in their mind almost automatically with "exploitation"—again an example of affects and resentments distorting the learner's ability objectively to recognize and understand the essence of social realities.

Another boy, who was definitely more of a neurotic than a re-

*Plural of Kibbutz.

tarded type, affectively protested against the educational policy of the Kibbutz, according to which children of the various age groups lived in groups in separate housing units under the supervision of trained counselors and not their parents. When the teacher tried to neutralize this affect by adding objective information (that each child saw his parents every day and that adequate care was taken of their needs, even when the parents were absent or engaged in work), his fears were *not* alleviated.*

It was the purpose of the teacher to make his pupils aware of the assets and the liabilities of a collective as against an individualistic life-style. One of the "regular" pupils understood the issue and the implications. "In the Kibbutz," he said, "all are equal, and everybody gets what the others get. This is justice. But they must also do what they are told to do; they are not free to decide, the group decides, the committee. Just like in Russia. And that is bad." Another said: "In the towns, everyone can do what he wants to do, but some are rich and some are poor. There is no equality. And no justice."

Here, a critical point was reached, from which "branching out" into social problem areas far beyond the specific topics of the lesson (the Kibbutz and the difference between life-styles) was indicated: a discussion of class clashes, discrimination, the objective and the subjective causes of poverty, and similar questions could not be avoided at this point. The feelings and affects known to accompany them are liable to distort objective thinking not only about them, but also about other issues; they are apt to impair the pupils' motivation to learn about those issues and certainly to think about them in abstract terms. A full discussion of the different forms and causes of poverty, for instance, should have ensued here; comparing with each other these forms and these causes is necessary to neutralize the (actually or potentially) distorting affects.

"If equality is possible in the Kibbutz, why can't it be in town?" one of the girls wanted to know. The others offered a variety of answers: "Perhaps they receive support from the government and

*He emphasized in particular the "cruelty" of separating the children from their parents *at night* (incidentally, a practice much criticized and discussed in the relevant educational literature!) and, as a result, was unable objectively to interpret and evaluate the ideas and ideals expressed in the educational practice of the Kibbutz.

therefore can afford giving everybody what he needs." "Perhaps, they work harder, because they have nothing else to do." "And there are less opportunities to waste as much as can be wasted in towns."

The teacher formulated what had been suggested at the end as an abstraction: "What you want to say is actually that one of the causes of social inequality is the abundance of what is called consumer goods in modern society—the more goods we see, the more we want to have. And sometimes we spend our money on nonessential goods and have not left enough for essentials. But this is, of course, only one cause of poverty. Can you think of another?" "Yes, bad luck." "Or there are no jobs, unemployment." "Or illness or accidents." "Or exploitation."

"Yes," said the teacher, "what you say, can be formulated as a general law: those who work for others, depend on them. One day, business may be bad and then the workers are dismissed. Even if they are industrious and well-skilled, they may find themselves one day without work." "That's why they make revolutions," said one. "And labor unions," added another. "You are right," summarized the teacher, "social inequality is, in your opinion, a result of the fact that some depend on others, the poor on the rich. This is the claim of those whom we call 'socialists.' Think also about the ways in which poverty is connected with overcrowding and how with schooling."

The two factors were then discussed in great detail, both as symptoms and as causes, or at least as aggravating causes of poverty, the pupils offering examples and partial answers and the teacher helping them translate their contributions into general statements.

The most meaningful result of the lesson was the gradual replacement of affective prejudices and generalizations by adequately formulated abstractions and objectively recognized causal connections between certain factors and the facts of poverty. When personal and affective resentment is translated into even the most radical theories, it ceases to be a cognitively harmful factor.*

When the teacher "returned" to his original topic, the comparison

---

*A word of warning may be properly placed here: the teacher must be prepared for what seems an almost absolute reversal of successful neutralization of affects (through translating them into their rational and conceptual equivalents)—in which case it is advisable to start the whole process again, though with the help of different examples.

between the collective life-style of the Kibbutz and the individualistic patterns of urban family life, one of the pupils from the majority group repeated what had already found expression before: "My father always says, this is nothing for him, the Kibbutz. He wants to earn money and to spend it as *he* decides, not the committee." "So, what your father says," remarked the teacher (again by way of translating—"noninductively"—the father's words into a more abstract and more generally valid statement), "actually means that he prefers what we have called the inequality and injustice and the lack of security of an independent life to the security of the life in a Kibbutz because there he would have to give up his freedom and do what he is told to do." "Yes," replied the boy, "my father says that he does not want to be exploited."

This last remark proved that he had *not* understood the essence of what had been discussed before, and that his thinking, his way of interpreting and evaluating the facts of social life, was still determined primarily by his deep-rooted resentments, that is, by his affects. And as if to confirm this presumption, the boy continued, "The Kibbutz is not bad, because there they give you everything you need, but why shouldn't they pay you for your work and leave you alone?"

It was obvious that in this case not only the father utterly failed to understand the essence of the collective ideology underlying the social order of the Kibbutz; the boy who identified with his father was not capable either of drawing the proper conclusions, that is, of learning from the analytic discussions through which the teacher had tried to neutralize the affective elements of cognitive distortions. The boy neither understood the personal implications of the individualistic ideals of economic independence, with its intrinsic and inevitable insecurity, nor the social implications of the collective ideals of security, with its intrinsic and inevitable element of personal dependence and limitation of personal freedom. Any attempt on the part of the teacher to correct this as a misinterpretation was bound to encounter strong resistance on the part of the boy because accepting such "corrective" interpretations of man's place in society would have required rejecting his father's attitude and value system.

The teacher decided to try again to neutralize this affective element in the boy's thinking by contrasting *as equally valid and acceptable* the two value systems, that of the boy's father with his individualistic orientation and that of the Kibbutz, where receiving services and full satisfaction of all basic needs required, to some extent, sacrifice of individual freedom.

But while still engaged in this "neutralizing" comparison between the assets and liabilities of two social life-styles, he was interrupted by the aggressive outburst of one of the *"regular"* pupils, who said, "They [meaning the underprivileged who regarded as exploitation working without pay in compensation for receiving services without pay] want presents; everything should be given to them; that is unfair." "My father is not a beggar and not a thief, you son of a bitch!" was the first boy's reaction, and the class was in uproar.

This incident shows that affectivity is far from being the privilege of the underprivileged, and that is is liable to produce cognitive distortions and thus to impair the intelligence of any student (a fact only too well, and painfully, known from the psychology of prejudice, dogmatism, or political indoctrination).

When a teacher wants to cope with this problem (of affective distortion), and certainly when he is faced not only with thinking about, but with an actual outbreak of, social clashes, neutralizing affects means two things: (a) to start with an unambiguous "identification against the attacker" and to analyze as objectively as possible the conditions that make a feeling of being discriminated against, or a seemingly aggressive expectation of help coming from the outside, almost inevitable; and (b) to leave sufficient time for discussing the liabilities of each of two opposed and, often enough, clashing social attitudes and life-styles.

The teacher, and certainly the teacher in a class in which most pupils come from underprivileged areas and families and need cognitive rehabilitation, must learn how to "put aside" his own political or social ideologies and convictions. He should remember that his primary commitment is to the restoration of impaired cognitive abilities, in the presently discussed context through helping the pupil replace his distorting affects and their "outcome" (false generalizations, stereotypes, prejudices) by their rational and conceptual equivalents.

"You have made a number of serious mistakes," said the teacher to the second boy. (It was a welcome opportunity for him to demonstrate the universality of the ways in which objective thinking is liable to be distorted by affects.) "First of all, you did not understand what A [the other boy] had said when he mentioned his father. His father rejects the Kibbutz because he prefers personal to collective responsibility. I am sure, if you ask your father, he will give you the same answer. And, incidentally, both have drawn the same conclusion: neither your father nor A's father lives in a Kibbutz [showing the partial identity of views between representatives of different classes and life-styles here serves a double purpose: deflating unjustified superiority complexes in the minority group—of the "regular" pupils—and teaching all the dynamics of relativization]. Your second mistake was that you used the word 'They.' As if there existed a group of persons living in a certain neighborhood and under certain social conditions, all of whom do not want to work but want to receive all they need as presents. This is a false statement because it is based on prejudices. You cannot prove that your statement is correct. All you could say is that there are some people in every neighborhood and in every class who are lazy and irresponsible. And thirdly, you do not know anything about the differences between the ways families of different income-groups live. We have already mentioned some of the ways in which poverty expresses itself and some of its causes."

The tendency to use dichotomizations and to refer to external signs only was as much in evidence at this stage of the discussion as it was at the beginning. Since it was repetition only, the teacher took the initiative by defining in his own words the mental attitude produced by the objective conditions of a life in poverty. He said:

"This time, I don't want you to discuss again in which ways social conditions manifest themselves, or what causes social differences. I want you to understand something much more difficult: Why do we have prejudices? Why do we say 'They'? All those uncritical, false generalizations? 'They', meaning: all the poor want everything free, as you said. 'They,' meaning: all the poor are exploited, are discriminated against, as others have said. We know, of course, it is not always correct; but we make no distinction, we say 'They,' all of them. Why is that so?"

"It is much more simple to say 'All of them,' than to say sometimes yes, sometimes no," answered one of the "better" pupils. "No," reacted one of the majority group, "not simpler. It is

true in most cases. And the few exceptions are not important."
"They hate each other, therefore they say 'They'," was the answer
given by one of the aggressive but relatively intelligent representatives of the majority group.

At this point, the teacher felt that he had reached the optimum
point and decided to bring the discussion to an end. He summed up:
"We have spoken about the Kibbutz, and, I hope, you have seen that
not everything is good, not everything bad there. Some people prefer
a life in the security of the Kibbutz, although it means giving up part
of their freedom; others prefer a life with their family in their neighborhood, to a life in groups, although it may mean inequality and injustice. Not all wealthy people exploit; not all poor people are exploited. Sometimes, parents take excellent care of their many
children; sometimes—bad care even if they have only one or two
children. We must beware of general statements. Instead, we should
always look at each individual case, ask about the people's character. Each one is different from each other person. And this is no less
important than to know whether he is poor or wealthy or to which
group he belongs."

The Right to Revolt

We have already discussed the intricacies of civics, when we tried to
answer the question of how to define good citizenship (see p. 80f).
The proclaimed purpose of civics as a subject matter of teaching is
the development of reliable citizenship qualities in the child growing
up in a democratic society. When teaching this subject matter in a
group of underprivileged junior or senior high school students (most
of whom will show clear signs of affectively impaired patterns of
thinking), the teacher will have to face the problem of genuine
democracy as against phraseological distortions. A pupil of normally functioning intelligence will have no difficulty in raising skep-
tical questions as to the limits of true democracy, will argue and
learn concepts even when their factual basis does not convince him.
Not so, we have already said, for the secondarily retarded child, for
whom aggressive protest against what he may consider the falsity of
democratic principles is of vital concern.

One of the most provocative questions in his mind is: Does true democracy give the individual the right not only to criticize but also forcefully to change the existing order when it proves to harbor injustice? Has the individual the right, guaranteed by democracy, to act, even violently and even without being permitted to do so by parliamentary consent, against the existing order? Rational arguments, based on definitions or on showing the danger of anarchy taking the place of democracy if every individual is granted the right to revolt, do not convince these people, as a rule, particularly because aggressiveness has already contaminated and impaired their thinking (so that "anarchy" is far from being a deterrent for them).

In a vocational school class of 15-year-old boys, one of the most aggressive and resentful spokesmen of violence was attacked by another boy, who said: "If you voiced your radical opinion in Russia, they would shoot you immediately." To which he replied: "Don't you worry! In Russia, I would do the killing, because I would have to protect the regime against those who want to destroy it."*

The teacher saw his task *not* in arguing about the objective justification of violence in revolutionary processes but in helping the boy become aware of the conditions under which aggressiveness is legitimate, as against purely subjective forms of (mostly destructive) aggressiveness. In other words, he tried to neutralize the aggressive affects, which prevented an objective evaluation of revolutionary protest in its legitimate and illegitimate manifestations.

"I agree with you," he said, "that under certain conditions aggressiveness may be legitimate. But it is exactly *because* I accept it that I ask: What is the opposite view? What would say someone who is against killing, but who, like you, is convinced that there is injustice in the world and that it must be changed? What would *he* do?" (Neutralization of affects, in this case, was based on two elements; on identification with the ideational equivalent of the boy's affects, that is, with his—presumed—rational considerations, and on trying to force him into confrontation with the "other" position, by way of hypothetical thinking.)

---

*It may be of some interest to add here that this boy, shortly before, had taken part very successfully in a simulation game about an election assembly. But at that time he had not yet reached his revolutionary mood.

The boy's first reaction was disappointing. He said: "Nothing. What can he do? If he does not eliminate them, they will kill him, and everything will again be as it was before." "But do you really like killing others?" asked the teacher, fully aware of the fact that this question was not less explosive than the boy's preceding aggressiveness. "No one likes killing," answered another one, and it could be felt clearly that, through his blunt question, the teacher had achieved what he had wanted to achieve—the creation of an atmosphere of uncertainty, as a counterweight against the hate and aggressiveness in the first boy's outburst.

In order to neutralize this aggressiveness still more effectively, the teacher thought that he himself should answer the question he had asked: What is the alternative to violence when we want to guarantee the effectiveness and the continuity of social change? Democracy, he said, means the rule of the people. But rule of the people can never be genuine unless each of us learns how to be considerate, how to think of the other and not only of himself. And this, he added, is the reason why true democracy is so rare. For, most people think only of themselves and are not considerate enough of others. And only those have the right to revolt who think of others more than they think of themselves or even of what is right in their eyes.

The teacher was aware that the level of his explanations was too high to reach every one of his pupils. But on the other hand, he had every reason to believe that he had succeeded in bringing down the level of *affective* tensions precisely through raising that of *intellectual* tensions.

"We have learned in history about revolutions against kings," said one of the girls. "After they have made a revolution, things are better; there is more justice. So they don't need any revolt now. And they need not be violent in a democracy." "No," said the boy whose initial aggressiveness had set into motion the discussion, "you yourself have said that it is rare to find a genuine democracy because there are always only few people who really care for the others. This means that there will always be cases in which it is justified to revolt against injustice, and I think that everybody must be ready for it, not simply attack or kill but . . . "

It was obvious that the boy's affects had lost much of their original violence, had turned into more rational feelings, although he was not quite able yet to formulate them in clear, conceptual language.

Feudalism and Social Mobility

The next example is of interest not only as a case of cognitive distortion as may result from affective contamination of thinking processes; it also shows a comparable process in the teacher, and therefore may serve as a lesson in teacher guidance (see later).

In a history class (of 15-year-old boys, all secondarily retarded) the problem of lack of social mobility in the feudalistic class system was discussed. One of the boys could not accept this fact (of limited mobility resulting from the absolute separation between nobility, clergy, artisans, merchants, peasants). Although the teacher gave some examples of relative mobility within each class (particularly among clergymen and among merchants), the boy was not ready to give up his rigid rejection of the historical fact as such. More, he saw the teacher as if she were personally responsible for that fact (of class immobility), because she had reported it objectively, as a historical fact, without personal involvement or protest.

The pupil's reaction was easy to understand: he identified with the underprivileged, that is, with those who were "condemned" to the social status into which they were born. This identification prevented him from accepting as such the essence of a "fact" that belonged to the historical past. For him, the past continued to be a painfully real present, and he considered it man's duty strongly to protest against its underlying injustice, as if even facts of the past could still be changed through such affective (protesting) intervention.

Here was a clear case of affects disturbing the learner's time-consciousness, that precondition of every adequate interpretation of history; neither could he understand the laws underlying certain historical constellations or developments. For him, every historical fact was the result of man's decisions only; everything could be different if only man behaved differently. However, this belief in man's power of absolute determination was not an expression of his belief in genuine freedom but, on the contrary, an expression of his belief in arbitrariness.

The teacher's reaction to the pupil's misinterpretation of her function and her attitude was interesting. It could be compared to a process of counter-transference in psychoanalytical treatment-relationships: just as a psychoanalyst, in spite of his theoretical knowledge about the nonpersonal nature of a patient's transference, sometimes reacts to it as if it justified personal reactions, our teacher felt herself "accused" by the pupil. She saw in the latter's failure to understand and accept objectively a historical fact (lack of mobility in the feudalistic class system) not only a result and reflection of her failure as a teacher but also of some kind of personal guilt: as if something in her felt that the pupil was right in his claim that she accepted the injustice and "discrimination" inherent in that system, merely because she had reported it without emotional involvement and without identification with the underprivileged.

If this interpretation of the teacher's reaction is correct, we can see in it signs of a "contamination" of thinking by feelings, comparable to that of the secondarily retarded pupil. (Perhaps it will be claimed that this use of the term is not justified: Is not *primary* inadequacy of the structural separation between the two functional areas, thinking and feeling, one of its essential, its "constituent" elements? Should the term not be reserved for an analysis of cognitive impairment resulting from the relative absence of regularity in the sequence of contradictory life experiences? Whereas we are faced here with a case of illegitimate interference of feelings with thinking processes, as it is liable to happen in the life of people who have gone through adequate functional differentiation? However, where such illegitimate interference takes place, for instance in cases of neurotic pseudo-feeblemindedness, it is, as a rule, structured and not an isolated occurrence as in the case we have in mind here. The latter comes to prove that no one can rely on his well-developed ability to differentiate and keep his feelings separate from his thinking; everyone can, from time to time, fall victim to spells of partial and passing "contamination.")

The teacher received the following advice from her didactic counselor:

She should try to see in the boy's protest against the finality and the factuality of lack of social mobility in the feudalistic class system not a mistake, but the reflection of a *Weltanschauung*, a belief in man's unlimited ability to determine the events of history.

She should try to make the boy see, as clearly as possible, the implications of his "philosophy." Mobility requires readiness to give up passiveness, requires the development of initiative, of responsibility for the individual's development, his progress, his fate. Such responsibility is not compatible with the tendency, frequently found in man, to accept his fate as something fixed, something "given from above," something into which he is born; and not everybody is prepared to give up the "comfortable laziness" underlying such a fatalistic attitude. Nor is responsible determination identical with arbitrary manipulation.

She should try to show the pupils that change of class-belonging is not the only possible form of social change, as the protesting boy seemed to think; that there exist many varieties of relative progress of man *within* his class, and that such changes require individual initiative not only in the feudalistic system but in every period of history (a fact which should and could be exemplified easily).

She should wholeheartedly agree with the boy in his condemnation of social injustice, of which the seeming or real immobility of the feudalistic class system is one example only; and that this injustice is particularly offending when one ruling class has the absolute right and power to determine the fate of all in a specific society. But she should add that transition from one class to another is not in itself a sufficient guarantee of social justice (since it is not at all certain that the individual will feel more comfortable or proud after such transition); that the decisive factor is not the transition but man's freedom to choose where he wants to be, and how he wants to define his social status.

She should conclude her explanations by asking the students that they should think *not* in terms of class and class-belonging, and certainly not *only* in such terms, but that they should concentrate on the conditions of man's conception of his possible development and status change. The pupils should come to recognize the social order into which man is born as a facilitating or an impeding factor of individual development rather than as its sole determinant.

In this case, the counselor said, not only the *pupils* might be helped to overcome their cognitive difficulties (of understanding the ways of interpreting facts in history, their causal connections and development); the teacher as well would learn how to relate more objectively to her teaching functions and her pupils' reactions.

When the teacher decided to conduct the following lesson in accordance with these principles, she found out something which she had not thought of before; the very fact that the class was homogeneous, composed of secondarily retarded children only (although they differed, of course, from each other in degree of intelligence and of cognitive impairment), helped alleviate the explosive nature of the topic under discussion. It was the "neutral" acceptance of the factuality of historical facts by many of the other pupils that helped neutralize the first boy's affective reactions and distortions. It was, of course, primarily the way in which she herself neutralized these affective reactions that determined the successful outcome of her interventions:

First of all, she said, she fully agreed with the boy's claim. History, indeed, is full of cases in which social injustice rules, the feudalistic class system being only one of them. However, she added, the fact that we learn about such cases and events in history does not mean that we agree with what has happened. On the contrary, because we want to condemn injustice, we must know the facts of history as objectively as possible. Furthermore, social injustice may make it difficult for the individual to develop personal initiative to improve his condition, but does not offer him an excuse for indulgence in passive, fatalistic indolence. On the contrary, he must learn all about the essential connections between a certain social order and its intrinsic conditions, on the one hand, and its implications for the individual, on the other.

(It is, to say the least, uncertain whether a similar effect could have been produced by the same didactic method had the class been heterogeneous. It is safe to presume that in this case resentment and tensions between the socially different parts of the class population would have aggravated the affective claims.)

Blood as a Life Force

A series of biology lessons in the first grade of senior high school (age 16) was devoted to the problems of blood circulation. After the dynamics of the physiology had been explained, emphasis shifted to a discussion of the blood components, their function and their pathology. One of the most meaningful topics proved to be that of the measurable quantity of blood. Several students wanted to know how much blood could be lost without endangering life. The affective nature of their question was self-evident (as was the restrictive and thus distorting influence of these affects on their motivation to relate (objectively) to the topic chosen by the teacher, that of blood components).

The teacher first thought that she could neutralize these affects by repeating the information she had already given, mainly about the replaceability of blood and about the techniques of blood transfusion. But she felt that the scientific aspects of the problem interested even the best among her pupils much less than its personal implications. They asked again and again about blood and dying or about the meaning of the terms "blood relationships" and "blood feud," about racial differences and similar culture-conditioned beliefs. The teacher's answers made it convincingly clear to them that a biologist and an anthropologist speak about different things altogether when they use the same word ("blood"). And yet, they were unable to accept a purely physiological view because of their ever present affective associations. The latter had nothing to do with the physiology of blood, but originated in, and reflected, their concern with identity,* on the one hand, and death-fear, on the other.

The teacher, therefore, saw her most important function in dealing with that existential fear (rather than in adding more information, for instance, on the blood plasma preserved in freezers for emergency interventions, or on the blood types and their compatibility or incompatibility independently of personal relationships). By branching out into areas of psychology and philosophical speculations about the nature of death, she hoped that she could neutralize their strongly personal affects and thus prepare the ground for a more adequate understanding of her objectives as a biology teacher.

---

*Whenever similar affective associations and fears appear in children of normally functioning intelligence, it is easy for them to recognize the metaphoric character of the word "blood" in nonphysiological expressions. And even when such associations seem to produce the same irrational fears (for instance, at the sight of blood), those fears are not rooted in culture-conditioned patterns and therefore do *not* impair their cognitive abilities.

In order to weaken the associative ties between "blood" as a biology topic and "blood" as a symbol of identity, on the one hand, and of dying, on the other, she joined hands with the school physician, who talked with the class about the process and the various causes of dying. He showed them the relative unimportance of "loss of blood" as against the importance of other pathologies as causes of death. He emphasized in particular those causes that are connected, directly or indirectly, with breathing. He took care not to transmit his information about death causes as "scientific facts," but accompanied every bit of information by medical advice as to prevention and care.

These explanations undoubtedly helped decrease the affective tensions, as they had resulted from irrational fears; the very fact that "loss of blood" was shown to be only one among many causes of death helped dilute, as it were, the intensity of fear, and thus increased the pupils' readiness for a more scientific, objective approach to their specific biology assignment.

Simultaneously, the teacher continued with her attempts to loosen the irrational and concretistic association of "blood" with "identity." She explained as "figures of speech only" such expressions as "blood relationships," "royal blood," or "in the blood" (instead of "in the personality").

"I understand," said one of the intelligent students, "that we do not mean here the same blood about which you and the doctor spoke. But why did they choose, for all that, the blood? Why not say simply 'family relationships,' 'royal families,' or 'that is in my character'?"

"You are perfectly right. Why, indeed, do we use these figures of speech in which the word 'blood' appears? The answer should actually be given in a language or a literature lesson. As far as I understand the problem, I would say: many figures of speech originate in ancient beliefs, which, in the meantime, have been proven to be erroneous interpretations of reality; and yet, they live on in those figures of speech. But we must be careful not to understand them literally or concretely. If we do that, we are liable to glide into all sorts of superstitions and fearful imaginations."

At this point, one of the students asked about the meaning of "blood feud" and vengenace. Since this was clearly a nonbiological problem, it was transferred to the history teacher, who agreed to devote one lesson to a discussion of this subject, based on the following deliberations:

We know of many historical periods and social systems in which individuals did not, or do not, consider anonymous (impersonal) authorities competent to punish the murderer of one of their family members. They considered, or consider, it their duty to kill the murderer, since only thus, that is, only through their personal involvement and responsibility, can the disturbed order of the family system be restored, and only then will the slain man's soul find peace.*

Here, blood is seen as identical with the soul: No one can see the soul, but everyone can see blood. Some people look for something that can be seen, that is concrete, like blood, to replace something that can *not* be seen, that is *not* concrete, but which we believe exists, e.g., the soul.

Therefore those people, particularly in ancient times, said that, if one of their family members was killed and his blood spilled, his soul was spilled, as it were, and demanded vengeance, justice, through the murderer's death. And his near-ones had to obey the demand and kill the murderer because only then would the slain man's soul find peace. His near-ones had to obey the order, even if they did not like killing and even if they did not particularly love their dead relative.

These facts were well known to many of the pupils because the pattern was still a reality in the ethnic groups from which they came, and cases of blood feud were reported frequently in the newspapers. Some, however, wanted to know what the *teacher* thought about it, and particularly whether our soul was "really" represented by our blood.

The teacher understood the explosive implications of these questions. On the one hand, he could not identify with the magic concretism underlying the blood-soul equation or the practice of blood feud and vengeance. And it was relatively easy to justify his

---

*A conception radically different from the idea prevailing in modern states, namely that the individual is not allowed to take the right into his hands, but has to leave the right to arrest, investigate, judge, and punish to the state authorities only.

objection; he could even refer to the remark made by one of the pupils who had said: "Well, then there will be no end to killing. The murderer's soul when they kill him will also not rest until *his* murderer was killed. No end." But on the other hand, he knew that such a critical attitude on his part might be contrary to certain ideas which were—perhaps—deeply rooted in family patterns. True enough, in rehabilitative teaching we must be prepared for alienation-conflicts and tensions, and we have already pointed out that the inevitability of their emergence requires treatment on a personal level, for instance by a social worker. But in the present case, it was not the danger of causing inner conflicts in some of his pupils that troubled the teacher when he thought about how to react to their questions; it was primarily a question of whether the discrepancy between patterned and critical thinking could not harm and impair the latter.

Neutralizing culture-conditioned affects that may impair cognitive abilities does not mean to take an unambiguous stand either for or against a patterned "truth"; it means showing the learner how to make use of different criteria. In our case, the implication is the coexistence of cultural traditions or beliefs and scientific research findings. The former are valid only when we decide to accept them as integral parts of a comprehensive value system; the latter may contradict the former, but they, too, will be valid only to the extent that we decide to accept critical, rational, differential thinking as a value. All depends on our decision: when we choose the way of scientific learning, we must be prepared to give up certain beliefs and patterns of thinking; when we choose the way of loyalty to tradition-sanctioned beliefs and patterns, we must be prepared to give up our loyalty to the ideals of logics and abstraction.

"I have chosen the way of critical thinking," said the history teacher, in answer to the pupils' questions. "Therefore, I believe that what we call man's soul is *not* identical with his blood. It is obvious that I am against the theory and practice of blood vengeance. But everyone must decide for himself and must choose what he wants to believe and what he refuses to accept."

The biology teacher reported that the discussion with the history teacher had apparently had the desired effect, of neutralizing affective elements. In any case, the class was much more ready for an objective analysis of the topics she had chosen (blood circulation and blood components).

It is safe to presume that undesirable trends, such as certain tendencies toward magical thinking, will be felt long after a relatively successful restoration of impaired cognitive potentials. The influence of cultural patterns transmitted through the family will remain a strongly determining factor even after rehabilitative thinking will have neutralized many of the dangerous affects that are liable to distort concepts and contents of learning. But to the extent that we bring secondarily retarded pupils at least to a point where they come *aware* of the incompatibility of affective patterns and rational thinking, to that extent we have made a significant contribution to the restoration of their potentials.

7
Analysis of Lessons

I. INTRODUCTORY REMARKS

On the following pages several lessons will be described and analyzed. The explanatory remarks accompanying the different phases of the lessons described will serve two purposes: to show how the teacher should react to the—faulty or correct—cognitive expressions of socially or culturally retarded students, and how rehabilitative teaching should be guided in each phase by tentative interpretations of "inadequate" answers.

We have tried to select some parts of lessons that could illustrate and clarify certain principles of rehabilitative teaching. For this reason, we have considered it legitimate to combine into one unit parts taken from a series of consecutive lessons.

We not only hope that the lessons described and analyzed will help the reader understand the method employed, but also that they can serve as basic material in teacher training, and particularly in training teachers for secondarily retarded adolescents. Such training (or in-service training and guidance) should be based on the analysis of lessons, and the analysis should be focused on (hypothetical) interpretations of cognitive processes and their conditions, on the one hand, and on discussing the rationale of didactical interventions, on the other. All theoretical explanations (in various fields such as psychology, sociology, anthropology, philosophy, and general didactics) that may be considered useful should grow out of discussing concrete learning-and-teaching situations. To separate theory from didactic application means: to let theory remain

209

irrelevant for the essential purpose of teacher training, that is, for sensitizing the teacher for the different learning needs of different individuals and different groups (see the last chapter).

If there is any chance of rehabilitating impaired intelligence, it depends on the teacher's readiness "to follow his students" and to believe in their potential cognitive abilities.

Some readers may ask whether the lessons described are not too much "idealized"; they may claim that we did not take into account the ordinary teacher's inability to mobilize that amount of differentiation and imagination which is required for teaching according to the principles here outlined and demonstrated. But we should keep in mind that the teachers who gave the lessons were not capable either, at the beginning, of using these methods properly. Only in the course of time and owing to constant guidance, did they learn how to apply them successfully. This is also the reason why we chose lessons given after the teachers had already had the benefit of a certain period of guidance.

Once again the question will be asked by primarily content-oriented teachers when they are confronted with the here-advocated teaching methods: Is it legitimate to use subject-matter contents for the purpose of trying to develop differentiation, rationality, and responsibility in the pupil's attitude towards their learning tasks? Do we not neglect their needs by emphasizing the functional aspects of learning more than the learning material as such, the reality-implications of a story or a problem more than the formal criteria of its structure, its immediate implications, its value aspects, and so on? Our answer is that the principles of "using" learning materials for the purpose of strengthening cognitive functions more than for enlarging the students' *massa apperceptiva* are valid, according to our experience, at least for the beginning years of junior and senior high school studies. Once a new orientation toward the learning activity as such is acquired, the intake of learning material proceeds at an accelerated pace, and most such students should be ready to face the—content-oriented—matriculation tests equally as well as all other students. Our experience has shown that most of the graduates succeed, and continue to succeed, in their later studies. It therefore seems justified to emphasize, during the beginning period of rehabilitative teaching, the functional aspects of learning more than the contents.

On the other hand, it is essential to base the functional aspects on subject-matter contents as "presented" in the curriculum, and not to use for this "preparatory" period non-curriculum "exercises in abstraction," as some suggest. It is important to give the pupil a feeling of being, at least potentially, equal to the others, the so-called regular students. Although it is usually difficult to convince second-arily retarded pupils at the beginning of the need to form separate classes for them (and this precisely for the purpose of having time enough to help them develop their cognitive functions toward the later learning assignments), most come to accept separation as an initial necessity when they see that finally their contents of learning are equal to those of all other pupils. (This is also the reason why we refuse to work our separate, "adapted" curricula or textbooks for them.)

II. EXAMPLES

Intention and Cause, Chance and Law

In a ninth grade biology class the teacher announced that she intended to discuss a number of general questions that had come up in previous lessons, in which the phenomena of pollination and germination had been studied.

Of the natural factors responsible for spreading pollen grains, the wind, the flow of water in a river, and insects had been mentioned; so had the differences between the outcome of the natural ways and the artificial ways of planned experiments. The teacher raised the question of whether waste of fertilizing material was essential to the creation and propagation of life. Was nature ruled by chance or by intention?

Abe: How does the water in the river or the wind know where to find the proper plant for the pollen grains?

Beni: They don't know; they just carry them. Some find a

	plant, by chance, but only very few; all the others fall down and die.
Dave:	Not true! They don't die; they fertilize the soil.
Teacher:	Let us first look at Abe's question. He thinks that the water and the wind must know what they are doing. Do you remember what we have said about the difference between man, on the one hand, and physical forces of inorganic material, on the other? That man has the ability to act according to plans and intentions, whereas physical forces move and inorganic materials. . . ?
Lea:	Are moved.
Abe:	Man can also change them and use them.
Dave:	But a stone can also kill me, so, it can also change things.
Beni:	A stone kills only when it falls down by chance. It does not *want* to kill me.
Teacher:	Right. It has no intention to kill me: it does not *want* to kill me. Beni was right when he used the words "by chance." Do you see now, Abe, what was incorrect in your question?
Abe:	Yes! The river and the wind do not look for plants; they have no intention to transmit the pollen grains. It just happens that some find a plant.
Teacher:	Find? When do we find something?
Abe:	When we look for something we have lost or for something we need.
Dave:	Or by chance. I once found a five-pound note lying on the street, by chance. I had not lost it; it belonged to someone else. But since it was lying there, I just took it, because. . . .
Teacher:	What you then did is not important in our present discussion. But what you said is important. The wind or the river reach or, as you said, find a plant by chance and then transmit to it the pollen grain, without "knowing" what they do; they do not *look* for plants. Man, too, sometimes finds things by chance without looking for them, without having any intention, just by chance.

Abe's first question reflected the use of personifications, of anthropomorphic thinking. Beni corrected him by mentioning the chance factor in causal processes. Dave was not ready to accept the idea, not so much because he objected to "determination by chances," as he rejected the ideas of dying and of waste. His personal experience of want and his orientation toward the havable did not allow him to accept "waste" as a fact of nature. Nature is good, as he says later, it does not waste; man is bad, he wastes. Aggressive tendencies (which were well-known characteristics of this boy) made him react with protest against any mention of death. Instead, the idea of soil fertilization was brought up, somehow connected with what the class had learned about the soil as part of the plant's environment.

The teacher postponed discussing the issue at this point because she was afraid emotional factors would come up that might interrupt the course of arguments she had in mind. So, she returned to the question of causation in the human and in the physical world. She considered the use of personification a threat to rational thinking and therefore tried to explain (again) the difference between cause and intention in the interpretation of processes and of behavior.

To what extent Abe's remark ("We can also change them") reflects a tendency to replace *processes* of causation by *actions* of manipulation, is not clear. To what extent is he ready to accept causation as a process? To what extent is the idea of manipulation still an essential element in his concept of causation? That this was the case with Dave can be seen from the fact that Abe's remark evokes in him affective associations of violence ("A stone can also kill me").

It is again Beni, one of the most intelligent boys in the class, who finds the proper connection: that we should distinguish between causation by chance factors and causation by intentional action.

The teacher did the right thing when she connected this correction with Abe's original question: wind and water may cause the pollen grain to fall on a plant, by chance, without being directed by any intention. Hence, fertilization of the plant is a process, in which chance factors are the causal determinants and not the result of an intentional action (with the exception of experimental interventions; see later).

Here, it would seem, the teacher made a mistake when she insisted too much on semantic accuracy. The pupils had used the word "find" (some pollen grains "find" a plant, by chance), which seemed to her too anthropomorphic. She made an issue out of an unessential speech form. She tried to use this inaccuracy to teach the class a lesson in differentiation; but since it was an issue of no importance, she did not succeed. She was, however, aware of her mistake and therefore gave up her demand for semantic differentiation in the following discussion with Dave.

It may be of interest to note here that aggressiveness in socially disadvantaged and secondarily retarded pupils makes them particularly sensitive to weaknesses in the teacher's argumentation. Dave reacted by bringing up another emotionally conditioned association: For him, chance is essentially connected with some exciting experience and—with the havable. The words "to find" and "by chance" were enough to bring up an entirely irrelevant event he remembered, irrelevant at least within the abstract context of the class discussion (the story of the five-pound note). The stream of highly emotional associations, which seemed to break through, could have diverted the discussion into a completely meaningless "talk," had it not been for the teacher's decision to use her authority and to interrupt the process at the beginning. She was well aware of the fact that her function differed from that of a therapist, who might have been interested in the release of affects and would perhaps have sacrificed the cognitive aim of the lesson to a possible therapeutic gain. But at the same time she knew that it might be harmful to interrupt the boy's associations without compensating him by some more legitimate satisfaction. She therefore made him feel that he had contributed something significant to the clarification of the problem under discussion: she *interpreted* what he had said as related to the question of pollen-grain distribution.

At this point, the teacher thought she should come back to the first remark that Dave had thrown into the discussion. She asked him, whether he still thought that the pollen grains which do not reach a *plant* to pollinate it enter the *soil* to fertilize it. She wanted to show her class that what seems to be waste in nature may have a function and is closely connected with the main issue, chance and cause. Dave reacted:

Dave: But it is a pity that so many should be lost.

Ruth: There are so many millions of them, and they are always produced again. So, what does it matter?

Joe: What does that mean? It *does* matter. Even a very rich man will not throw away his money, even when he has more than he needs.

Lea: In the reproduction of animals, there are also many more sperm cells than there are eggs.

Ruth: And there are always many more eggs than are fertilized.

Dave: But the sperm cells are always in the majority.

The associations brought up here are of a potentially disruptive nature, at least in a class of children whose secondarily impaired intelligence often reflects their affect-laden experiences and phantasies, their aggressive or sexual preoccupations.

It may well be that when Dave was concerned with the "fate" of fertilizing material, he had in mind the sperm cells rather than the pollen grains. Sperm cells should not be wasted, he says later, when he makes a clear distinction between pollen grains of plants and sperm cells of men and animals, and even adds a moral value judgment ("it is very bad"). He knows, of course, the Bible story about Onan, who lets his semen fall to the ground. "Fertilizing the soil" may, therefore, be for him a kind of "losing" the sperm cells.

Another association is that of "male superiority," strangely contrasted with his preceding fear of sperm loss: the number of wasted male sperm cells, he declares proudly, is much greater than that of nonfertilized eggs. Only an externalized person can so easily exchange his affects, in our case guilt and fear for pride and superiority feelings. (It may well be that similar feelings found their expression in what the two girls contributed, as if they wanted to say: the female is worth more than the male, it has the advantage of singularity.)

Another line of emotional associations can be seen in Joe's remarks about waste of money: no one should waste his resources; man should keep what he has. Here, it is the experience of want and the feeling accompanying "having" and "having not" that determines his affective protest against waste.

What should the teacher do when strong emotions and affects not only accompany but determine his pupil's cognitive activity? We should bear in mind that we do not speak here of emotionally disturbed children, who may need a therapy-oriented discussion group in which all those fears and desires, aggressive tendencies and repressed feelings could be brought to the surface, at the cost of cognitive advancement. This is *not* the task of rehabilitative teaching. Children and adolescents whose intelligence is secondarily impaired as a result of growing up under externalizing life conditions, are *not* neurotics, although they may be similarly preoccupied; they do not suffer from the results of repression, but of too much affect in their consciousness. Their concepts, in our case, of cause and causation, of process and chance, of intention and manipulation, are in constant danger of being contaminated by affective associations. Hence, the teacher must constantly be on guard to bring them back to formal thinking, to eliminate affective and affect-producing associations.

Our teacher, therefore, decided to state in her own terms what she had to say about chance and causation, about laws of nature and laws of human behavior. She knew, of course, that this could only be a beginning and that she should, after making her statement, guide her pupils toward finding adequate applications of her principles.

Teacher: Let us return to the main question: How do we explain that so much fertilizing material is wasted, as some of you feel. Joe has compared processes of nature with the behavior of men, who, he says, should not waste their resources either. He blames nature for behaving so badly. Dave, too, regrets this waste. Ruth, on the other hand, says there are so many pollen grains and sperm cells that it does not matter that so much is lost in the process of transmission.

Ruth: Yes, and the more there is, the better are the chances of one grain finding a plant and of one sperm cell finding an egg.

Teacher: That's right. You remember what we have said before: it just happens, by chance, that some of the many pollen grains find plants. Well, if chance determines the transmission of pollen grains (through the wind, through the water, or through insects), it is quite useful that large quantities are available.

Dave: Maybe what you say is right for the pollen grains of the plants, but not for the sperm cells. They must not be wasted. It's very bad.

Teacher: I understand what you want to say, Dave. But you must understand that when we speak of good and bad, we have human beings and their behavior in mind, not processes in nature which are neither good nor bad. There, the process simply goes on, step by step, one fact being the cause, the other being the result or the outcome. Laws of nature are different from the laws of human behavior: Laws of nature say: If something happens by chance or otherwise, then something else is likely or bound to happen. Laws of human behavior say: If I *want* that something should happen, or should *not* happen, I must do something or *not* do something. In other words, in nature, whatever happens is the cause of something else; in human life, not only what happens by chance is the cause of something else but also and mainly, what we *decide* to do, according to our plans and intentions. Do you understand now, why we say nature is not "bad" even if great damage and death is caused, for instance, by an earthquake or by floods, and it is not "good" even if the weather is nice and the soil is fertile?

There is no need to comment on this part of the lesson, since the teacher's intention was obvious.* She lectured to the class for a short time, stating her basic thesis (which, among other things, was meant to neutralize affects). This noninductive method is indicated in rehabilitative teaching, so we have said, to satisfy the children's needs for reliability and security, provided the teacher strengthens at the same time their independence and cognitive responsibility

---

*Note the excellent reaction to what Dave had said. Without venturing into the psychological comments, which would have been entirely disruptive in a class situation, she gave the boy to understand that she was with him and that she knew what worried him.

through giving them chances to find, or to discuss, areas of application of the principles learned from the teacher's statements.

In our case, the teacher suggested, as a first area of application, the problem of germination that had been discussed both in the classroom and in the laboratory.

Teacher: We are trying today to remember a number of problems we discussed in previous lessons, and to ask ourselves what we can learn from them better to understand the meaning of "chance" and "cause" in nature. I remember, Naomi once asked how the farmer, when sowing his field, could prevent his seeds from falling down "by chance" with their roots pointing upwards. In this case, she said, the seeds would have great difficulties with the intake of water, without which germination would be impossible. And what about round seeds, she had added at that time, when we could never know where the roots were? One boy, I don't remember who it was, had answered that when he lived in a Kibbutz for a while, he saw a machine sowing the fields, throwing out the seeds. There must have been thousands which *by chance* did fall in a wrong direction, and yet, the whole field was soon after covered with wheat. Since it could not possibly be that *by chance* every seed fell with the root downwards, we asked what law was regulating the germination processes of plants and also experimented with the problem in the laboratory. Do you remember?

Naomi: We studied the processes of geotropism and phototropism: the roots always find their way downwards and the stems always upwards.

Teacher: Always?

Several: No, not always. The soil may be unsuitable, too dry, too salty, too stony. And the seed may be ill, may have been kept too long, may have been injured by insects, may have lost its vitality.

Teacher: That's right. We, therefore, spoke of *external* causes (like soil conditions or injuries inflicted by insects) and *internal* conditions (like inner tendencies in the seed to develop in specific directions or, on the other hand, a defective heredity that prevents germination). Do you remember how we summarized the facts so far mentioned into a law?

Beni: We said: Geotropism and phototropism guarantee the growth of plants, provided the soil conditions are suitable and the seed is not defective.

Teacher: And what determines soil conditions, on the one hand, and the nature of the seed, on the other?

Several: In one country, there is too little rain, in another too much. There are goats to eat up all plants, and the soil becomes a desert. There are earthquakes.

Teacher: And what about *internal* causes?

Joe: A bad heredity.

Dave: Bad luck and good luck. What kind of law is this? Lottery?

Teacher: Have you forgotten what I told you just now about chance in nature? How seeds fall on the soil with their roots turned upwards and yet, after a while, they grow with the roots downwards, owing to the tendencies we call geotropism.

Dave: All the time, I wanted to say that there are good laws and there are bad laws: chance is bad law, and geotropism is a good law.

Teacher: If I understand correctly what you want to say, it seems that you would like everything in life to be understandable and logical and regular and reliable. Nothing should exist by chance only. Am I right?

Dave: It would be much easier.

On her way to explaining causal constellations in nature, the teacher was again confronted with the complicated task of satisfying the cognitive needs of one difficult boy. Such cases will be found in every class of secondarily retarded students with their strong tendencies towards externalization and their concepts being contaminated by feeling elements. It would be easy to try to solve the problem by throwing him out. It can, of course, be done, since the behavior of such a student—boy or girl—always lends itself without difficulty to a diagnosis of deep personality disorders. However, it is a wrong diagnosis, since it is based on a misinterpretation of externalized patterns; few things are as rewarding for a teacher as the intellectual rehabilitation of precisely such a student. It can be done, without damaging the interests of the rest, since he is actually only an "extreme representative" of all the others; and whatever attention is given to him is of benefit to all.

The aggressive note in the boy's comment ("What kind of law is this?") betrayed deep anxieties and security needs. The teacher was, therefore, right in confronting him directly with his need for trust in a trustworthy reality. Good luck and bad luck are only too well known to him from his day-to-day life experiences and from the external successes and failures of his family. He wants the world of science to behave differently, as it were, in a more orderly way, more reliably—hence his affective rejection of chance; hence his difficulties in causal thinking; hence his tendency to replace formal and objective thinking tasks by affective reactions and associations. Dichotomizations and stereotypes, manipulative and anthropomorphic distortions, are the typical concomitants of this disordered cognitive attitude. Aggressiveness is ever present, manifest or latent. And, strangely enough, opposition to chance factors in the explanation of events and processes appears together with chance-addiction in a day-to-day behavior.

However, the teacher cannot possibly play the role of a therapist. Her means of dealing with aggressive preoccupations and tendencies are of a cognitive order only. And yet, the choice of her interpretations can have a near-therapeutic effect. It was sufficient for her to give expression to some kind of personal uncertainty ("If I understood correctly what you want to say"), and add the emotionally charged word "reliable" to the cognitive terms "understandable" and "logical." The boy's reaction ("It would be much easier") seems to prove that she had touched on one of the roots of his vulnerability. Her words "Nothing should exist by chance only" were, in any case, meaningful for all pupils in this class.

It was therefore most important to conclude the discussion of chance in processes of causation with some remarks on man's role in these processes.

Teacher: We have said, nature is neither bad nor good, things just happen, by chance, sometimes positive, sometimes negative things, from our point of view. But we must not forget that man can also interfere with what simply happens in nature and can thereby change nature, create more favorable conditions: Can you give examples in the two areas with which we have dealt today, pollination and germination, examples which could prove that man is not so bad as Dave seems to think, and that chance factors also can be changed by man? As Abe has has said at the beginning of the lesson (that we can also change things).

Abe: For instance, desalination of sea water, to make deserts fertile. Or what they did near the Dead Sea to make the arid soil suitable for plantations. Also what was done with the swamps.

Beni: We also discussed artificial insemination to improve the stock.

Teacher: All these are examples of man's attempts to control chance factors in nature. It is true that man often acts stupidly and spoils nature. You have mentioned the cutting of trees or the goat herds that are allowed to eat up all plants and thereby spoil the earth. But here you have mentioned the opposite: how man feels responsible to act scientifically (and we could mention many more examples) in order to improve conditions of living.

Dave: Like what you said about the laws of nature and the laws of human behavior.

Teacher: That's right. When we speak of "causes," we should always ask ourselves, what is the part of chance factors, and what is the part of man's intervention? Both may be good, as you said, Dave, and both may be bad.

Again, there is no need for comment. What seems to be particularly encouraging in this lesson is the fact that even a severely disturbed and affective boy like Dave was able to bring into one whole-context the various parts of what had been discussed and explained. It is self-evident that there must be a continuity of lessons given in the manner outlined here if we want to produce essential and lasting changes in the pattern of thinking and in the learning attitudes of children or adolescents whose intelligence is functioning below the level of their potentials.

Associations and Analogies

In another ninth grade biology class, problems of germination are discussed. The teacher asks about the functions of the capsule surrounding the seed.

Ralph: It protects the germ against all sorts of dangers coming from without, for instance, from insects in the earth or from bacteria or from blows.

Edna: To prevent too much water from entering so it would rot.

Alice: It is like the skin around the skeleton.

Mark: But when a blow is very heavy, the skin cannot protect the skeleton either, and a deep wound is caused and the bones can break.

Teacher: Which means that the skin cannot fulfill its functions of protection under all conditions. Can we say the same about the capsule? When does it cease to protect?

Edna: When it is too thin, so that too much water enters. This can ruin the seed.

Ralph: Also when it is too thick and does not allow the water to enter.

Teacher: And why is this dangerous?

Ralph: Because the germ needs water to develop, to grow, to expand.

Teacher: So, you see that the capsule has other functions, too, not only that of protecting the seed, but also to let water in, so that the germ can inflate. We can say that the capsule also has the function of regulating the water supply of the seed, to make its growth possible.

Edna: But this, too, is a protection; there is the danger of rotting inside.

Teacher: You are right. But these are rare exceptions, and we need not be afraid of them. As a rule, the capsule does its job. Water enters through it only to the extent that is required for the growth of the seed until the latter is ready to break through and germinate.

The two cognitive peculiarities that require the teacher's attention, particularly in a class of secondarily retarded pupils, are the following: They tend to bring up, by way of associative thinking, something they have learned and which seems identical with something else and then identify the two sets of facts instead of comparing them with each other. And they are afraid of dangers symbolized by a frightening word (such as "rotting," or "blows," or "death"), and thus are liable to lose their sense of proportion in the objective evaluation of facts in their intrinsic causal contexts. The didactical intervention with the first pattern is: correcting the erroneous identification of two somehow similar phenomena, pointing out the differences between them and thus strengthening the pupil's general ability to differentiate. Neutralization of affects, particularly of fears and aggressive feelings, through realistic interpretations (and *not* through psychological "treatment" actions) is the proper intervention with the other pattern.

Mary: . . . just like the eggshell around the chicken. It is also protected by the shell until it comes out.

Teacher: Is this comparison really correct from all points of view? What are the differences between the capsule of a seed and the eggshell? We have not yet learned about the chicken eggs or about the shell and its functions.

Alice: From where does the chicken in the shell receive its food, from outside or from inside?

Teacher: Let us not go here into discussing the growth of the chicken within the shell. Comparisons do not always help us understand a problem; on the contrary, sometimes they only take us away from the subject we want to discuss. I'll give you an example. You have mentioned the skin. We said that both the capsule of the seed and the skin have two functions; but only one is common to both, the function of protecting against external dangers. The second is different: Through the capsule enters the water which the seed needs to grow. And through the skin . . . ?

Ruth: . . . water evaporates.

Teacher: Perhaps you want to explain?

Ruth: We have learned that the water leaves the body through the pores of the skin and evaporates, which is important for the regulation of temperature.

Gabi: But all this comes from within and not from without.

Teacher: You want to say that the example which Ruth mentioned is not suitable because it refers to the functions of the skin in getting something *out* of the organism but not in getting something in.

Gabi: No, the skin, too, lets something important in, air. And this helps the skin protect the body from all sorts of bacteria and other damage.

Anne: The seed capsule does not expel materials as does the skin. It only protects the seed until it is ready to break through and germinate.

Albert: And then the root of the seed stretches and gets strong and pierces the capsule.

Rebecca: No. The whole seed grows and presses until the capsule is broken.

Teacher: That's better; the rootlet has no special part in the process of breaking the capsule.

Anne: I think that the comparison between the seed capsule and the skin is unnecessary, just like the one with the eggshell. The skin is not broken from within when the skeleton grows—on the contrary, the skin grows with it; and the skeleton cannot be compared with the seed. The skeleton is much stronger than the skin, not like the seed which is not stronger than the capsule. And also the functions of the skeleton are different from those of the seed. So, why should we compare the two at all?

Teacher: Good that you made this comment. When we compare with each other two facts of nature, it is not enough to ask in which respect they are similar and in which they differ. We should also ask: for which purpose do we need the comparison? Is it perhaps unnecessary? Or even misleading? True, we have said that both the skin and the capsule have similar functions insofar as they protect against external dangers and transmit materials vital to growth. But you have rightly pointed out a number of essential differences. Besides, we can understand each of the two equally well *without* the comparison; it does not add anything.

As the lesson progressed, two problems came up with which the teacher dealt adequately, the problem of analogies and the problem of "external versus internal" forces. She used the comparison suggested by the pupils in order to strengthen their ability to differentiate, for all and not just those who had made the suggestions. And she tried, in different ways, to make them see the ambiguity of the concept "external." Socially and intellectually disadvantaged children, with their marked tendencies toward externalization in behavior and evaluation, see the environment, as a rule, as accidental and threatening, a source of danger. They, therefore, see the inner world (if it is at all permissible to use this word with regard to them), their weak ego, as being in need of protection. But their basic insecurity makes them experience protection as external, as coming from the outside only; they are incapable of seeing positive forces in what we can call inner realities.

It is because of this world perception that the teacher found it necessary to emphasize the nourishing function of water penetrating through the seed capsule, as well as the meaning of inner activity in the organism: the inner world not as an object, a possible victim of threats and dangers coming from external realities, but also as a source of growth and protection.

On the other hand, it would seem to us that the teacher did *not* deal adequately with a third problem, that of the fears which made their appearance here and there, and particularly in Edna's recurrent remarks on the danger of "rotting." Such fears are important in the light of their irrational and symbolic nature. The dangers of receiving blows, of getting sick, of being attacked, for instance by insects, all belong to the area of rational reality experiences, particularly in the life of a disadvantaged child: he knows that injuries through such "aggression" will pass. But the process of rotting does not only symbolize illness and weakness, but also, and mainly, the process of decay and of incomprehensible and irretrievable disappearance. The fact that this girl returns several times to the very same association proves that she is somehow "fixated" to the frightening image of decay. Even though the other pupils did not ,eem to react, the teacher should, in such a case, try to neutralize the affect that can be supposed to lie at the basis of such an association. (It may be that the power of imagination through which this morbid thought is brought up time and again, is indicative of some neurotic disturbance; it may be that it is produced by aggressive tendencies; or maybe it is but an accompanying symptom of externalization. In each of these cases it is worthwhile for the teacher to try to neutralize the underlying affects.)

Yet another association did not receive the teacher's attention: Albert said, as will be remembered, that the rootlet stretches and grows until it pierces the capsule. This remark was apparently the outcome of his sexual fantasies: implied was a comparison of the rootlet with the male sex organ. Needless to add, it would be dangerous to deal with this kind of association in a class of adolescent boys and girls. Moreover, the fact that Albert's remark did not produce any reaction in the others proves that, by chance, it was insignificant for them. And yet, every teacher of socially disadvantaged and externalized adolescents must be aware of the possibly disruptive effect that strongly emotional sexual fantasies may have on cognitive processes. He must be prepared to relate to these manifestations of disturbed thinking, if not in a group discussion, at least in individual contacts.

(By the way, discussing such associations is much more important in a class of secondarily retarded than in one of ordinary adolescents. True enough, the latter are no less often disturbed by sexual activities and fantasies, but they rarely "allow" them to distort their thinking processes—although they may restrict their general ability to concentrate and their general involvement in thinking. The socially disadvantaged adolescent, on the other hand, with his secondarily impaired intelligence, is liable to be drawn by such sexual associations into irrelevant thought processes, and thus be drawn away from his learning assignment.)

Some time later, the class was given a test in which one of the questions was: "Although the wheat seeds received optimal environmental conditions, some did not germinate. What could be the reason?" After the teacher had examined the pupil's written answers, she wrote on the blackboard the answers, organized in four groups, according to what seemed to her to be adequate criteria of classification. In most answers it was evident that the pupils had thought about defects in the seeds, of a constitutional or a traumatic nature.

1) *Doubt in the optimality of conditions.* "Perhaps not *all* conditions had been so good, after all?" asked Albert; and Mark suggested, "Some seeds fell by chance on a soil that was not so good, not optimal." To the same group the teacher added Mary's answer: "The seeds fell too deep into the soil and there they were suffocated."

2) *Example instead of generalization.* "Perhaps the capsule was too thick and therefore the water could not penetrate," said Ralph. "Perhaps the seed died before it was sown," suggested Alice. "It may be, that the capsule was too thin and too much water entered so that the seed got rotten," wrote Edna.

3) *General and abstract formulation* (appeared in two answers only). Anne wrote, "Perhaps the seeds that did not germinate were the offspring of defective seeds so that heredity was bad." And Ruth suggested, "The seeds were spoiled."

4) *Relativization.* Harry wrote, "Optimal condition can be bad for a certain seed, which needed something different from what this soil could offer." Rebecca suggested, "Some of the seeds were too small, they therefore developed too slowly and when they came out they were too weak and therefore did not survive, like some premature babies."

(The other pupils gave similar or even identical answers, and we therefore did not copy them here, although the teacher included them in her list.)

Obviously, another form of classification could have been used as well. However, we are not concerned here with an analysis of criteria for the classification of problematic answers, but rather with a description of the teacher's interventions and an examination of their adequacy.

Teacher: I have divided your answers into four groups to help you in our discussion. First, I would like to find out, with your help, in which ways you have thought about what we had learned about germination. What was common to the ways in which Albert, Mark, and Mary answered, in contrast to all the others?

Harry: All said that the soil is guilty.

Teacher: And what was the question?

Harry: What causes disturbances in the germination process when conditions are *optimal*?

Teacher: I believe I understand what you, Albert, Mark, and Mary, wanted to say. You do not want to accept the fact of something *within* being responsible for defects in germination. Perhaps you were thinking: All that is inside must be good and healthy and advancing and supporting growth and development; only the environment is liable to spoil what nature created. There are many who tend to interpret life in this way. But even they cannot overlook the fact that in certain cases something may be spoiled at the moment of birth.

Ruth: For instance children who are born with a defect.

Teacher: Right. And defects may be found in all areas of life. However, as we have already said several times, these are relatively rare and therefore we call them "exceptions." Usually, environmental conditions are to blame for them. But in our case, we presumed that even if the soil conditions are optimal, it may be that this or that seed will not germinate. In these cases we must look for something internal that may be responsible for the defect. By the way, why is the expression "They are guilty" not adequate?

Rebecca: Because only men can be guilty for what they do or do not do.

Teacher: That's correct. When we say something in nature is guilty for an outcome, we sort of turn nature into man, as is done in fairy tales or sometimes in poems. We call this form of expression "personification." We should beware of using it when we deal with science. But let us now return to our table. What is common to the answers given by Ralph, Alice, and Edna against those suggested by Anne and Ruth?

Albert: It is written there: "Example instead of generalization" and "General and abstract formulation."

Teacher: What is the difference between the two?

Harry: When we say that "something" in the seed is spoiled, we cannot know *what* it is and *how* it is spoiled. This means all sorts of defects: perhaps the seed is dead; perhaps it is weak; perhaps it is too small.

Albert: And perhaps the capsule is too thick or too thin.

Anne: And all this is the outcome of bad heredity.

Teacher: This is, indeed, the intention of a "general" formulation. The general concept, for instance the concept "spoiled," includes all possibilities, those that we think about in a certain moment as well as those that we did *not* think about, by chance, but we could. On the other hand, any example that we may give is only accidental.

Harry: Now, I want to know: I said that optimal conditions are not optimal for every seed. And Rebecca said, development may be slow. Are these generalizations or examples?

Teacher: What you said was a general statement. You intended to say that not only impairment of the seed owing to bad heredity or to damage by the environment explains why sometimes a seed will not germinate in spite of optimal conditions; but that there may also be a specific seed and certain good conditions, but they are not good for a specific seed and therefore this seed will *not* germinate. We can call what you have said a "law." Usually, we will not meet with this law because, as a rule, there is "agreement" between seeds and environment. But today we speak all the time of exceptional cases, among them also seeds that are in need of different soil conditions.

They are not defective but they can develop only under certain conditions which are not the same as those called optimal for most of the seeds. I think you would say that the concept of "optimal conditions" requires the addition "optimal for . . . ."

Ralph: And what about the slow-growing seeds? Is this not a defect? Are they not spoiled?

Alice: But when we give such a seed more time, it can find its place and germinate and a plant will grow, only a little later. It is only a question of time until it will be normal.

The following patterns of faulty thinking, which became manifest in this lesson, were dealt with by the teacher in one way or the other: interference of irrelevant emotional *associations* with cognitive processes; prefering *examples* to concepts; weakness of *differentiation*; misinterpretation of *analogies* as statements on reality; inadequate use of *personifications* ("guilty"), indiscriminate use of *scientific terms* ("offspring") or overdependence on *authority* ("it is written on the blackboard").

The teacher dealt with all these patterns in two ways: She tried to neutralize affects of fear and aggressiveness where they appeared, through rational explanations. She tried to define, as simply and as clearly as possible, the cognitive acts required, to make her pupils aware of the difference between their erroneous thinking and more adequate operations.

Thus she tried to give the first three pupils to understand that even their faulty answers (which referred to environmental rather than to internal factors) were based on scientifically legitimate principles of interpretation, those of behaviorism; and that she understood the motivation of their thinking, their wish to see as "good" all that belonged to inner reality, to nature, to constitution, as against the bad, the negative, influences of the environment. We should mention in particular that the teacher was not afraid of pointing out the differences between students. She could do it without hurting any one of them because she could show them that their answers, though incorrect, were based on comprehensible considerations. This is a most important element in rehabilitative teaching: positive or negative judgments should be replaced, as much as possible, by explaining the (presumed) rationale of the correct or the faulty answer given.

Another method of intervention that deserves special mention is the way in which this teacher dealt with her pupils' affects, especially their anxieties. No doubt many will claim that her interpretations of certain answers as indicating affects are not convincing, and that they are certainly not based on any scientific evidence. We could not argue with such a claim, since the here-advocated method as such is built on the "principle of presumption."

We claim that, in rehabilitative teaching, the teacher must learn how to relate to factors *presumed* to determine the child's way of faulty thinking. Thus, we claim that the externalized child suffers from the relative absence of experiences of regularity in his life, for which reason he shrinks from recognizing exceptional facts. This fear may cause premature, hasty generalizations and the overlooking of differential factors. We therefore claim that the very act of developing and strengthening the child's ability to differentiate has cognitive as well as emotional functions: raising the level of intelligence and allaying fears. We have already mentioned fears of symptoms of aggressiveness or of decay; the perception of the environment as hostile to the inner world; fears of the exceptional. (We could add the last-mentioned answer given by Alice as indicating her fears of the learning progress being too quick for her, fears of having to compete with the others in her class.)

All these fears are liable to disturb the mind of regular pupils as well. But unlike the disadvantaged pupil who is driven by such affects into faulty thinking, the ordinary pupil usually remains capable of thinking without being determined by fears in his thinking (unless he is neurotic and, as such, needs therapy before being free for any learning assignment).

And finally, mention should be made of the way our teacher handled the expressions of personification, dependence on authority, or indiscriminate use of pseudoscientific terms: she considered it worthwhile to explain in detail what was wrong with personifications and also what were the limits of analogy. On the other hand, she almost did not react to the other expressions of faulty thinking. Here, too, we can see an important principle of rehabilitative teaching: the teacher must be aware of all symptoms of cognitive distortion but he must not deal with all of them in every lesson. On the contrary, concentration on a few is better than diffusion for the sake of completeness.

Simultaneity of Different Aspects

In a ninth grade literature lesson, a story is analyzed in which a group of soldiers has been sent out on a reconnaissance mission, to find out details about the enemy position in a frontier village. When the officer in charge recognizes that the terrain and the activities of the villagers would make a smooth reconnaisance action impossible and would therefore be likely to prejudice more serious military operations, he prefers to return. However, he feels that he could not possibly return empty-handed and therefore decides to "capture" a shepherd. This capture is described ironically, as a successfully planned and executed military operation. Once the shepherd is in their hands, the officer has another "great idea": to take the sheep too. The soldiers consider this an excellent joke; but when they react in a merry mood, the officer orders them to behave in a soldierly way—a rather ridiculous request in light of the obvious discrepancy between the "action" and true soldierly qualities.

The purpose of this first part is to deflate ideals of military heroism. The second part of the story, in which the "prisoner" is interrogated, continues in the same vein: the stupidity and the rather inhuman manner in which the interrogation is handled are no longer ridiculous only, but there is an element of bitter criticism in it, from a humanistic viewpoint.

The third part deals with the inner conflict of the soldier, the imagined writer of this story, who has to accompany the "prisoner" to headquarters and considers very seriously letting him go free. He weighs the pros and cons against each other, and the man's inability to decide is shown convincingly.

The teacher's primary aim in the lesson is to make his pupils understand the expressions of irony rather than take every statement at face value. Ordinarily, this is not too difficult a task when the ability to differentiate and to think in terms of "As-If" or in terms of "the possible," "the meaning behind the facts," is well developed. The absence or weakness of this ability, however, is, as we have emphasized repeatedly, one of the essentials of secondary retardation, impaired intelligence, the externalized ways of thinking and feeling.

Teacher: You have all read the story. Now, let me ask you: What do you think about the officer? Was he a good one or a bad one? [Such a dichotomous formulation is contraindicated in any case, but certainly in a class of secondarily retarded adolescents, whose tendency to use dichotomies is one of their cognitive handicaps.]

Misha: He was excellent. He knew how to give orders, and he was tough.

Isaac: And he always had new ideas, one after the other, brilliant ideas.

Arthur: For instance, when he thought of the sheep, to take them with him, for the soldiers at the camp, for a big feast.

Teacher: But remember that he was sent out for a military action, a reconnaissance.

Isaac: How he planned the capture of the shepherd. This was real planning, like for a battle.

Billy: And how he insisted on good order when they returned to camp. He know how soldiers must behave.

Teacher: All of you feel that he was a good officer who fulfilled his duties well enough: he was tough, insisted on soldierly behavior, knew how to plan an action, and thought of his men. But none of you has asked himself whether the whole action which he had planned and carried out successfully was really what he was expected to do. Was this really a military action?

Elizabeth: To take the shepherd, perhaps, He could give valuable information. But not the flock. This was ridiculous: soldiers with rifles and hand grenades guiding sheep to a military camp.

Fred: Why not? When Saul beat the Philistines, he also took their flocks and all their other property.

Teacher: What is the difference between the Bible story you have in mind and a present-day war?

Juliana: That times have changed. We no longer live in ancient

history. Customs have changed. People behave dif-
.ferently.

Teacher: Right. We evaluate and judge people's behavior according to different criteria, or, as we also say, the values
have changed. Therefore, we can say that, in our times, it
is *not* considered soldierly behavior to "capture" sheep.

Anton: I think the officer was simply making himself important.
He was sent out with his men to find out how strong the
enemy was. He could not do it because it would have
meant a fight, and they were not strong enough for a
fight. So why not return and say so?

Gerd: That's right. He was not so intelligent as his soldiers
thought. When the shepherd did not return, the enemies
could imagine that the other side was planning some action. It was therefore a big mistake to have captured the
shepherd and his flock.

Misha: But nothing happened. They did *not* move. The officer
was too clever for them. Before they heard anything, he
had already returned to his base, with the shepherd and
the flock.

Billy: Because he forced his men to keep discipline.

Margaret: But now, I don't understand why the author wrote the
whole story. Did he want to confuse us? What does he
want us to believe? That the officer knew his job, or that
he was simply a pompous man, who made himself and
the whole Army ridiculous?

Teacher: You have asked a right question: What does the author
want us to believe? No one likes "his" Army to be
ridiculed. The author, too, is one of us and perhaps he,
too, was an officer in the Army. So it is difficult to
believe that he wanted to belittle the Army. And yet, as
Elizabeth has said, it is all rather ridiculous. . . .

Let us look at this part of the discussion and try to answer two
questions: What typical patterns of faulty thinking have manifested
themselves so far, and what has the teacher done so far to counteract
them?

We have already mentioned that he should not have used a

dichotomous formulation when asking about the officer's qualities. It elicited "absolute" answers, first from those who considered the officer to be highly competent. Their arguments were typically externalized; they did not ask themselves what a certain behavior *meant*: "planning" for them, meant simply that—planning the capture of a shepherd or planning a battle; demanding order and discipline was simply that—whether in taking care of sheep or in a military action.

The teacher tried to make them aware of their lack of differentiation by throwing in the idea of the different contexts in which an action should be seen. His mentioning the discrepancy between a military action and capturing a shepherd and his flock (thereby giving his students to understand that he did *not* share the view so far expressed) was enough to elicit another tendency, no less typical of secondarily retarded children, in one of the girls: she took the hint and even went so far as to use the word, "ridiculous" to characterize the action. In such a case, the teachers reinforce a more or less correct answer and thereby help the students internalize what they *may* have found simply by way of imitating a teacher's trend of thought. Here he was helped, indirectly, by Fred's attempt to support the opposite claim, that of the others who had justified the action from a military point of view. When this boy quoted an event related in the Bible, the teacher used the opportunity to strengthen the pupils' weakly developed sense of differentiation by discussing the problem of value differences between past and present. He did not hesitate to apply the principle formulated by Juliana to the case under discussion.

This helped Anton and Gerd bring up arguments *against* the officer, who now appeared as unintelligent, heedless, pompous. When two of the more externalized pupils, Misha and Billy, then again brought arguments in *favor* of the officer, one of the better-functioning girls, Margaret, felt prompted to ask the "right question," as the teacher said, that is, the question that he considered essential for the understanding of the story: What was the author's intention when he confused us with contradictions between the storyteller's whole-hearted acceptance of the officer's "positive" qualities and clear hints at the "ridiculous" nature of the action? By adding that the author certainly did not want simply to ridicule his nation's army, the teacher wanted to block the way out into a simplifying perception of the author as one interested in criticizing and attacking *per se.*

In this way, he tried to prepare the ground for an analysis of the concept of "irony": Not only the possibility of different and even contradictory points of view should be discussed, but also the uncertainty as to "who says what."

Margaret: I think what confuses us is that we don't know what the author thinks. He has invented the soldier who tells the whole story. But we don't know whether he agrees with all the soldier says. The soldier uses such beautiful language that we think he must be a writer. But then he says all those stupid things about the officer.

Teacher: For instance?

Margaret: For instance, that he has brilliant ideas, and how he planned a big military action to capture a poor shepherd and all that.

Lotte: The author was not stupid. A stupid man cannot write stories. So, he invented a stupid soldier.

Rosa: And the soldier did not realize how ridiculous it was, soldiers capturing sheep instead of enemies and then acting like shepherds, with rifles and hand grenades.

Teacher: Well, the difficulty, you feel, is that, in order to understand the story, we must understand the author's intentions. But in order to understand his intentions, we must think on two levels at one and the same time: on the one level we have the story as the soldier tells it. On the other level is the fact that the author does not disclose clearly his own view, but leaves it to us, the readers, to guess what he meant.

Selma: But how can we know what he really thought? If we only guess, we may be wrong.

Teacher: Yes, we may be wrong. But a story can always be explained in different ways. We know, for instance, that all historical documents have been interpreted by many commentators, each one in his way. How can we know who is right?

Anton:	They are all right. Everyone sees one side. But when he thinks much and writes well, we are convinced that he is right. And when we read another one, we also feel that he is right. The one comment makes sense and the other, too.
Clara:	A story is not like algebra.
Teacher:	Well, to come back to our story: In order to understand it, we must have the courage to guess what the author wanted to say. And when, in the end, we understand all the details of the story better than we did at the beginning, we can say: It makes sense. What do you think was the author's intention?
Louis:	He wanted to show us that soldiers are not always big heroes but are like everyone else.
Felix:	They did not like war, they wanted to be at home and work the fields; he says so at the beginning.
Teacher:	This was certainly one of the author's intentions: to show us human beings as they really are—without exaggerations and without phrases. But there was yet another intention. You said, the action was ridiculous. How do we react to something ridiculous?
Bob:	We laugh.
Teacher:	Well—did you laugh when you read about the soldiers doing the job of shepherds?
Fred:	No, but then we thought the author meant it seriously.
Teacher:	As long as we do not understand the author's intention, our reactions are bound to be inadequate. How did you react?
Juliana:	Misha and Isaac accepted what the soldier had said and thought the officer was a big man. The others called him stupid and ridiculous.
Isaac:	And now you say he was neither big nor stupid? What, then, *is* he?
Teacher:	If we accept what we have said about the author's first intention, we don't admire the officer and we are not angry at him. We just smile at what we see before us, shepherd soldiers. This is what we call "irony." In literature, it means that an author makes someone say something

positive, while he, the author, means the opposite: the soldier speaks of the officer's cleverness, and about his "strategies," as if he were a great man; but what the author means is the opposite. So we laugh a little; we smile.

Laura: And when we smile, we are not angry and we don't admire?

Teacher: That's right. Irony is also criticism, but more human, not so aggressive.

Margaret had been aware of the contradictions between the story-telling soldier's literary style and the primitiveness of his value judgments, between the soldier's military actions and their non-military meaning. But she did *not* understand that this play with contradictions was part of the author's intention in this first part of his story—was, in fact, an intrinsic element of his irony. To understand irony, we must be willing and able mentally to move on two levels of meaning simultaneously—an attitude unknown to the externalized mind. But didactically it is most important to make a secondarily retarded pupil sensitive to irony and to make him understand its dynamics. He will learn in this way to differentiate between levels of meaning, a variety of viewpoints, different values, different attitudes; he will learn in this way to see the futility of dichotomization; he will experience simultaneity and coexistence of seeming (or real) contradictions. In brief, understanding the dynamics of irony is both an important *milestone* on the externalized child's way to internalization and one of the *symptoms* of internalization.

The teaching process in this part of the lesson is a good example of what we have called "the noninductive approach to rehabilitating impaired intelligence": the teacher elicits answers and, after a while, offers a clue to the solution or even a definition. In our case he was able to elicit a negative evaluation of the officer's personality, at least in a number of students, after some others had at first naively and uncritically accepted the "externalized" evaluation as expressed by the story-telling soldier. This experience of opposite views was in itself highly important. It made possible a discussion of different value criteria and different aspects of a problem.

Not all the pupils *did* follow the teacher. Misha and Billy continued to "defend" the officer's cleverness. Most characteristic of the unaltered externalization and secondary retardation was Isaac's question: What remains if dichotomy is rejected? What is a man when we say he is neither good nor bad? (The teacher, incidentally, did not pay adequate attention to this question, which proved that the boy had failed to understand his interventions; it is most likely that there were others in the class who did not follow him either.)

The teacher spoke of the courage needed to guess the author's intentions, and he explained that the only proof for the correctness of our guesses is that we understand more details of the story. This is an excellent example of what rehabilitative teaching should be: dealing with the emotional components of cognitive processes whenever possible. Another example is his reference to the affective elements in the pupils' reactions to the story at the beginning, to the affective nature of their value judgments. The method will probably help ordinary students as well, but for the rehabilitation of impaired intelligence it is indispensable; it is the rational counterpart of the irrational "contamination" of cognitive by emotional elements, in which we have seen the essential characteristic of secondary retardation.

At the end of this part of the lesson, the teacher summed up the discussion by introducing, and trying to define, a new concept, that of "irony." Laura's remark proved that she at least had understood the interpretation, and with her, undoubtedly others, too, could now see the meaning of the story more clearly.

In the second part of the story, the "prisoner" is interrogated by some rather inefficient men who know but one method of interrogation—roughness. The stupidity of their questions is matched only by their lack of human feelings. At the end, it is decided to send the shepherd to regional headquarters, and the story-telling soldier is ordered to accompany him.

Much time was devoted to a class discussion of nationalist feelings and prejudices. But in this problem area, the difference between ordinary and externalized pupils is one of sophistication only, and not one of the essence; and sophistication tends to make prejudices—perhaps—more radical but not more intelligent. On the other hand, secondarily retarded and externalized youngsters are liable to substitute aggressive prejudices for well-meant, but meaningless phrases, under the influence of explanations given by a teacher whom they like and therefore want to imitate. He must then be careful to subject not only prejudices but also arguments *against* prejudices to questioning, analysis, and conceptualization; distorting affects may hide in the latter arguments no less than they are manifest in aggressive prejudices.

Without going into a detailed discussion of this second part of the lesson, we can say that it was evident that in the end the teacher succeeded in making most of the pupils see the differences, and the possible clashes, between true and false nationalism, between nationalism and humanism, between prejudices and critical evaluation of opinions. It was, however, equally evident that many more discussions of this kind would have to be added to make the insights gained durable and applicable.

The third part of the story, which was discussed in the following lesson, deals with the conflicts of the story-telling soldier while he accompanies the prisoner and asks himself whether he should be humane and let the shepherd go free, or obey the orders he was given and be—inhuman. Here are parts of the class discussions concerning these conflicts.

Teacher: Why does the soldier think he should let the prisoner free?

Heddi: The soldier is a traitor.

Dan: He does not behave like a soldier.

Bill: He is stupid when he thinks that he can let him go free. The others in the Jeep would kill him immediately.

Teacher: Well—maybe you are right when you say that a soldier must obey the orders he receives. But, first of all, he does not let him go free, he only *thinks* about it. So, he is not a traitor. Besides, I asked a different question Why does the soldier think he *should* let the prisoner go free? Or, as we asked before: What was the *author's* intention when he described the soldier's deliberations?

Clara: This is a man who does not know what he wants.

Laura: He pities the prisoner and his family, but is afraid they will put him in prison when he helps him escape.

Misha: He is an idiot.

Teacher: This is what *you* feel about him, but it certainly was not the *author's* intention to show the soldier as simply stupid. What Laura has said is what we call a "conflict." It is a struggle between two wishes or between two feelings.

Bill: But also between two countries.

Gerd: This too, is a conflict between two feelings: one wants peace and the other wants war.

Arthur: Why should the soldier, then, think about one enemy?

Teacher: Here we are back at our last discussion, of different ideals, of identification with our nation and of general human values. You remember that we had agreed in the end that it is very difficult to evaluate and to compare with each other these ideals or these values; and we said that we must use different criteria to judge different persons' behavior. From one point of view a behavior may seem to be bad, and from another point of view it may seem to be good.

Elizabeth: Does this mean that the soldier's conflict also was one between two points of view?

Dan: He is a coward.

Teacher: Now you see what it means to use two different criteria. Before, you said he was a bad soldier, for the mere reason that he considered the possibility of disobeying the order he had received. And now you say he is a coward because he is unable to break the orders he had received.

Rosa: Perhaps we can say, as a soldier he is bad, but as a civilian he is good.

Anton: No, as a civilian he is not good either, because he cannot make up his mind.

Elizabeth: It all depends on our point of view.

Teacher: We now understand better the author's intention: he describes the soldier as someone unable to decide. The author feels that it is good to be human, to think of others, even if they are enemies, to imagine what you, yourself, would feel, were you in the other person's

	place. And the author feels, it is bad to hesitate in carrying out what you consider your duty. Do something, he says, and be human.
Ellen:	But how can it be good to decide to do something bad, such as disobeying a military order?
Anton:	I know: It is good to obey an order; but the results are bad—people are killed, this is war. It is bad to disobey orders; but the results are good—the shepherd can live.
Billy:	But I want to know, was it good or was it bad? What do *you* say?
Teacher:	Don't ask *me*! Everyone must give his own answer to such a question. Don't rely on books or on teachers, when it comes to such questions or opinions. But one thing is clear, I believe: the author thinks that the soldier was a *weak* person, not a *bad* person.

At the beginning, most pupils showed little, if any, understanding for, or insight into, the inner world of motivations and feelings. Their judgments were typical of the externalized child's mentality: affectively negative, referring to the surface manifestations of the behavior only. It was therefore important to help them see the difference between "the world within" and the "world without," as it is represented, for instance, by that between thinking and acting, or between the author's intention and the described sequence of events. The students' answers did not yet indicate full understanding of what the teacher wanted to attain, but they at least referred now to inner qualities, such as pity, inability to decide, inner conflicts. Only the most problematic among the pupils (a boy known for his aggressive and even destructive tendencies and his negative leadership qualities) remained "faithful" to his nondifferentiated, summary judgments (of rejection). (It might be interesting to note, that, as a rule, girls are superior to boys in those mental operations that require differentiation between processes in "the world within." This is true for secondarily retarded no less than for normally developed adolescents. On the other hand, girls are also more prone to use concepts "without full cover," such as the concept "point of view" in the remarks of Elizabeth.)

To counteract this affective distortion, the teacher tried again to make clear to his pupils the principle of relativization through using different criteria. (He used the easier and better-known terms of "points of view".) It was a fortunate coincidence that one of the boys had made two contradictory statements, each of which made sense, though each from a different "point of view." This convinced the class of the justification of the principle better than any theoretical discussion would have done. And yet—relativization is not easily learned; it requires considerably more courage and mental mobility than a secondarily retarded pupil usually is capable of mustering. After several more or less successful attempts to define the principle of different criteria, one of the boys very definitely demanded to receive an *absolute* answer, which would satisfy him in his basic insecurity. And he demanded the answer from the teacher as the source of authority.

This was a good opportunity for the latter to act against the pupil's dependence-needs, which one of them had expressed but most of the others undoubtedly had felt no less acutely. It is one of the teacher's tasks in rehabilitative teaching to weaken these dependence-needs as much as possible (while at the same time helping his pupils towards a more adequate orientation in a world of differences).

It will perhaps be argued that the discussions here related are, in part at least, much more sophisticated than one would expect to find in a class of socially retarded adolescents. It is, however, a prejudice of those who identify socially or culturally impaired intelligence with genuine retardation, to think that a sense of nuances *cannot* be developed in them. On the contrary, it is precisely through stimulating concept formation, differentiation, and defining principles that these students are helped to overcome their externalization, and that their impaired intelligence can be rehabilitated. And it is precisely their readiness to react to and to learn from the teacher's attempt to stimulate their conceptual differentiation that makes possible a proper diagnosis and a distinction between secondary and genuine retardation.

8

On Teacher Training and Guidance

I. INTRODUCTORY REMARKS

Wherever the methods of rehabilitative teaching were employed in elementary and in junior or senior high schools, two seemingly contradictory experiences could be found among the teachers. On the one hand, every one of them, even those who had studied the psychology of secondary retardation and the theory of rehabilitative teaching, required intensive guidance to bring out the necessary didactic reorientation, from a purely intellectual, content-oriented attitude to a combination of analytical thinking with imagination. On the other hand, many complained that rehabilitative teaching required of them too much intellectual effort. Thus, they proved that they distinguished between their self-image as intellectuals and what seemed to them to lie beyond the reach of their intelligence: logical, analytical thinking combined with imagination, that is, constant openness to the dimension of "the mere possible".[19]

The conventional method of teacher training is, indeed, conducive to such a definition of intelligence as "mastery of knowable contents" rather than to a more comprehensive conception of intelligence, as suggested, among others, by K. Goldstein.[19] The conventional training is divided into four, more or less independent, parts.

1. General knowledge of some basic facts in psychology and

sociology meant to prepare the future teachers for a deeper understanding of their pupils' different individual and cultural backgrounds, though this knowledge is rarely translated into significant case-analyses.

2. Some basic information about the history and the philosophies of education and teaching meant to prepare them for the application of differential methods of education and teaching, but rarely followed by adequate translation into practice.

3. A large "bloc" of subject-matter studies claiming to make the graduates of the training courses capable of intelligently transmitting the knowledge required of the students by the curriculum, however the latter may be constructed; but rarely taught in a *didactically* relevant way, that is, in a way which would enable the teachers to show their pupils the interconnectedness of the various areas of knowledge and their personal relevance, functionally or otherwise.

4. Teaching methods, usually taught in addition to, and not integrated with, the subject matter studied and as a rule with emphasis on one universally valid ("preferable") method rather than on differential ways, that is, on adaptation to the cognitive and emotional needs of different groups of pupils (class populations).

Sometimes, bits of "practical" psychology are added loosely, claiming to develop the future teachers' understanding for differential diagnosis and/or for the children's mental health needs. But rarely, if ever, are teachers taught the ways of *cognitive* diagnosis or of *intellectual* hygiene; how to discover in the pupils' reactions and answers indicators of specifically determining (overt or covert) patterns of thinking, how to distinguish accordingly between different intellectual syndromes, and how to use thinking and learning processes for strengthening the learners' self-esteem, trust, and autonomy.

Teacher-training programs can undoubtedly be constructed in a way in which some of the mistakes inherent in the generally accepted approach can be avoided:

Thus, subject matter can be taught not in a science-oriented manner, as accepted in most university courses, but as a sum total of educationally relevant topics focused on the school-learners' foreseeable associations and interests. (This may necessitate teaching subject matter to future teachers in a separate setting, whether inside or outside a university.*)

Even at the training stage, branching out into adjacent fields of knowledge or into actualizations of a personal or a social variety can be practiced. It is only logical to presume that in this way the teacher will have fewer difficulties later, when it comes to applying the same matter in his class teaching.

Psychology and sociology can be taught simultaneously on a theoretical and an applicative level; in the theoretical part, the emphasis is to be placed on human development and human differences, as well as on presenting basic concepts in a way in which they relate to development and to individual differences. In their applicative aspects, psychology and sociology appear as case-analyses, in the broadest sense of the term: behavior of different children or adults and behavior of different groups are to be compared with each other; teacher behavior must be discussed and explained; class events and lessons should be analyzed as exemplifications of what is ordinarily known as psychology of thinking, learning, and teaching.

Of particular importance are group discussions of affect-laden problems, as they come up in connection with a certain subject matter or a specific behavior of children, parents, teachers, groups, or political figures—behavior experienced directly or indirectly, i.e., in actualities reported through the mass media.

Before going into a detailed description of such a teacher-training program, we should answer two questions asked by the advocates of a different approach: the advocates of the "classical" approach, with its emphasis on content-learning with auxiliary subjects, such as psychology or sociology, loosely attached and with "didactics" added, as if it were a monolithic piece of one universally valid methodology. They ask whether intelligent and gifted pupils do not

---

*It is well known that many attempts made all over the world to liberate teacher training from (pseudo-) scientific ambitions, ideals, and prejudices have failed because society has not yet agreed to give equal status to graduates of science-oriented university courses and those of teaching-oriented training courses. The reason for this discrimination is much less the lower standard of the subject-matter teaching than it is the inadequate integration of subject matter with didactics. As a result of this deficiency, the teaching-oriented training courses are indeed, objectively, inferior to the university courses (although the latter, far from preparing adequately functioning teachers, produce many frustrated "scientists," who accept teaching only because they have no alternative left).

need a different kind of teacher, a teacher who masters his subject matter sufficiently well to make his lessons stimulating precisely *because* they are based on scientifically well-founded knowledge. Is not for these children the *content* to be learned more important than the manner in which it is taught? Because they feel the challenge of both, acquiring objective knowledge (whatever that may mean) and drawing their own personally relevant conclusions? Because they know not only how to internalize what they learn but also how to do it in their individual way? Do not *their* teachers require primarily science-oriented training?

Paradoxically, the same claim is made by the advocates of individualized and progressive teaching, as far as the gifted pupils' cognitive needs are concerned. But it is precisely in the light of their claim that the here-suggested approach to teacher training seems to be justified as a *general* program, valid for *all* teachers: A secondarily retarded child needs teachers capable of using their teaching material for strengthening his ability to differentiate, to think rationally and responsibly, and, at the same time, capable of making it personally relevant. A gifted child may *not* need functional strengthening, but he certainly needs the experience of knowledge and skills acquired as being personally relevant. This is why his teachers emphasize so much self-expression, self-confrontation, in the learning process or in applying knowledge to behavior.

True enough—neither the one nor the other can learn in a science-oriented university course how to teach subject matter in a way conducive to personal involvement. But the questions each one has to ask himself as a teacher are different, according to the different meaning of "involvement" for the gifted and for the secondarily retarded child. On the other hand, both can benefit from teaching-oriented subject-matter courses. To the extent that a teacher of normally functioning or gifted pupils feels that he needs a wider and a deeper orientation in his specific teaching-subjects, he can easily acquire it through additional university studies.

But since many students, at the beginning of their university studies are likely to overestimate their chances of success in a scientific career, and others are uncertain about their ability or their willingness to teach, it is almost impossible to direct all suitable candidates into either the scientific or the teaching trend of subject-matter studies. Moreover, scientific studies offer many applicative careers *in addition* to teaching; in these cases, too, the teaching trend would not be indicated.

In spite of these and similar reservations, it will become evident from the details of study programs as outlined later in this chapter that a teaching-oriented trend of studies can be, and should be, planned and carried out on a high level of intellectual differentiation. Thus, it will be no less attractive for highly intelligent students than a science-oriented study trend. This is also the only way to raise the prestige value of the teaching profession. Economic and social recognition will then be an almost natural outcome of that rise in the students' quality and in that of the profession's prestige value.

But whatever the orientation and the quality may have been of the basic training that the teacher received, the type of class population with which he comes in contact in his practice no less determines his attitude to teaching. This results so often in a sort of "dyscrasia," a discrepancy between principles learned and preferential reactions, that the resulting tension is almost inevitable. It happens frequently that a teacher, in spite of all he may have learned about differential didactics, chooses a method unsuitable for a specific class population. Here, then, starts the well-known vicious circle between natural preferences, choosing unsuitable methods (in one case too much "inductiveness," in another too little consideration for individually or culturally determined affects, and so on), class failure, teachers' frustration, and affective identification with irrational preferences.

Hence, the vital need for in-service training and didactic counseling services as integral parts of any basic teacher training! This becomes particularly evident where the class population is heterogeneous, but also where a teacher gives up teaching a "regular" class and starts teaching a class of secondarily retarded pupils.

In the same context, the question may be asked whether "relearning," following a teacher's transition from a regular to a secondarily retarded class population, is better for him than to start with the second type of pupils, *without* prior experience with "regular" students. The answer is that both ways have their advantages and their disadvantages: the advantages of re-learning lie in the acute awareness of differences between methods; the disadvantage, in the need for overcoming resistances and prejudices. The advantage of the second way lies in the fact that exclusive experience with secondarily retarded pupils and the methods of rehabilitative teaching makes the use of the latter methods "natural"; the disadvantage lies in the fact that the teacher is liable to lose his flexibility and to overlook an ordinary pupil's cognitive needs.

A strong objection to the training program as recommended here (and as outlined on the following pages) is based on the claim that the intellectual level of most teachers, and particularly of most elementary school teachers, is too low to allow them to benefit from what seems to be a highly sophisticated training (and guidance) program, one based on that rare combination of analytical thinking and imagination which it requires. Can the average teacher ever be taught clearly and exactly to define concepts or phenomena (in noninductive ways of teaching), to master the knowledge required for "branching out" from his subject into relevant adjacent fields, to understand the covert meaning of affects and their presumed distorting influence on thinking processes, to deal with them effectively on a cognitive level?

But it has been our experience that even an average level of intelligence in the participants of a teacher-training program, as recommended here, is sufficient to translate basic concepts of the theory used into teaching practice, provided they are accompanied by detailed descriptions of processes of teaching specific subject matters, recorded or projected.

II. SOME SUGGESTIONS FOR A TEACHER-TRAINING CURRICULUM

On Psychology Teaching

The first part of this section will be devoted to the analysis of a psychology training program for teachers. We shall try to show how each topic contained in the program differs essentially in its significance and the ways of its presentation, when it is meant for teachers and when it is meant for research students.

1. Unless teaching is understood to be a well-planned series of conditionings, psychology for the teacher means a theory of *subject-object relationships*. Separation between subject and object is the precondition of reacting and experiencing. This process of separation, already starting at the beginning of life, depends on the individual's structural tendencies* and on the quality of his environment. All through his life, relationships to his objects, be they persons or tasks or happenings, are determined by the extent to which he feels himself as an acting and reacting, a responsible subject confronting an independent object. All personality peculiarities, attitudes, minor or major pathologies and deficiencies, can be expressed in terms of adequate or inadequate separation between subject and object.

2. A second topic of psychology, which is equally important for understanding human behavior, relationships, differences, and developments, as well as for any theory and practice of intervention, is that of *structurization*, meaning the gradual transformation of experiences and reactions into parts of man's structure, normal or pathological. This transformation constitutes a third dimension of interpretation of human behavior, in addition to "nature and nurture"; and, still more important, it concerns the therapist, the social worker, the educator, the teacher, when they ask themselves to what extent attitudes or properties resulting from such processes of structurization are reversible.

3. The intimate connection between psychological theory and educational practice becomes even more convincing in a third topic of psychology teaching: if intervention means change in a "desirable" direction or supporting "desirable" properties and attitudes, the *value question* becomes relevant. How do we define the aims of education? As a well-balanced personality? Or as readiness and ability to serve ego-transcending tasks? Or as internalization of learning contents and values? Or as relative autonomy? What is the meaning, what are the implications, what are the structural, what are the educational preconditions in attaining each of these alternative aims? What is their place in a change-oriented, what in a

---

*Known as "types," "thresholds," "reaction patterns," "openness" versus "organizational strength," "type and level of intelligence," and so on.

tradition-directed, what in a totalitarian society? And what is the role, what are the dangers, of suppression and repression in each case?

It is obvious that the approaches to teaching these issues as part of a psychology program are essentially different, when we consider it auxiliary to preparing future teachers for their educational tasks, or when we consider psychology training a first step toward specialization in research or even in diagnosis or therapy. For the teacher and the educator, confrontation of values with psychodynamics is of the essence, and it is this confrontation that should determine the way of teaching this complex of topics.

4. The latter, in turn, is connected with a fourth problem area, that of *causal interpretation* of individual differences. Here again, the scientific approach essentially differs from the educational. The first places emphasis on measurement, the second on change, and the methods of inquiry are determined accordingly.

The teacher often uses measurement techniques comparable to those used in research: he evaluates and rates his pupils' achievements in quantitative rather than in qualitative terms. For this purpose he divides a whole into parts, since only partial factors are measurable. In this respect, his methods resemble those of factor analysis in research. On the other hand, he knows (at least when he is a good teacher) that no individual can be understood adequately through fragmentation and pluralistic analyses. He needs an opposite, a holistic or, better, a configurational approach, not only in his attempts to do justice to the individual child but also in his attempts to reconstruct his development.

It is in this context that the principles and the limits of a factorial and a configurational approach to the problem of cause[9] must be explained, with emphasis on the second (according to which each causal factor is considered a partial factor only and receives its specific causal meaning only through configuration with other partial factors, including its antecedents and its results). When this topic is accompanied by case-analyses, psychology teaching, again, becomes a significant part of the future teacher's preparation for his educational function (precisely *because* the emphasis is not on "scientific proof" but on hypothetical thinking, imagination, and practical conclusions).

5. Another chapter of psychology teaching is that of *developmental phases*. While the analysis of each of these phases in the various schools of (normal and abnormal) personality psychology is an attempt to reconstruct, as it were, the development of either cognitive or emotional and relational functions, it has a different function in psychology teaching for teachers. Here, it means demonstrating how each "phasal achievement" manifests itself in thinking *and* in relationships, which cognitive elements emerge in feelings, which emotional elements in conceptualization, phase by phase:[7,10,11]

—How the basic experience of regularity in the sequence of tensions and satisfactions, in a family atmosphere of personal intentionality, helps establish a sense of trust in the reliability of persons and of facts, a sense of nearness in both cognitive and interpersonal relations;

—How the early experience of mutuality marks the beginning of an adequate understanding of causality;

—How trust and mutuality strengthen a sense of autonomy and responsibility as conditions of internalization of learning (as against the automatic processuality of conditioning and habit formation);

—In which way aggressiveness in relationships and in behavior is linked with intentionality in thinking;

—How oedipal conflicts are responsible for differentiation in feelings and in thinking;

—Under which conditions ambivalence tensions are conducive to differentiation and internalization and under which conditions they are not;

—How to explain the normative and the pathological limits to internalization in behavior, in feelings, in relationships, and in thinking (see also point 7);

—In which way dependence and independence are interrelated;

—In which way adolescent conflicts are cognitively relevant;

—When identity is an asset, and when it is a liability.

It is obvious that when "development" is taught in this way, it is much easier to make the future teacher aware of the didactic and educational significance of the concepts used.

6. The five topics mentioned so far make meaningful a comparison of cognitive and relational *behavior manifestations* in the

ordinary child during each of his developmental phases with those appearing *in a neurotic, an aggressive, an "externalized," a mentally retarded child* of the same age group.

The psychology teacher should be aware of the dangers inherent in this part of his program; a class teacher is neither a clinical diagnostician nor a therapist, although he should know enough about their functions to understand *why* he should not even try to do their jobs. And yet, only too often do we find teachers misusing whatever scanty knowledge of diagnostic or therapeutic techniques they may have acquired during their study course and playing the roles of clinical psychologists.

We suggest the following teaching methods to prevent such undesirable distortions:

—When explaining and discussing diagnostic techniques, one should avoid every semblance of systematic teaching; the mathematical aspects should be mentioned but not explained; test results should be interpreted in alternative ways; clinical pictures should be demonstrated by way of comparing with each other one symptom that appears in each but has, in each, a completely different meaning.

—When dealing with various ways of intervention (such as group work, social work treatment, counseling, therapy, and so forth), it again is important to present processes, describe them in detail, and explain the essential differences between each of them and teaching in its uniqueness. Unsuccessful or only partly successful treatment cases should be described to discourage seeking solutions for every "problem" in methods outside the teachers' competence and responsibility.

—At the same time, however, the information given to the teacher-students in the area of clinical psychology has the purpose of preparing them for readiness and ability to cooperate with school social workers or school psychologists and counselors, or for referral of problem cases to specialists for examination and treatment. This point is of particular importance for the teacher of secondarily retarded pupils. As said in Chapter 3, among them are likely to be found not a few severely disrupting behavior-disorder cases.

7. An analysis of the *psycho-dynamics and the symptomatology*

of externalization in its various forms (compare with Chapter 1) should constitute an important part of psychology teaching within every teacher-training program. It is indispensable in our era when teachers are bound to encounter in their teaching practice many classes of secondarily retarded pupils. True enough: the teacher should also learn how to face the implications of an externalized value system that may result from a variety of social or cultural conditions prejudicious to internalization but *not* to intellectual differentiation or the normal development of cognitive potentials. Here, we can see again the contribution psychology training can make to value education as such. But still more essential is an analysis of externalization as it may result from growing up in poverty, want, neglect, or cultural ambiguity. It is here that the teacher-student should learn all about patterns of normal and distorted thinking, as they appear in the learning processes of ordinary as against neurotic or socially or culturally retarded pupils. (This part of the program could be called: applied psychology of thinking and learning, as against the theories of thinking and learning in a science-oriented program of psychology studies.)

These are the main topics of a teacher-oriented psychology program. To what extent information on various schools of depth-psychology or anthropological psychology should be included as a teaching and reading subject, depends on the students' level of intelligence, involvement, and interest in theorizing. But even *when* it is decided to include them, the planners should be careful not to burden the regular curriculum with time-consuming discussions, which, if at all, become meaningful only after extensive reading. It therefore seems advisable to relegate these topics to continuation-studies, as additions to case-analyses and didactic guidance. (We shall see in a later part of the present chapter how most of the teaching subjects mentioned in our list reappear in connection with such guidance.)

The program is meaningful also for the training of psychological and educational counselors and for special education experts, within a total training program specially designed to meet their needs.

The number of hours to be devoted to each part of the program depends on the framework and the specific needs of a given population. In any case, it is essential to supplement each part with guided observations of, and active participation in, field work and not just with analyses of cases and "events." It is precisely this addition that makes the above-mentioned topics meaningful for every training course in which representatives of different levels of intelligence and experience are bound to appear. And although most of the subjects are formulated in an abstract way, emphasis on the educational implications of each problem to be discussed should guarantee its concretization.

On Sociology Teaching

The following program is meant for the training of teachers and teaching-counselors, but also of school social workers and group-counselors who work with underprivileged children and adolescents. (It is needless to add that in the training of school psychologists, special education workers, and headmasters similar courses are required.)

Whereas in science-oriented sociology courses emphasis is on defining "objective" factors and on techniques to measure their intensity in specific cases, in teacher training it is on making their *subjective* meaning understandable. Here, measurability is of importance only to the extent that it allows us to show that degrees of intensity are *not* responsible automatically for more severe symptoms, but that the influence of any social factor on the individual's behavior depends on the configuration of a number of environmental and personality factors much more than on the measurable degree of intensity of each.

This is what we have in mind when we speak of the subjective meaning of objective factors. It can also be defined as a kind of psychologization, or, better, humanization, of sociology. It is in this form that sociology teaching becomes also the basis of subject-matter training in civics, as we shall try to show later, in any cases of civics-courses for teachers of secondarily retarded pupils with their needs for actualization and for neutralization of affective reactions (more than for information on "democratic institutions" or for training in what is called, rather uncritically, "democratic behavior").

The following is a tentative list of topics to be dealt with in a sociology course for teachers and teaching-counselors. The first items seem to be of a more theoretical character (though where to put the emphasis depends, of course, on the sociology teacher). They should *not* remain lessons in the definition of basic concepts, and it is important *not* to concentrate them in a closed unit but to intersperse them, as much as possible, among the discussions of more specific issues.

1. The meaning of absolute and relative poverty, of economic stability or instability as a function of the individual's attitude toward the objective conditions of life, with emphasis on their educational implications, as reflected in the parents' and the family's adequate or inadequate attitudes toward their interpersonal relationships, their children, their occupational roles, their status conception, and so on.

2. The conditions of change in social status and its impact on educational and interpersonal relationships and on the upbringing of children.

3. The different meanings of plenty as an economic condition and a life-style, related to the extent to which the conditions of plenty are based on tradition or on recent changes.

4. The various conditions of value-changes and value-clashes, social gap, justice and injustice, and the resulting tensions; their meaning in a primarily class-divided society as against their meaning in an ethnically heterogeneous population. The essential differences between a democratic ideal of pluralism and tolerance, the socialist ideal of equality, the liberal idea of equal opportunities (again connected with pluralism), the messianistic or pseudomessianistic ideal of eschatological or secular nationalistic elimination of differences. The social pathologies emanating from each of these ideals and their specific influence on the individual and his reactive pathologies.

5. The so-called objective factors usually correlated with individual behavior: living-conditions, the occupational and the age structure of specific families, as against that of the total population, the parents' level of schooling, the languages spoken at home, birth rate and the number of children in a family, the personal or impersonal character of the family atmosphere as a function of each of these "objective" factors; the neighborhood, the community organization or dissolution, the religious institutions and their im-

pact on the family's life-style; each of these factors to be analyzed in relation to the parents' expectations and demands, the child's motivation for learning, his achievement drives, his perception of the future, his value-orientation, his rules of behavior (as much as possible, each analysis to be accompanied by case descriptions).

6. The impact of social intervention with a "family in distress"; individual interventions of the social welfare variety, as against the impact of social planning and social policy on the family's life-style. It is important for the teacher to have understanding in this area, for which purpose he should at least receive a minimum of information on the principles and the methods of such interventions. This part of the sociology curriculum, in addition to its theoretical and informational function (with which a science-oriented sociology teaching program may be satisfied), aims at correcting a number of widespread prejudices against so-called dependent families.

7. In connection with (6), the frequently raised question of to what extent it is essential to supply the student with information on demographic data, on the structure of the national economy, on the availability and the function of the various social services (in the comprehensive meaning of the term), on the structure and the legal data of social and educational, medical, and other institutions, on the legal rights and duties of the citizen, on political, cultural, and religious ideologies prevailing in the society. To what extent do these factors determine the quality of educational trends and processes, on the one hand, and family life, on the other?

Here, again, it may be preferable to relegate at least part of such information to continuation courses, and this not only to save time for other training tasks but also, and mainly, to guarantee that the data will not remain informational only, but will be related to teaching-experience. As parts of a subject-matter course in civics they should be included in the basic training. Several topics (such as the structure of government, stages in the processes of law giving and law execution, election procedures, and so forth), which usually are given prominence in any civics program, are omitted on purpose, not only because we consider them of very limited value in civics or in training for good citizenship, but also because they are not essential parts of a sociology program, nor do they contribute anything to teacher training as such and certainly not to rehabilitative teaching.

(We shall return later to suggesting a program for civics teaching as part of a teacher training program.)

8. The bureaucratization of social service as a result of certain ideologies and of certain socio-cultural developments in our technological era, and its impact on the distributor as well as on the recipient of the services. This is a very peculiar subject, insofar as it stands between culture analysis and sociology, on the one hand, and teacher psychology, on the other (since the teaching profession does not differ much from other social services in its trend toward bureaucratization).

This, then, is an additional subject of a sociology program for teachers (although it could have been included equally well in a psychology program). Its practical significance for teaching training becomes evident when we ask two questions with regard to reversibility: Should it be one of the teacher-counselors' functions to help the individual teacher overcome a culture-conditioned trend toward bureaucratization of his professional self-image by strengthening his personal involvement in his teaching? Can the school, can the teacher, do anything for the humanization of services through a planned development of service-orientation in school children?

It is obvious that, whenever such subjects *are* considered parts of a practical sociology training program, the delineations between sociology and psychology become flexible. But it is equally obvious that—and in this respect a sociology program so conceived differs essentially from a science-oriented teaching program—whatever changes can or may be brought about will undoubtedly never become accessible to scientific proof and measurement.

A number of subjects have not been included here because they are meant for representatives of other professions—school social workers, group-counsellors or leaders of group discussions with children, teachers, or parents (particularly discussions on "explosive issues," such as social gap, discrimination, cultural patterns, intergroup tensions, and so on). Although the sociology program outlined here is meaningful for the training of such workers, they need a number of additional courses; these should *not* be given to teachers or teacher-counselors, in order not to divert their attention from their main concern—teaching (which reminds us of what we said above about psychology topics that should *not* be included in a training program for teachers).

Some Ideas about Didactics

It would not be appropriate here to summarize what has been said in a variety of textbooks on the teaching of didactics in teacher-training courses. Nor do we intend to compare traditional with progressive teaching methods at the various age levels of the learner, from kindergarden through elementary and junior high schools to academic or vocational senior high schools. Also, the principles of teaching through activity programs, the so-called discovery method, or stimulation of creativity are generally known, and many excellent analyses are available from which their theory and practice can be studied.

As regards the method of rehabilitative teaching, we refer to the Chapter 2 of the present study. It is only through detailed descriptions of lessons or isolated class events (as illustrated in the preceding chapters) and through analyzing the rationale of every didactic step taken that a course in rehabilitative teaching becomes meaningful. Comparing these methods with their "counterparts" in regular teaching, on the one hand, and in teaching slow learners or emotionally disturbed children, on the other, serves as a means to make the teacher-student aware of the multitude of possible approaches to teaching and thus to make him flexible enough for experimentation with different methods.

However, it is precisely the multitude of methods (and particularly of the so-called innovations in teaching), each of which often claims the right to exclusive validity, or, at least, to superiority, that makes it imperative to raise a number of questions when we deal with a didactic course for rehabilitative teaching, as part of either basic teacher training or continuation courses or in-service training. There is one common denominator to all these questions: to what extent are methods that may have proved their validity and their efficacy also valid for the teaching of secondarily retarded children?

In addition, a number of other questions refer specifically to this variety of teaching:

1. How does a teacher learn the art of defining concepts or phenomena (which, as we said in the Chapter 2, are of particular importance in noninductive teaching, in each of its phases)?

2. How can we develop the teacher's ability to react to his pupils' faulty answers in alternative ways (that is, according to their reactions to his reactions)? To what extent can he be sensitized to the hypothetical meanings of a faulty answer? How can he be trained in flexibility, that is, in the art of passing from one diagnosis of that answer to another and from one intervention to another?

3. How does the teacher learn to translate "concretizations" (examples, illustrations, formal symbols, and so forth) into concepts?

4. How does he teach his pupils to explain in exact terms their choice of a correct answer to test questions or exercise assignments meant to strengthen their ability to think in abstract terms?

5. How can teaching-contents be made relevant for the formulation (and not only the "experience") of values? How can culture-alien values (that is values contrary to those of the family, the neighborhood, the ethnic subgroup) be made comprehensible through the teaching of such contents?

6. What is the place of using different criteria in learning about seemingly or truly contradictory values?

7. Does there exist an affinity of types or inclinations of individual teachers to specifically "preferred" methods of teaching?*

We are now going to supplement what we have said briefly on didactics as a subject in a training program for rehabilitative teaching by comparing its principles with those of a different—in fact, opposite—approach. We have in mind teaching the underprivileged jointly with well-functioning middle-class children. Many classes all over the world are conducted according to the prin-

---

*Some may be so strongly opposed to leaving the area of concrete and provable givens and to venturing into the "dimension of the mere possible" that they never will be able to learn the ways of rehabilitative teaching. Others may be deeply convinced of their pupils' inability to think in abstract terms and therefore may be inclined to misunderstand rehabilitative teaching as if it meant simplification and concretization only.

Still more problematic are the cases of those teaching candidates or teachers in the field who are convinced that they know the art of defining as well as that of imagining, but actually do not but imitate the external expressions of abstraction and of empathy.

In such cases the didactics course should include intensive guidance on a personal basis though care must be taken not to let such guidance "glide" into misconceived therapy.

ciples of heterogeneity and integration as recommended by Coleman.[6] Often this type of teaching is based on activity programs and on the use of small groups, and we are told that the better achievements of underprivileged pupils in mixed groups justify the method.

However, rarely, if ever, is the question asked of to what extent the knowledge acquired by these pupils will be available to them in different learning situations and for different learning tasks, or to what extent it will remain associated with the specific content and subject matter through which it was established. We have found that in some seemingly successful projects of this kind, the well-functioning and the underprivileged learners differed from each other in this respect, and that most of the latter showed considerably less "mobility" than their socially more fortunate classmates, even though the ordinary means of measuring achievements did *not* reveal this difference in the quality of the knowledge acquired and applied.

The positive effect of mixed groups is often explained as the result of a change in the pupil's self-image, from that of being a failure to that of being "one who can learn like others." But again: we should be careful not to overestimate the real change that may have taken place. We should ask: Does the child indulge in an externalized and externalizing illusion, namely: that the very fact of his sitting together with others who *are* able to learn freely, is for him proof of his ability to learn as well? Or is the changed self-image real, internalized, independent of the situation in which it took place? Is the pupil able, to the same extent as his "normal" classmate, to preserve an objective ability to master his learning assignments, even when they bore him?

More often than not, we could observe† that the secondarily retarded pupils remained, almost tragically, isolated—less interested in finding "their" solutions, often copying their "more gifted" friends (and thus indulging in the illusion that they *were* their equals), much more dependent on "authoritarian" textbooks, in which unambiguous answers were given or expected. To the extent

†See a not yet published report on "Integrational Schooling Programs", prepared by the Hebrew University Department of Continuation Courses, under the direction of Mrs. Hava Salmon.

that these shortcomings were *not* in evidence and the pupils were able objectively to compete with the others, they invariably belonged to the higher intelligence level.

On the other hand, active support on the part of the teacher ("reacting to his pupils' reactions") proved much more effective. Activation undoubtedly stimulates, but stimulation is not sufficient. Nor is working in small groups. Here, we should beware of another dangerous illusion: Not always do the more active and more advanced pupils in such a group offer *genuine* help; they may serve as examples only, to be imitated externally; they may "give" their help uncritically and even if it is not appropriate, because it takes the place of constructive activation.

Reality-orientation to be developed through observation and participation may be a similar illusion: even when small groups are well planned as heterogeneous groups, it is not always the more developed in abstract thinking who can help properly prepare the visit to an institution or enterprise, or draw the proper conclusions from their observations, since they may be *less* developed in understanding the implications of reality-observations. Nor can we rely for this purpose on the underprivileged pupils' presumably wider range of social involvement, since the latter does not mean that it is accompanied by an adequate understanding of the *essentials* in an observable situation. And since the life experiences of middle-class and of underprivileged children have little in common, we cannot rely on their cooperation either, when it comes to preparing observational contacts with the environment or to summarizing their results.

At a higher age level, when such contacts usually form the basis of studying a social problem (for instance, in a civics course), insufficient ability to differentiate between essential and inessential (or less essential) details to be observed and questions to be asked is often aggravated by an illegitimate interference of affective stereotypes or prejudices, which are liable to distort what has been observed unless a teacher is available to correct such distortions. Such correction, by the way, is important for *both* parts of a mixed group, the middle-class *and* the underprivileged, since *both* are likely to be handicapped by social misconceptions and prejudices.

And once again, it becomes evident that it is not the coexistence of pupils from different backgrounds or their interaction within a so-called integrated class that accounts for the weaker class members' relatively better learning achievements, but the teacher's adequate intervention. He must interpret the social facts that make understandable the functioning of any institution, enterprise, or activity observed, irrespective of the observer's cultural associations. It is only on the basis of such "introduction to social meaning" that observations become meaningful, that intelligent questions can be expected, that correct conclusions are likely to be drawn.

Curriculum Planning in Rehabilitative Teaching — Some Guidelines

It is generally agreed that the purposes of teaching should be defined as:

—Establishing basic skills;

—Gradual enlargement of the child's *massa apperceptiva*, causal understanding, and time-consciousness;

—Mediating personal experiences through objective contents and, in most cases, translating them into concepts;

—Helping the learner understand ideas and meaning behind facts;

—Training him in formal (operational) thinking through gradual replacement of concrete contents and realities by forms and formulas, symbols and concepts.

—Strengthening his ability to differentiate, through showing him or making him discover nuances and alternatives.

In rehabilitative teaching the last purpose is so important that contents are liable to become instruments only for functional development:

—Knowledge, causal connections, and time-sequences remain meaningless unless systematically developed by the teacher's intentional interventions.

—The distinction between facts and meaning, or between concrete data and concepts, is the outcome of a prolonged process of rehabilitative teaching.

—Personal experiences are not as easily elicited through objective contents in secondarily retarded (and externalized), as in ordinary pupils; and to the extent that they *do* emerge, they tend to be elicited by affective associations (see what we said in the Chapter 2 about "neutralizing affects").

—When bringing up personal experiences, the teacher must in any case be careful not to include experiences that have no reality-significance for his secondarily retarded pupils.

—The latter consideration should also determine the selection of interpretations (of texts, events, processes, life phenomena, and so on) that have optimal chances of appealing to the learners' past life experiences.

—Here we come back to our starting point, though in a different formulation: it would be a mistake to conceive of the functional approach to teaching, that is, of using contents as tools for cognitive rehabilitation, as if it excluded and contradicted faithfulness to the subject matter taught: selection of certain aspects must be justifiable objectively and should never be "forced upon" that subject matter, as it were. But since every content (not only in history or literature but also in the sciences) permits a variety of interpretations and accentuations, it is perfectly legitimate to select *that* interpretation, *that* emphasis, which offers the best chances of reaching the individual pupil. He must be reached in those layers of his cognitive structure that it is most important to reach when we want to bring about attitude changes desirable for the restoration of his impaired potentials.

—The contents taught do not lose their raison d'être as part of a well-structured body of knowledge just because rehabilitative teaching selects certain aspects or interpretations for didactic reasons; the learners' associations do not lose their didactic significance, as expressions of personal involvement and as possible bridges to the revelation of essentials, just because, uncontrolled by the teacher's interventions, they are liable to *distort* the essentials and to play havoc with thinking. These are the intrinsic paradoxes of rehabilitative teaching. They can be solved to the extent that the teacher is aware of his role as selector and interpreter.

Rehabilitative teaching is based on the presumption that the suitability of a certain teaching content depends on the way in which the teacher uses it and not on its adaptation to the "inferior" abilities of the secondarily retarded pupil, that is, on its simplification in style, extent, and complexity. Simplification means perpetuation of the cognitive handicaps. On the other hand, if we believe in the possibility of rehabilitation, that is, of restoring impaired cognitive abilities to their original level of normalcy, no content can be too complex to be included as such in the curriculum.

We have already mentioned that the *number* of curriculum items to be taught may have to be reduced: noninductiveness, branching out, neutralizing affects—the three principles of rehabilitative teaching—require time, and time to be added to the learner's day is not unlimited. Hence, cuts in the number of teaching items taught are inevitable. However, cutting down their number has no negative influence whatsoever on the process of functional restoration, and the irrelevance of the *quantity* of curriculum items has long been proved beyond all doubt.

All the more important becomes a thorough and intelligent analysis of the representative nature of each curriculum item (which may, of course, be exchangeable, as long as it remains representative of one of the basic, the "constitutive," ideas of a well-planned curriculum). To give a few examples, what are the fundamental ideas which should be covered by a literature, a history, a civics, a biology program in the six years of the secondarily retarded and externalized pupil's junior and senior high school studies (not taking into account the culture-conditioned and -determined choice of representative creations)?

Curriculum Suggestions (Literature)

The educationally relevant ideas illustrated through any literature curriculum can be divided into the following groups:

The Individual

(a) Changes taking place as the result of step-by-step developments (the problem of personality-integration) or of suddenly occurring ("irruptive") events (the problem of conversion or of traumatization). The purpose of analyzing poems, stories, or dramas in which such changes are reflected is twofold: to teach the externalized pupil something about the complexity of causal thinking and help him discover the dimension of the individual as a reality.

(b) Fate and individual responsibility. This is a problem of particular importance for the correction of the externalized child's distorting patterns of either fatalistic or manipulative thinking about man's life.

(c) The diary not as a piece of art but as a personal confession. Again, this is a topic of particular significance in rehabilitative teaching, because of the extreme weakness in an externalized child's self-perception and sense of continuity.

(d) Courage and doubt, in action and in suffering; active and passive heroism. Many literary creations lend themselves to a discussion of the differences between an internalized and an externalized version of courage and heroism (although it is, of course, doubtful to what extent insights thus gained will have a direct bearing on the pupils' behavior).

The Social Idea

(a) Growth of ideas or movements. This is a topic common to the teaching of literature and of history. Its peculiar function as a topic of literature teaching is its contribution to a *dynamic* understanding of ideas in their development and in their dependence on man's decision and action. In rehabilitative teaching such a dynamic understanding serves as a means to counteract concretistic misinterpretations of ideas, as if they were parts of an external reality.

(b) Equality and justice in their (false) realistic interpretation as unconditional equality and as externally identified with automatic reward and punishment; as against equality as dependent on personal involvement, and justice as an inner reality and certainty. Here, again, the difference between the topic in literature teaching and in history teaching is comparable to that of the aforementioned subject.

Form and Content

(a) Information on the different forms of poetry, novels, and theatrical plays should be given and illustrated, though the educational and cognitive importance of such information must not be overestimated. Stronger emphasis should be placed on the intrinsic relationship between certain forms and ideas (not contents). The question of why an author has chosen a specific form to express his ideas and intentions may not always be easy to answer but should at least be asked. Its purpose is to help develop the learner's, and particularly the secondarily retarded pupil's, sensitivity to different forms of literary creation.

(b) Allusions of meaning through description of landscapes, moods, gestures, verbal behavior, actions—all require translation from the "covert" into the "overt." To what extent is it the purpose of the author to produce tensions and greater involvement and mental activity in his readers, and to what extent is the allusion involuntary and unintentional? In rehabilitative teaching the "deciphering" of allusions is particularly important, both for a more adequate understanding of the creation and for the development of the pupil's ability to think in terms of the As-If.

(c) Ambiguity, as a way to add a dimension of depth to the content and its underlying ideas and intentions, finds its expression in comparisons, metaphors, analogies, symbols, paradoxes, irony, or wit, as well as in the aforementioned allusions. It is one of the most important functions of literature teaching, particularly when we think of rehabilitative teaching, to explain ambiguity (though it should be clear to every teacher that it will often take lengthy, continually repeated analysis to increase the pupils' readiness to "tolerate," and to accept as legitimate, expressions of ambiguity).

(d) One of the areas in which allusion and ambiguity should be demonstrated is that of literary creations dealing with conflicts, and particularly with intrapersonal (rather than interpersonal, hence external) conflicts. It is in this area that the secondarily retarded pupil will experience, through the medium of his learning, the meaning of inner realities.

Although we have emphasized here the functional approach to literature teaching, it should be obvious from our brief analysis that this approach does not contradict "loyalty" to the objective content of each creation. The main difference between the here-suggested teaching method and the one generally used in ordinary teaching of the same material to normally functioning pupils is that purely formal analyses are neglected here. It seems doubtful that such analyses are of great value in ordinary teaching; but there can be no doubt that they are bound to remain utterly meaningless in the learning processes of the pupils we have in mind. Those pupils' strong orientation toward the reality-significance of every content learned and their relative inability (and weak motivation) to think in purely formal categories make the functional approach (with its frequent attempts at actualization) seem preferable, provided, of course, that the objective meaning of the literary creation taught is not neglected.

One additional remark: We did *not* mention among the aims of literature teaching one that is often given prominence—the development of aesthetic differentiation. This omission is based on the presumption that a "sense of beauty," an ability to differentiate between styles, and the emergence of personal preferences depend on a number of *personality* factors (such as increased rule of rationality over distorting affects, identity-formation, or objective enlargement of experience and knowledge). It therefore would seem advisable not to put too much emphasis on aesthetic differentiation as an aim of literature teaching, if we want to avoid the risks of phraseologies, externalization, imitation, and falsity.

Curriculum Suggestions (History)

Instead of teaching selected history periods or, better, selected aspects of each of these periods, and trying to build up in this way a sense of sequence, it seems preferable to teach history as a comparison between "ideas in development" or between life-styles. The importance of data, then, becomes, of course, negligible; they serve as illustrations only in the teacher's hands. And at the termination of a course or a learning period, it is not recall of data and not even their accuracy that should be examined, but the individual student's ability to see them in proper, and changeable, contexts; in other words, historical thinking rather than knowledge is the aim of a history course, as suggested here.

Examples (Subjects)

(a) Not "ancient history" but "varieties of ancient man" should be defined as one subject; or, "the concept of national expansion as a power ideal versus culture transmission as a motive for political expansion."

(b) Not "medieval history" as such should be taught, but "religious ideologies versus statehood" should be illustrated in various movements and crystallizations. To the extent that inter-state conflicts and struggles for supremacy resulted, they should not be treated as primary but as secondary and peripheral issues only.

(c) The French revolution can be taught as "standing" between etatism and Napoleonic nationalism, and Napoleon as "standing" between the French revolution and European nation-formation in the nineteenth century.

(d) Industrialization should be treated as a precursor of modern technology in its economic, anthropological, and political aspects, and at the same time as the basis of socialist ideologies, reform movements, welfare state ideals, and revolutions, in Germany and in Russia. (And the often overemphasized history of world wars and the ensuing changes in political constellations would then appear to be of lesser importance.)

(e) The upheavals in Asia, with Russia belonging to Asia *and* Europe, should be taught as a radical change in the concept of man, determining, as it does, the fate of the world. The same applies, of course, to the "atomic age" as a subject of political history, anthropology, and futurology.

(f) This would inevitably lead to a course in "democracies compared": not only would it necessitate an analysis of the "democratic idea" in its varieties (from Rome via England to France and America, and to Weimarian Germany and Russia), but also a "value-oriented discussion of the criteria of authenticity and falsity" and a survey of what could be called "the vicissitudes of the democratic idea and ideal."

Other meaningful topics of history teaching are still more removed from data learning and data remembering than those mentioned so far. We have in mind subjects such as:

(g) National value systems compared;

(h) Religious systems (beliefs and practices) compared;

(i) The history of an ideology, its sources within the national or cultural unit and outside influences well adapted or integrated and externally attached, its periods of crystallization and decay;

(j) Identification with the culture's value system (in a nationalistically imitative way) as against the individual's ability to relate to it objectively and critically;

(k) Assimilation versus internalization as group processes.

General Considerations

It will probably be argued that such a curriculum requires a much higher level of differentiation than can be expected of secondarily retarded children; does it not transform history as a teaching subject into "philosophy of history"? However, all depends on the teacher's way of dealing with his topics. Discussions of the principles of events and of interpretation require condensation of data into short information presentations as the basis of theoretical discussions.

These data can be presented in the form of coherent accounts and descriptions of sequences or in the form of novelistic elaborations. In the latter case (in which the teaching of history is combined with that of literature), historical events and developments appear in two dimensions simultaneously: in that of objective occurrences regulated by intrinsic laws and logics, and in that of objective occurrences regulated by intrinsic laws and logics, and in that of subjective interpretations, that is, as material meant to arouse the reader's imagination in personally relevant reflections and speculations, as an intentional subjectivization of factual data.

All this does not mean, of course, that knowledge of basic facts in proper time sequences is irrelevant for history teaching. But we do believe that the motivation to learn about facts and sequences (as a means to understand historical contexts) increases to the extent that the pupil learns to look at them from the vantage point of general viewpoints. It may sound paradoxical when we say that such concepts are more meaningful for the secondarily retarded pupil than data and facts. An ordinary pupil, through increasing acquaintance with the facts of history, arrives at asking questions of meaning, inductively, as it were. The secondarily retarded pupil, in his concretistic dependence on realities, finds it difficult to attribute such reality-character to facts of the past. National or religious values, patterns, beliefs, and practices, however, form part of his actuality, his reality; hence his tendency to see history in the light of such seemingly abstract and generally defined aspects, of which we have given some examples. (He needs this form of translating the past into ideas, of permanent actuality, in order to take a historical past seriously.)

Curriculum Suggestions (Civics)

Practically every textbook contains details of the legislative procedures of the country for whose pupils it is written. Sometimes, the procedures are compared with those of other countries, but more often this comparative aspect is neglected or is included in a separate course of political science. Similarly, an analysis of the principles underlying court procedures, that is, legal practice and a description of law execution and of the services available for the enforcement of the law invariably forms another part of such textbooks. A third chapter usually is devoted to a description of the services maintained by the state, on a central or a local level, as well as by the citizens (on a voluntary basis). Social, economic, technical, and defense services and the ways of financing such services are explained.

A comparison of the philosophy of services underlying the practice in different countries is rarely included in a "civics" course, at least not on a practical descriptive level. It may, and in fact often does, form part of a political science or a law-philosophy course on a University level, but usually is considered beyond the field of interest of junior or senior high school students. This, however, is a mistake, since it is precisely such a comparative description of services that gives meaning to the concepts of civics and civic responsibility, as well as to a differential definition of democracy (a subject already mentioned as part of the history curriculum).

At the same time, it should serve as the basis for a discussion of genuineness versus falsity of the democratic idea. To what extent are the citizen's rights in a democracy to criticize the social and political system and to elect its representatives taken seriously in all its consequences; to what extent are they used as phraseologies only: to what extent do they serve as outlets for demagogical self-inflation, on the one hand, and for aggressive drives, on the other? Which internal and external controls are built into the social and political system, and to what extent do the executive organs and the public services take seriously the findings of such control agencies? What is their impact on changes and development?

The second part of a meaningful civics curriculum deals with the criteria of *good citizenship*. The aforementioned analyses undoubtedly are likely to make substantial contributions to the genuineness of later political convictions, but they do not determine the quality of the grown-up individual's citizenship. Neither can the latter be developed by such frequently recommended training practices as simulating civic actions—for instance, by "playing" election or parliamentary discussion, or by voluntary participation in services rendered to individuals or to the public. The latter may favorably influence the individual child's development, but have little to do with his later ways of citizenship. Not only are they usually lacking in continuity and genuine involvement (particularly when organized by the school as part of its curriculum), they are rarely if ever related to the many factors that determine the individual's real growth into his community.

What are the essential criteria of good citizenship, and what can the school, more specifically, what can teaching (for instance, teaching citizenship as a course), do to become relevant for its functional development? (Reference is made to the examples of Chapter 5 and 6.)

—Good citizenship means man's readiness and ability faithfully and adequately to perform a multitude of "small" assignments with which he may be faced day in, day out, within contexts of anonymity, that is, without being motivated by personal bonds of nearness (in his family, in his neighborhood, with friends, and so on).

—Good citizenship means man's readiness and ability to consider the needs of others, to give without expectation of reward, simply because it is "the thing to do"; means readiness to volunteer, and again beyond the bonds of knownness, that is, of personal relationship.

—Good citizenship means man's tendency to eliminate injustice inflicted upon others, *not* out of resentment or self-inflation, but out of a natural urge to identify with justice as the basis of human existence.

—Good citizenship means man's readiness to accept universal and anonymous laws as limits to his individual freedom, and this even in cases in which he rejects a certain social order for ideological reasons. He may decide to become a fighter and to give up his good citizenship, when his "cause" becomes more important to him than thinking of others as personal members of "his" community. We can even say, paradoxically, that even voluntary and conscious rejection of citizenship proves its existence.

—Similar conflicts may arise out of the contradiction between the behavioral values and demands of the dominant culture to which a person belongs and those of his social or cultural subgroup, to which he may feel himself bound irrationally. In many cases loyalty to the principles of good citizenship as defined by the dominant culture *requires* disloyalty to the values of the subculture, and loyalty to the latter contradicts the former, as long as the subculture has not become dominant. In other words, the concepts of citizen and citizenship are valid under certain cultural conditions only.

—Good citizenship is not identical with good character qualities. Many unselfish, good-hearted and devoted men and women are known to function rather poorly as citizens. They may be much too indolent to understand, or to take an interest in, the demands and expectations of society's anonymous representatives or to observe the generally prescribed order of things. They may be negligent and forgetful of the "small duties of the day." They may be introverts unable to establish contact with others, through *not* egotistically secluded in empty shells of selfhood.

On the other side of the fence we find those "excellent citizens" whose very observance of social demands, whose ability to live up to society's expectations, indicate no more than extreme adaptability. These are "the good citizens" out of selfishness, whose all-determining motive is to exploit to their own advantage the good impression they try and succeed to make.

Hence, we should distinguish between the phenotype of good citizenship and the underlying motivations; we must know the latter properly to evaluate the different moral levels of citizenship.

A third part of a meaningful citizenship curriculum, meaningful particularly for secondarily retarded pupils, deals with topics that usually are excluded from it, topics considered not to be definable in cognitive terms. We have in mind such *"explosive issues"* in the area of social and interpersonal behavior as cultural differences, social inequality and injustice, social gap, discrimination and prejudices, political controversies and rivalries, and so forth. Their very explosiveness prevents an objective, affect-free, analytical treatment. It is for this reason that teachers, as a rule, are reluctant to touch at their emotional aspects. The teachers maintain that it may well be appropriate for well-trained social psychologists or mental health workers to conduct discussions on these subjects, preferably in groups in which various intellectual and social levels are represented. But they feel that it is beyond their competence as teachers to deal with the strong affects that are likely to express themselves in such discussions.

This, however, is the most meaningful task of citizenship teaching: to sensitize both the socially established (middle-class) and the underprivileged and therefore often secondarily retarded pupils to the problem of differences and its implications, in the area of social coexistence as well as in the area of patterns of cognitive, personal, and interpersonal behavior.

What can a training seminar for teachers do to prepare them for making intelligent use of such a civics curriculum? (A similar question can, of course, be asked about the training of teachers in history, literature, biology, and so forth.)

It is relatively easy to define the details of knowledge required for final examinations and to compile them in textbooks (as it is done in various forms all over the world). But for the purpose of comparing with each other legal systems, "styles" of democracy, ideologies of service, forms of bureaucratization versus humanization of services, a civics curriculum for training seminars depends on philosophical studies. The "translation" of the abstract language of such studies into applicative terms is not easy, and the danger of using empty phrases should be carefully avoided. The best way of preparing the teacher-students for their future function in this field is to analyze records of actually given or model lessons, in regular and in rehabilitative teaching.

The most important training task is that of preparing the students for the ways of dealing with secondarily retarded pupils' affective reactions, not only to some of those theoretical issues but also, and primarily, to the manifestations of good or bad citizenship as illustrated by case descriptions. It is one of the most urgent needs of teacher training in civics to prepare such case descriptions and analyses, based on historical or literary documents as well as on reported actualities. At the same time, however, a training course in civics must contain an individual, psychological analysis of the students' observable and expressed reactions to these cases and manifestations, and in particular to the so-called explosive issues. (The analysis of such reactions often requires individual contacts between one of the students and one of the teachers.)

In the end, we repeat what has been said before: we must not expect too much of a real impact of civics lessons, whatever their content or their structure may be, on the pupils' quality of citizenship, on their immediate or later behavior. The only real gain that should and could be hoped for is the learners' increased awareness of affective elements that are liable to distort their judgments and result in the emergence of prejudices in their personal relationships. It is obvious that what we have defined as the third part of the curriculum is the most relevant of the three parts, and that the least effective, in this respect, is the first part.

Curriculum Suggestions (Biology)

When we want to compose a biology curriculum for junior and senior high school pupils who are secondarily retarded, we should bear in mind the following:

(a) That the value of experimentation is restricted, in their case, because of their tendency to relate the outcome of each experiment to the particular case rather than to proceed from it to proper generalizations; and that the latter, to the extent that the teacher wants to "produce" them in the pupils' mind, should in any case be formulated by the teacher himself, according to the principles of the noninductive method;

(b) That for them the manipulative, and even the play-character of experimentation is a source of immediate satisfaction, so much so that the pre-experimentation questions of methodology (the why and the how of planning adequate experiments) do not interest them at all; and that the rationale of a specific experiment must therefore be given by the teacher himself, for each experiment separately, instead of being learned "through" experimenting;

(c) That the number of problems (or problem areas) to be included in the curriculum is limited, not only because the knowledge of adjacent fields (such as biochemistry or enzymology) is practically absent, but also because much of the available time must be used for making the pupils see and understand the cognitive implications of the general issues, the essential questions of life sciences.

Here are a number of such essential questions, which determine a possible selection of teaching subjects:

1. What is the essence of life? Does the differentiation between inorganic and organic modes of existence give an answer to that question? In which sense is inorganic matter "living"; in which sense is it not?

2. Closely connected with this first question is the second one, concerning the beginning of life: Can this beginning be explained as "rooted in lifelessness"?

3. Here arises the question of complex versus simple forms of life, in plants and in animals: In what sense is the cell, is a one-cell being already "complex"? And in what sense does the concept have a different meaning, when we consider the structure of developed organs and bodies? Can the forms of complexity of life be shown as a developmental sequence or not?

4. What are the basic functions of life without which it would not be possible? And what are the different forms in which these functions "function"? Of breathing, food intake, food digestion and transformation, procreation, perception and apperception as against stimulus reception and reaction? And again, what are the essential differences between these functions in plants and in animals (and what are the chemical equivalents in inorganic matter)?

5. Another form of dealing with the same problem is by asking: What is meant by "learning," by "experience," by "being conditioned," as against "learning of functions" and "learning through structurization"? What are the roles of instincts and organic tendencies (such as the tendency toward homeostasis and equilibration) as against the role of experience in the processes of adaptation to a changing environment? (With illustrations from the

life of plants and animals, their forms, their functions, their movements, their interaction with the environment.)

6. Can these processes of adaptation (and gradual transformation as a result of it) be explained satisfactorily as a series of causes and results, or does the scientist need concepts of finalistic explanation? Or are the latter "façons de parler" only? What are some of the ideological consequences of each of the two methods of explanation?

7. A closely connected question: Is everything in life determined by laws of expediency, or is there any justification for concepts (or "images") such as "the luxury of life" or "the playfulness of nature"?

8. The most problematic areas are those of genetics and evolution. It may sound paradoxical to say that a biology curriculum could be built up without dealing with these subjects, but in rehabilitative teaching, experience has shown that an adequate treatment of them requires more time than is usually available. It has therefore been suggested that information given on the basic laws of genetics should be confined to a minimum, making possible some understanding of the phenomena of mutation and, through them, of evolution. A secondarily retarded pupil, even more than a so-called regular one, needs a correction of the simplifying perception of development as a harmonistic sequence, needs confrontation with the unforeseeable as part of causal and developmental laws, and this precisely because of his overstrong tendencies toward simplification, automaticity, and lack of differentiation.

9. Some fundamental information on man's organism, its systems, and their functions should be given (accompanied by a maximum of illustrations), not only as a means of helping develop rational behavior and understanding conditions of health and illness, but also as a preparation for the following problem in biology teaching.

10. In which ways does the life of man depend on the development of modern technology? (Ecology in its positive and negative meanings.)

11. As a last, and often neglected, subject of a biology curriculum for secondarily retarded pupils we should mention one that, in general terms, could be called "the psychological implications of

biology teaching.'' In this connection, reference should be made to the multitude of affective reactions that are liable to be elicited by topics such as: ''fear of the struggle for survival or of evading the ever-present danger of falling victim to the survival needs of other, stronger, beings''; ''nothingness and death as the beginning and the end of life''; ''fear of complexity and the inability to function well in complex organic or environmental conditions''; ''fear of autonomy as against strong dependence needs'' (that is, preferring automatic modes of existence); ''deterministic beliefs as signs of strength or of weakness''; ''superstitious associations with organic processes such as bleeding or blood transfusion.''

12. One of the most complex affective problems connected with the teaching of biology is that of ''sex education.'' It is obvious that we do not refer here to the latter's purely informative aspects. The emotional concomitants of sexual satisfaction through normal or abnormal intercourse or through masturbation are much more important for preadolescent and adolescent girls and boys than to understand the processes of contumescence and detumescence. Culturally or individually conditioned fears of defloration or masturbation, of venereal diseases or birth-control procedures must be dealt with on a level far transcending physiological or biological information.

The general age-conditioned discrepancy between knowledge and experience, the often incomprehensible coexistence of physiological and emotional components in sexual activities, the differences between individual pupils (of different backgrounds) in maturation, experience, associations, and interests, the differences between teachers in dealing with sex problems without inhibition or affects, and many similar problems have little, if anything, to do with biology teaching pure and simple. Every biology teacher should know that, when dealing with such issues, he faces general, educational, and psychological problems that require intensive cooperation with others—psychologists, social workers, educators.

Once again, it should be emphasized that what we have said here about the biology curriculum is valid for the training of teachers more than it refers to the actual teaching of junior and senior high school students. It was our intention to formulate some guidelines for the preparation of biology teachers in classes of secondarily retarded pupils. We have, therefore, included in our presentation general issues rather than details of teaching items. The latter are exchangeable, provided they allow for neutralizing affective reactions and for branching out into "adjacent" problem areas. But the most important point in using any specific content for teacher training is that teachers must be shown how to present it in a noninductive way, that is, they must be trained in summarizing the essential points of a specific subject matter by clearly defining whatever they want to explain and asking questions of relevant application and modification.

III. THE ORGANIZATION OF TEACHER TRAINING

We have suggested here some of the basic ideas that, in our opinion, should guide curriculum planners for junior and senior high schools. We have presented these guidelines as identical with the basic ideas according to which teachers should learn their specific subject matter. It is needless to add that this way of teaching literature, history, civics, biology, or any other subject essentially differs from the way in which they are taught in science-oriented university departments.

It is not in the specific, teaching-directed, selection of problems in each of the various bodies of knowledge that this basic difference becomes visible (every university course is selective in some way and requires supplementation through the student's individual reading and research). It is the attempt to connect each specific study topic with its didactic implications that requires, as we have already said, a separate setting and a separate method for subject-matter courses in the training of teachers, whether as part of their basic training or as part of their re-learning for rehabilitative teaching.

We have emphasized before that in teacher training each subject matter taught should be integrated as often as possible with recognizing, and referring to, the psychological, sociological, or philosophical implications of that specific problem or content. This means that the course material of the above-specified psychology or sociology curricula must not only be supported by varied subject matter; the latter must also refer, as frequently as possible to what has been taught in these courses.

It is in this way that the teacher-student learns from the method of relevant branching out when teaching a specific topic, that he learns the art of recognizing affective interventions in the pupil's thinking processes. The same subject matter should also be taught, in teacher-training courses, as teachable in different ways, using different methods. Obviously, this cannot be done in an ordinary science-oriented university program.

The training approach here recommended does not exclude separation of didactic "applicative," from purely informational subject-matter teaching; but they should not be split into two, more or less independent, units of training, as is done in most training courses. Each piece of information given on a partial, narrow, well-circumscribed teaching topic should be followed immediately by didactic illustrations. The latter may be elaborate or brief and limited, may be accompanied by demonstrations or not; but every effort should be made to develop and strengthen the teacher-student's sense of didactic obligation toward every piece of subject matter he learns in his relevant courses.

They can, of course, be represented by a number of other content areas as well. These principles are of equal importance in training programs in which various methods (such as those of regular and of rehabilitative teaching) are taught simultaneously and in which they are taught consecutively. It may well be that even though non-separation of subject matter from teaching methods is justified in the second case (when rehabilitative teaching is taught in specialization courses), it may be contraindicated in the first case: here, it could produce confusion in the mind of the teacher-student; he would perhaps be unable to acquire adequate mastery in his field of knowledge and, as a result, would be unable to teach effectively in any class, of regular and of secondarily retarded pupils.

Obviously, the development of differentiation, responsibility, and rationality of thinking is a central purpose of teaching in every case. But only in "regular" teaching are *contents* capable of achieving that purpose. This is the reason why in the training for regular teaching, learning of contents and learning of methods are in no way contradictory. Therefore, the teaching of contents and the teaching of methods, as it is practiced ordinarily in teacher-training programs, is definitely unnecessary and may even be detrimental to the formation of a good teacher. Inductiveness, concentration on a specific content, and value education can be learned well when the study of contents is integrated with method-teaching.

The same cannot be said about the training of teachers for rehabilitative teaching. Here are a few suggestions as to the organization of such training (a slightly different version of a program presented by the author in a previous publication; see reference 11, pp. 225f.):

(a) Some kind of "preliminary" life experience is essential before the candidate enters a teacher-training course. The desirable age for admission would seem to be 21. This holds good for elementary as well as for secondary school teachers.

(b) The first year of studies should include courses in which the candidates participate together. Here, information would be given—illustrated as much as possible by case stories—on the child's general and functional growth and development, on the demographic, cultural, and economic structure, and on the ideologies of the society for which they will work, as well as its typical pathologies (under the aspect of their educational significance and implications) and its available social services.

(c) Another part of the first year's program should be organized in separate units: we refer to the contents of teaching, which, in the elementary school, are "basic skills" and "general orientation," and are clearly defined subject matter in junior and senior high schools. In the training of elementary school teachers more emphasis is placed, even at this initial stage, on connecting skill training with methods—here called "techniques"—than in the training of secondary school teachers. The latters' first encounter with their specific subject matter may be almost exclusively content-oriented, particularly since it is one of the functions of this initial stage to familiarize them with the ways of finding proper source material, for the purposes of self-learning.

(d) In the second year of training, the need for separating the two types of teachers becomes still more evident. It is true enough that both must learn their teaching-methods as applied to teaching-contents and their contents as teachable contents. Besides that, to the extent that a distinction is made between teaching "regular" and "secondarily retarded" pupils, elementary and high school teachers will find that there are more common elements in rehabilitative teaching at the various age levels than there are content-conditioned differences, and that these common (didactic) elements can certainly be taught jointly to elementary and high school teachers of secondarily retarded pupils. And yet, even this would not make redundant their separation into different learning-units for the study of their learning-contents.

(e) In the third year of studies, the difference between training of elementary and high school teachers becomes still more evident. It is suggested that the candidates for elementary school teaching now go out into the field and start teaching, while receiving method-oriented guidance. Candidates for high school teaching should go on studying their subject matter, while receiving guidance when practice-teaching in regular classes. Furthermore, it is suggested that discussions of general educational problems, such as value-internalization, participation in social tasks, stimulation of interests, behavioral issues, sex education, parent-child relationships, and so forth, should be considered part of the third year curriculum for high school teacher candidates, while parallel discussions—though on different aspects of such general educational problems, according to the younger age of the pupils—should form part of the in-service training and the individual guidance given to third year elementary school teachers in practice.

(f) A fourth year should be devoted to further training for specialization, particularly but not exclusively in rehabilitative teaching. Conditions prevailing in our technological era—conditions of anonymity, impersonality, insecurity, competition, and value-ambiguity—explain the dangers of ever increasing externalization and secondary retardation. It is therefore of the utmost importance to make as many elementary school teachers as possible aware of the difference between teaching according to the principles of inductiveness, content-orientation, and personal experience stimulation, and teaching according to the opposite principles, of noninductiveness, branching out, and neutralization of affects. But this can be achieved, in their case, through in-service training and concentrated continuation courses, all based on the analysis of processes of thinking, learning, and teaching.

(g) It is not so in the case of training teachers for secondarily retarded pupils in (homogeneous or heterogeneous) classes in junior and senior high schools: there will always be many teachers whose genuine involvement in the subject of their studies will make them feel they should arouse a similar involvement in their pupils, and particularly in the most intelligent among them. These teachers will see their fourth year of studies as a year of preparing themselves for teaching their subject matter as effectively and as scientifically as possible. They will certainly be unsuitable for rehabilitative teaching on a high school level. But others will take an equally genuine interest in teaching their subject matter to secondarily retarded high school pupils in order to help them in their cognitive development toward optimal functioning. For them, the fourth year will be a year of specialization in the methods of rehabilitative teaching as related to "their" specific field of interest and knowledge. They will now face the extremely complex problem of "double loyalty," loyalty to the contents of their teaching as such and loyalty to their functional significance (the question of when to give preference to which aspect of any teachable content).

(h) One thing should be clear to everyone engaged in rehabilitative teaching, at whatever age level: just as physical or cognitive rehabilitation requires permanent aftercare (see p.105f.), learning how to rehabilitate a secondarily retarded pupil's socially or culturally impaired ability to think differentially, responsibly, and rationally requires "aftercare," that is: didactic guidance. At the end of the above-quoted study, we said: "The teacher, too, should learn, how to differentiate, how to react individually to his pupils' manifestations of thinking, how to think rationally, how to become free of stereotypes and of dependence-needs, how to take upon himself full responsibility for his teaching-acts and his educational interventions, how to improvise without losing sight of his main trend of teaching, how to handle different methods according to the changing needs of the class or of an individual pupil, how to be spontaneous and how to act spontaneously." (11, p. 133)

For all this, the teacher needs the help of a counselor, with whom he can discuss class events and his reactions, his overt and covert fears, and his expectations (and all this, of course, without gliding into pseudotherapeutic activities).

IV. ON TEACHER GUIDANCE

In different parts of this book, we have mentioned that the teacher of secondarily retarded children, particularly in junior and senior high school classes, must receive constant guidance in the methods of teaching such children. Noninductiveness, branching out, and neutralizing affects are not only liable to frighten the teacher, since they are contrary to the generally accepted ideals and principles of "teaching-through-doing" or of "activating the learner" or of "learning as discovery"; they also require that an unusual amount of mental effort be invested by the teacher in preparing his lessons and in his teaching activities. They require much more inner freedom and courage, readiness to improvise and to guess, ability to play with the unknown, than an ordinary teacher is helped to develop in himself as a student in training centers or as the recipient of educational guidance made available to him—if at all—in the field.

Actually, all that has been said in this book related to the contents of didactic—as against psychological—guidance can and should be translated into such guidance (or counseling) language. But where do we start when we want to establish in the teachers awareness of the need for special training methods when they deal with secondarily retarded children? How do we prepare understanding of, and motivation for, rehabilitative teaching? It is only too well-known that most teachers connect the terms "guidance" or "counseling" with problems of behavior disorders and class discipline, and expect from a counselor practical advice on how to deal with such cases, or how to provide treatment services for them outside the class environment. It is all the more important to find an answer to our questions.

The answer looks like a vicious circle: we cannot explain to the teachers in the field the essence of rehabilitative teaching without analyzing their actual observed teaching activities; and we cannot analyze them meaningfully, without using properly prepared didactic counselors; the latter, however, must be experienced teachers who have had an opportunity to use different teaching methods, first in regular classes, then in classes of secondarily retarded pupils; for this purpose, they must be exposed not only to sound theoretical training in the etiology and symptomatology of secondary retardation, but also to a clear demonstration of noninductiveness, branching out, and neutralization of affects, those main characteristics of rehabilitative teaching. Who will be able to offer such training of counselors, that *they* could bring about didactic attitude-changes in the teachers in the field?

It is precisely in this last question that we find a way out of our vicious circle according to the present writer's experience: after a small number of students in the University's School of Education had gone through a seminar especially planned for this purpose, they took part in teaching-experiments set up by the author and one of his colleagues (Dr. Hinda Eiger). They formed the staff of the first training units for teachers in rehabilitative teaching. In the beginning, these took the form of relatively short in-service courses, financed and organized jointly by the Education Ministry and the University. The teacher-participants came from all over the country (three times a year during vacation time). They were housed in a small hotel where the lectures and seminars took place, their class observations were analyzed, and many personal teaching experiences could be exchanged during mealtimes or in the evenings.

Much time was devoted to a discussion of their difficulties and doubts, in groups or individual interviews: many of them were afraid of curtailing the child's intellectual initiative by interrupting and shortening the question-and-answer period and by offering, instead, the correct answer, by exactly formulating a principle, a law, a solution; were afraid of causing a lesson to become diffuse, as a result of branching out into adjacent fields of knowledge without knowing how to return to the original subject of the lesson. All feared overpsychologization, particularly through thinking about the possible causes and meaning of an erroneous answer. And they wanted to know how the teacher could use relating himself to one specific pupil for the benefit of the whole class. And, of course, all brought up, again and again, fears that the here-recommended method might cause serious achievement gaps precisely in children who so much needed the experience of equality. Was the emphasis on the functional aspects of teaching really justified, when it was bound to lead to a lesser emphasis on the material, the content aspects?

Some of them thought that it would be inadequate to deal with such and similar problems on a purely intellectual level only, that is, by analyzing their rationale, on the one hand, and the psychodynamics of individual reactions, on the other. They claimed that these fears and doubts should be transformed into conscious experiences by encountering them, "concretely" acted out, in role playing and simulation games. However, since the time available in this first type of reorientation courses (three times seven to twelve days during the year) was much too short to allot enough hours to such "concretizations" of inner conflicts, doubts and fears, the achievement was disappointing (increased insecurity in some, aggressive rejection in others, and in only a few of the teacher-participants increased awareness and readiness to translate the specific group experience into terms of attitude change when they returned to work).

However, some of those responsible for the courses decided to learn the techniques of controlled group discussions, of acting out (playing) class situations, of interpreting the meaning of their and group members' reactions. In due time they became sufficiently well acquainted with the method to be able to use it later, in their guidance work with teachers, of course as an auxiliary service only.

But we must come back to the teacher-participants and their achievements and disappointments: they felt sufficiently "touched" by the message of the brief reorientation training, in all its facets, to become aware of what they really needed: permanent, optimally daily, opportunities to be in contact with a didactic counselor, who would, at least for some considerable time to come, use their observable classroom performances for the purpose of critical (and essential) evaluation and for a consistent presentation of alternatives. However, the manpower required for such intensive follow up and continued guidance in their day-to-day work was not, at least not yet, available—hence the teachers' disappointment and their relatively quick return to previous routine-practice.

The organizers and teachers in these short reorientation courses, however, arrived at another conclusion: to resist the ever repeated demands coming from the Education Ministry as well as from local authorities and *not* to repeat brief reorientation courses; to organize, instead, a counseling service in which they themselves would go out into the field, and particularly into some of these areas in which the majority of the school population belonged to the underprivileged and were secondarily retarded; to receive the Ministry's financial support and recognition, as a result of which the schools and their principals made the arrangements required for a smooth running of the guidance service.

Here again, the quantitative insufficiency of the service offered was painfully in evidence: the relatively small number of well-trained counselors (and the time-consuming traveling from one place to another) reduced the frequency and intensity of guidance contacts to a regrettable minimum. Some tried to overcome this handicap by forming local groups of teachers, mostly from one school and one class level. These groups were sometimes used by some counselors (who believed in the value of role playing) for simulation games, but most of the meeting time was used by all for discussing class events and teacher behavior.*

The next step was to try out another approach: to choose suitable teachers with a variety of different teaching experiences and problems from among the most afflicted areas and schools and to train them over a period of one year. During this year, they continued to teach but came for one day every week (40 weeks), for six to eight hours, to the training center, which happened to be connected with the University School of Education. The idea was that they would remain in their localities and would be able to give more effective teacher-guidance in their local schools than a counselor who would come to the place for one day every week.

During their 40 training days, one-third of the time was devoted to theoretical issues (whereas less time was taken up for this purpose in the above-mentioned reorientation courses); the rest of the time was spent on the analysis of "class events," mostly faulty answers given by children in different age groups to questions referring to various subject matters, and the teachers' adequate or inadequate reactions to such answers. Some of these class events had been prepared beforehand by some members of the training staff, based on ob-

---

*Here, a word of warning would seem to be appropriate: Not a few school principals, although they had themselves asked for the service, did *not* cooperate, once it was established, the main reason being that they saw in the counselors a threat to their own educational authority; and since the Ministry had made available a number of new methods, they preferred those that seemed to them to be the least "threatening."

servations and recordings of what had actually happened in classes, but elaborated in order to focus the discussion on the essentials. Others were brought to the seminars by their participants. Although emphasis was laid on the didactics in the teaching-learning process, examples of the counselor's intervention were not excluded. (Care was taken to establish as many cross-references as possible between the theoretical and the applicative parts of the course.)

All participants in the training course were also in contact with those counselors who worked in their schools. There, they joined them from time to time in the groups of teachers or even in individual guidance contacts to observe the process of guidance and, later, to discuss the dynamics of what had happened.

In this way, they were prepared for the next following year, when they started giving—closely supervised—counseling services to other teachers in their school or locality. Obviously, not all succeeded to the same extent. (As a rule, one-third were found to be suitable to undertake guidance functions independently, one-third were assigned as assistants to more experienced counselors, and one-third were found in need of one more year of intensive in-service training while engaged in teaching.)

References

1. Aichhorn, August. *Wayward Youth*. London: Putnam & Co., 1944.
2. Ainsworth, Mary D. The Effects of Maternal Deprivation. In: *Deprivation of Maternal Care*. Geneva: World Health Organization, 1962.
3. Ausubel, David, P. How Reversible Are the Cognitive and Motivation Effects of Cultural Deprivation? In: Passow, H. M., Goldberg, M. and Tannenbaum, A. J. (eds.), *Education of the Disadvantaged Pupil*. Springfield, Ill.: Charles C. Thomas Publishers, 1965.
4. Bernstein, Basil. *Class, Codes and Control*. London: Routledge, 1974.
5. Bowlby, John. *Maternal Care and Mental Health*. Geneva: World Health Organization, 1951.
6. Coleman, James S. et al. *Equality of Educational Opportunity*. Washington, D.C.: U. S. Government Printing Office, 1966.
7. Erikson, Eric H. *Childhood and Society*. London: Imago Publishing Company, 1950.
8. Frankenstein, Carl. *Persönlichkeitswandel*. München: Urban und Schwarzenberg, 1964.
9. Frankenstein, Carl. *The Roots of the Ego*. Baltimore: Williams & Wilkins, 1966.
10. Frankenstein, Carl. *Psychodynamics of Externalization*. Baltimore: Williams & Wilkins, 1968.
11. Frankenstein, Carl. *Impaired Intelligence*. New York: Gordon & Breach, 1970.
12. Frankenstein, Carl. *Varieties of Juvenile Delinquency*. New York: Gordon & Breach, 1970.
13. Frankenstein, Carl. The Complexity of the Concept of Integration. In: Frankenstein, C. (ed.), *Teaching as a Social Challenge*. Jerusalem: School of Education of the Hebrew University, 1976.
14. Frankenstein, Carl. *The Liberation of Thinking* (in Hebrew). Jerusalem: School of Education of the Hebrew University, 1972.
15. Frankenstein, Carl. *Genuineness and Equality* (in Hebrew). Tel-Aviv: Sifriat Hapoalim, 1977.

16. Freud, Anna. *The Ego and the Defence Mechanisms*. London: Hogarth Press, 1954.
17. Freud, Sigmund. *A General Introduction*. New York: Garden City, 1943.
18. Goldfarb, William. Various papers (1943–1949). In: *Amer. J. Orthopsychiatry* 14:441–447; 15:247–255; 19:624–633.
19. Goldstein, Kurt. *Language and Language Disturbances*. New York: Grune & Stratton, 1948.
20. Gordon, E. W. a.d. (eds.) Compensatory Education for the Disadvantaged, New York: College Entrance Examinations Board, 1966.
21. Jensen, A. R. The Culturally Deprived: Psychological and Educational Aspects. In: *Ed. Res.* 1967, 10:1, 4–20.
22. Jung, Carl G. *Psychological Types*. Princeton: Princeton University Press, 1974.
23. Jung, Carl G. *Symbols of Transformation*. Princeton: Princeton University Press, 1974.
24. Kirk, Samuel, A. An Evaluation of the Study by Bernadine G. Schmidt. *Psychological Bulletin*, 1948, 45:321–333.
25. Minkowich, Abraham. *The Disadvantaged Child* (in Hebrew). Jerusalem: School of Education of the Hebrew University, 1969.
26. Minkowich, Abraham. Failures and Risks in the Education of the Disadvantaged. In Frankenstein, C. (ed.), *Teaching as a Social Challenge*. Jerusalem: School of Education of the Hebrew University, 1976.
27. Nunberg, Hermann. The Synthetic Function of the Ego. In: *International Psychoanalysis*, 1931, XII.
28. Ophuijsen, John H. W. Primary Conduct Disturbances. In: Lewis, N. D. C. and Pacella, B. L. (eds.), *Modern Trends in Child Psychiatry*. New York: International Universities Press, 1950.
29. Passow, A. H., Opening Opportunities for Disadvantaged Learners. New York: Teachers College Press, 1972.
30. Piaget, Jean. *The Origin of Intelligence in Children*. New York: International Universities Press, 1952.
31. Piaget, Jean. *The Language and Thought of the Child*. New York: Meridian Books, 1955.
32. Rosenthal, Robert and Jacobson, Leonore. *Pygmalion in the Classroom*. New York: Holt, Rinehart & Winston, 1968.
33. Rothschild, Fritz S. *Das Ich und die Regulationen des Erlebnisvorganges*. Basel: S. Karger, 1950.
34. Sarason, Seymour B. *Psychological Problems in Mental Deficiency*. New York: Harper, 1949.

35. Schmidt, Bernadine, G. Changes in Personal, Social and Intellectual Behavior of Children Originally Classified as Feebleminded. In: *Psychological Monographs* 1946, 60, No. 5.
36. Spitz, René, A. Hospitalism. In: *The Psychoanalytical Study of the Child*. New York: International Universities Press, 1945.
37. Stoddard, George, D. *The Meaning of Intelligence*. New York: The Macmillan Nompany, 1951.
38. Tannenbaum, Abraham J. (ed.). *Special Education and Programs for Disadvantaged Children and Youth*. Washington: Council for Exceptional Children, 1968.
39. Thorndike, Edward L. et al *The Measurement of Intelligence*. New York: Teachers' College, Columbia University, 1927.

Index

Index